The
Road
Is
How

The Road Is How

A Prairie Pilgrimage through Nature, Desire, and Soul

Trevor Herriot

PATRICK CREAN EDITIONS
HarperCollins*Publishers*Ltd

Published by Patrick Crean Editions,
an imprint of HarperCollins Publishers Ltd.

First Edition

HarperCollins books may be purchased for educational, business, or sales promotional
use through our Special Markets Department.

HarperCollins Publishers Ltd
2 Bloor Street East, 20th Floor
Toronto, Ontario, Canada
M4W 1A8

www.harpercollins.ca

Library and Archives Canada Cataloguing in Publication
information is available upon request.

ISBN 978-1-44341-791-4

Printed and bound in the United States of America
RRD 9 8 7 6 5 4 3 2 1

For Olive Jeanne

To compare life to a road can indeed be fruitful in many ways, but we must consider how life is unlike a road. In a physical sense a road is an external actuality, no matter whether anyone is walking on it or not, no matter how the individual travels on it—the road is the road. But in the spiritual sense, the road comes into existence only when we walk on it. That is, the road is how it is walked.

—Søren Kierkegaard, *Provocations*

Contents

An Introduction: *Homo Viator*

A YOUNG MAN WALKS FOR A YOUNG MAN'S REASONS. In the summer of 1691, twenty-three-year-old Henry Kelsey, looking for beaver and friendly Indians who might be persuaded to trap them, left his canoe on the Saskatchewan River and began walking south through muskeg and bog. Within three days, he stepped out of aspen forest and onto the northern edge of the Great Plains. Historians say he was the first European to walk on the Canadian prairie. First to sit with its hunting people, to see its buffalo and grizzly bears, and to ramble through its unploughed world of grass.

Three hundred and some years later—grass ploughed up, buffalo and grizzly gone—young men go to the mountains to walk. The cultivated plains, the fields and road allowances where GPS-guided machines seed, supplement, and harvest the soil quarter mile by quarter mile, seldom feel the footsteps of any man, young or old. Such a subdued and woebegone landscape will never make the roster of great places to walk. Looking back on it now, the thought that no one walks this land anymore may have been what first made me want to try.

~

French existentialist and playwright Gabriel Marcel once suggested that instead of *Homo sapiens* we might call our-selves *Homo viator*, "man the pilgrim," the wayfarer. We are the oddball creatures who will walk two hundred miles along a river to find the headwaters, across a continent to honour a dying friend, or to the sea to scrape salt from the sand and found a nation. Most of us try simpler journeys, but the seeking is the same: a search for heart, a steadfast spirit, peace of mind, a soul worthy of an altar, or an altar worthy of the soul.

We are fond of our big brains but sometimes forget the wayfarer in us whose restless seeking may well have mapped our course as the hominid who wants to know things. Our intricate neural networks may have developed as our ancestors found food and fostered social linkages, but it all started with our feet following ever more complex pathways across the surface of the earth. To remember our wayfaring origins is to wield a metaphysics of hope against the dogma that we are aimless wanderers in a world whose chaotic surface is the sum total of reality. The wayfaring animal suspects there is something else going on and walks with an eye out for signs and symbols. Moving through the ever-patient land, we hope to connect mind to body to earth, begin the descent from outward to inward, and find a way for even our neuroses and distractions to belong. Spiritual writers say that when you take your consciousness down to the territory where your soul waits for you to wake up, it can be like finding a small door in your house you never knew about. You can't open it yourself, but just knowing it's there is reassuring, because from the other side comes the scent of a wind that holds everything together in its wide embrace—the broken and the whole, shame and forgiveness, despair and gratitude.

In the first days of September, as school and work rang bells to end another summer, I left home and headed east of the city to find that door. Events at the other end of summer had me looking for a better foothold, trying to understand a new feeling of being off balance, of questioning everything I once held as certainty.

There were many questions obsessing me, but none more vexing than the matter of what to do with desire. I used to be happy with the standard explanation: when your eye is drawn by the arc of a woman's foot swinging from a sidewalk through a doorway and the pang hits you, it's nothing more than hormones, a physical response programmed by selfish genes looking for more opportunities to join in the random sorting out of traits that may or may not be well adapted to the unfolding universe in which they operate. But the more I observe that call and response, the more I wonder. Dismissing the desire inside us—sexual and otherwise—as nothing more than biological programming is about as satisfactory as explaining music by referring to sexual and social bonding. I have every respect for evolutionary biology but have trouble seeing Verdi, Mozart, and Chopin as elaborate forms of courtship adaptation, like deer antlers. Never mind music, are we certain we know what antlers are for?

The obsessing over imponderables seemed to start early in the summer when I realized I'd become even crankier than usual with my family and the rest of humanity. If you have spent any time defending wild places and animals, you may know what I mean. Helpless to stop it, you watch a favourite stretch of valley vivisectioned by ranchette development, or a wood once filled with warblers and thrushes knocked down to grow soybeans. Each year, more shorelines, pastures, meadows, woodlots, marshes, and hedgerows slide into the jaws of that monstrosity we prefer to think of as the demon spawn of corporate and private greed—other people's, of course, not ours. What is wrong with them? we ask, turning our eyes toward the heavens, or toward Ronald Wright, Jared Diamond, or anyone with an answer. For a time, there is some comfort in that generalizing inquiry, the soothing intellectual grasp on reality that comes from holding on to something as big as a civilization and then pronouncing it innately flawed. But it eventually grows out to a bitterness that won't go away until you grab the other end of the truth and look at the particular by asking instead, *What is wrong with me?*

I knew I was sunk when I could no longer separate my own motivations from those belonging to the technologists, political leaders, and corporate decision-makers I like to blame. From the right distance, all egocentric, manipulative behaviour begins to look the same, whether you are bulldozing a woodlot or trying to get your wife to make dinner when you think it should be made.

Perhaps worse, for all of my time with birds and the prairie, I was beginning to feel that something was missing in the way I encountered and imagined the other creatures in this windblown land. It was as though my years as the know-it-all naturalist had rendered me deaf to the very spirits that might be able to help me grow up or heal or whatever it is I am supposed to do at this stage of life.

With luck, I might have twenty or thirty years left to find the gentleness and sensitivity that will let me listen more deeply, respond more gracefully. But winter would be here soon. I wanted to go now, to walk out of the city and into the land, following a descent that began three months earlier with a single step off the roof of our house.

On the June morning when the ladder disappeared and I found myself airborne, I put my arms out to see if I could grab on to something or at least protect my head and neck from the impact. My left hand hit first, then my ribs and shoulder on that side landed on something edgier than lawn—the ladder, it turned out—and my head only came to earth when I laid it down to try to yell for help. It was a modest yell—my lungs were in spasm—but when I stopped wincing from the pain and looked up to see who was talking to me, it was a policeman.

As I lay on the grass, trying to breathe within the clenching in my ribs and shoulder, and pondering the possibility I'd broken some bones and done damage I might be living with for a long time, a feeling of calm seeped into my body. I was no more than five or six when I found the little floating creatures that swirled across the sky if I lay down and looked at the clouds. Bits of vitreous jelly in the back of my eye were casting figures onto my retina, but to me it was my own shadow puppet show, and it taught me the pleasure of being a body held by the earth. *I need to do more of this*. I used to do it all the time. A memory of that pleasure invaded my pain, as I watched the floaters mime their tale of a ladder-wielding man operating on the world, now brought low, to get a new perspective on things.

The previous autumn, pigeons that had been coming to get scraps from my bird feeders in the city had begun to nest in a nook beside a dormer on top of our house that was easy for pigeons but difficult for me to reach. I pondered ways to install a mesh barrier but was in no rush to dangle from the eaves of our rooftop. A few weeks later, our oldest daughter, Kate, who sleeps in that dormer, began to find small things on her body the size of a period. Worse, the periods were biting her.

This news came to me via my wife, Karen. The bird mites were all over Kate's room and she had spotted one in the bathroom. Karen started to look for advice online, landing, as one inevitably does, in those online forums written by people whose levels of hysteria match those of no other human being you have encountered in actual life. The bird mite forum strongly advised fumigation—you only have to leave for a few days—though in some cases it does not work and unfortunately some homes simply have to be condemned. Karen had a resolute look in her eye that said, *Homeland Security is under direct threat.*

Thus began my career as a pigeon killer. I do not like killing things, particularly if I am not planning to eat them, so I started with chasing them away, removing the eggs, and putting up some page wire to block access to the nook. Bad feelings when I discarded the eggs, but things were at Orange Alert and heading to Red.

The pigeons rapidly re-nested, and Kate's room had to be sealed off from the rest of the house. This is the spot where desire intervenes between reality and response. Somewhere in the murky reaches of my hindbrain was a dim little sub-thought telling me that if I handled this well, I would score points with Karen and that would, with any luck, lead to you-know-what. Now, outside in the real world undistorted by my delusions, Karen is just wanting the pigeons to be gone. She doesn't use you-know-what as reward or penalty, and besides, there might actually be ways to woo my wife that don't require fighting with pigeons.

That winter and spring, I was up and down ladders so often that I became careless, not to mention a hardened killer. By mid-winter, I was stalking pigeons in the early hours of the morning with an air pistol, hoping to escape the notice of neighbours. I saw headlines: BIRD LOVER ARRESTED FOR SHOOTING PIGEONS WITH HANDGUN. My friend Nathan had located the pistol (I know a guy who knows a guy), which looked pretty much like the kind of Luger I saw in war movies as a boy. I shot four pigeons, but they kept on coming. More bad feelings. I wasn't that hardened after all. These are doves. We used to call them rock doves. People release them at armistice ceremonies. They fell into the snow like representatives of an avian Satyagraha campaign. There was a gentle soul-force there resisting my violence, but at the time

I did not want to think about that. I had to protect the house and Karen might be watching me.

The bloodshed continued into the spring, when pigeons got through the page wire and began nesting again. The day of the accident I was on the roof with a hose, using it to spray a nest full of eggs and knock it over the edge. I flushed away the pigeon droppings and twigs and headed back to the ladder. Thinking back, I don't believe it was the static of guilt and self-loathing in my head that made me careless; my step onto the ladder was careful enough. The ground was wet from two weeks of steady rain, though, and what I needed was someone to hold the bottom of the ladder, but I was a man acting alone, needing no one.

"I've got a ladder accident here. Male, middle-aged. He is conscious, not bleeding. . . ."

Not bleeding, but definitely wondering, *How did this cop get here so fast?* Later, Karen would tell me that the policeman had been driving past when he saw me perform my rooftop slapstick. A minute or two after he called in, I heard an ambulance coming. They had me on the spine board and loaded up in another minute and we were on our way, searching for every pothole and lump on the road en route to the hospital.

I went home later that day, everyone telling me I was lucky, and I guess I was. I had some ribs cracked and out of place, a fracture on the tip of my shoulder, and about half a body of aggravated tissue. Painkillers helped with the throbbing all down my left side, but the inflammation in my brain raged on.

I spend half my life trying to defend birds and their habitat, talking and writing about them, drawing and photographing them, and now I nearly break my neck trying to kill them. Anger that I had always been able to employ usefully by directing it at people—Karen, my children, Stephen Harper—seemed particularly bootless when turned on birds. Blaming was equally unsatisfying. The pigeons were just being pigeons. Worst of all, it would be weeks before I could escape the clamour in my head by digging in the garden or building the deck I had been planning. That only left self-pity, which had its usual consolations but wore thin as the days of bedrest merged into a kind of convalescent purgatory.

Eventually, and not without some resistance, I picked up a book I had been avoiding since a friend had passed it on to me a few months earlier. It was Bill Plotkin's *Soulcraft: Crossing into the Mysteries of Nature and Psyche*, a how-to guide on the spiritual journey using wilderness psychology and rites in nature. I had recently sworn off grand theories that explain the malaise of modernity and how to heal from it. I had decided that with the first grey strands appearing among my thinning hair, I should become more sophisticated and nuanced in my regard for the advancing doomsday. Halfway into the foreword by eco-theologian Thomas Berry, though, I gave in. Over the next couple of days, I downed Plotkin's spellbinding mix of story, theory, poetry, and prescription in great thirsty gulps, rereading and marking passages that made sense as I looked at my own life.

After reading the introduction, I set the book down and turned out the light, hoping to get comfortable enough for real sleep. Instead, I stewed in half-awake, triple-Tylenol hallucinations that mashed together memories from the Qu'Appelle Valley with shreds of a recurrent dream where I am a falcon gliding down a long slope covered with short-grass, rocks, and juniper.

I was travelling through the valley looking for an old lime kiln in the wall of a coulee. But it wasn't just the lime kiln. With the looking came as strong a pang of nostalgia as I have had in a long time, as though I were trying to recover something lost—my ideals of rural community, or perhaps days when I have felt completely at ease and happy on a hillside. And then I was on the rim looking down on the land from a great height. It was the falcon dream, where I always see myself as two, from within and without. Letting myself fall from a hilltop perch, I unfold my wings and glide down, watching my other off to one side moving in parallel, and the clumps of grass and juniper blurring beneath me as I fly faster and faster, rising just above boulders that could kill me at the wrong turn of a feather. I spot a red bird at the foot of the slope, a cardinal, and lift a wing to steer toward it, but when I pounce, it changes in my grasp to a wooden replica, its dead eye looking blankly at the sky.

The next morning, reading the first chapter in Plotkin's book, I came across a Rilke poem I'd seen before:

How surely gravity's law
strong as an ocean current,
takes hold of even the smallest thing
and pulls it toward the heart of the world. . . .

This is what the things can teach us:
to fall,
patiently to trust our heaviness.
Even a bird has to do that
before he can fly.

I doubt Rilke ever went on his roof to kill pigeons, but he knew a thing or two about flying: "patiently to trust our heaviness." Recalling my dream and wanting to feel that trust again, I read on.

The soul, according to Plotkin, is the wildest part of us. It is born and renewed in nature, he says, and we can count on nature to reflect the soul back to us. As a depth psychologist who leads eco-therapy initiation programs in wilderness, he says that we mature only in the womb of nature. Without its guidance and nurturing, we get stuck in a chronic adolescence that destroys families, community, and ecology. At its heart, the book promises that when your soul is awakened in nature and supported by elders, it can undergo a transformation that allows you to set aside egotistical ways, compulsions, and addictions, and finally grow up, discovering the life purpose and gift you were born to bear into the world.

As I made my way through the pages, I decided I had to go for a walk. Plotkin actually recommends wilderness fasts and finding an elder you can trust. All good ideas, I thought, but a journey requires motion. I'm going to walk. That way I can eat while I develop. As for elders, I could talk to my friend Daniel. If I call him an elder, he might take a swing at me, but he has been a patient listener and guide, gently nudging me to answer the stirrings and invitations I've been ignoring for years. He would have some thoughts on the walk.

A week or two after I fell, we met at a café we like to use when I have questions to ask or excuses to make. We are about the same age, but Daniel is one of the few men I know who seems to have actually grown up. The spiritual world of the Grandfathers is as near and real to him as his own beating heart. The guidance he receives in the heat of the lodge, during the hours at the Sun Dance, or fasting on hilltops keeps him aware of that dimension even as he works at his corporate job in the city or seeds cropland on the reserve.

Over cups of tea, I told Daniel about the accident, and the restlessness I'd been feeling. I said I needed to do something, and since my legs were good and I'd be able to carry a light pack in a few weeks, I thought I'd go for a walk somewhere. Nothing big, just a few days, but I needed to figure out what was bothering me.

Daniel gave me the smile he reserves for moments when white people aren't getting it, and looked out the window over the city's industrial zone. I was hoping he'd like the idea, might even join me, but I could tell he was dubious.

"This thing has happened for a reason. Walking is good, but you have to figure out why you want to walk. You need to go sit on a hill for a few days."

"No way. . . . How long?"

"As long as it takes—just you and the hill."

"No food and water?"

"Nope."

"Yeah, well. That's easy for you to say. I'm not an Indian,

just a confused white guy who wants to go for a walk. I could have liver failure or something. You probably have some kind of Nakota gene for vision quests. I have a gene for tolerating bagpipes. Besides, you always said, 'You are put down here to do a walk, and your job is to find out what that is.'"

"That's just a figure of speech. You should go sit first— then, when you take your walk, things might make more sense. You might even learn why you are here."

I went home and started googling for information on the dangers of wilderness fasting and anything else that would let me off the hook. Two weeks later, I met Daniel again. This time his brother was there, a man with those soft-spoken Aboriginal ways and that gentle, unassuming gaze that makes you wish you could shut up, because while you blather on, you know he never speaks unless his heart is open enough to say something worth breaking the silence for. Over a meal, we discussed the fast, with me doing too much of the talking, but Daniel's brother told me how to prepare by coming with one or two questions I want answers for, and to be open to the things I see and hear, not only in nature but in dreams and in my heart. As he spoke, I could feel myself giving in to the strength woven into gentleness in his voice. I was in too far to back out now. The two of them would drive out on the weekend to help me choose a site and show me how to make the circle.

That Sunday, we met at Cherry Lake, the place out on the prairie we share with two other families. There are several hills covered with native grass that I could have chosen, but Daniel pointed up to the one that overlooked three lakes in the valley, a couple of hundred paces past a spot we have sometimes called Vision Hill because it was where we stood when we decided to form our little group and buy the land.

"That hill should be good. You'll be able to see a long way from there. And your wife can keep an eye on you from the valley bottom. She should check on you once a day, but don't speak to her, just wave or give her a sign that you are okay."

"What's the sign for liver failure?"

Then we went down the hill and he showed me how to cut the buffalo sage plants I would need to make the circle. From a bundle in his hands, he laid the plants on the grass and then showed me how to make a door in the circle. "You open and close it behind you just like that."

Before they drove away, I had one last question. "How do I know when I am done?"

"You'll know."

"How?"

"You'll just know."

There was no getting out of it now. If I jammed out, I'd have trouble looking Daniel in the eye. He was right, of course. I would have to sit still and face my demons, if for no other reason than to find out why I was planning the walk.

The first three days were about what you'd expect—boredom and misery punctuated by moments of dread and anxiety. On the last night and the morning of the fourth day, though, things happened. I knew it was time to leave the circle, just as Daniel said I would. I floated down the hill, buzzing with a mix of sunstroke, hunger-induced euphoria, and enough of the Moses complex to convince me that I might have a few nuggets of truth to carry the nations through the next phase of history. Later that morning, when I found myself arguing with our teenaged daughter about the merits of cooked oatmeal versus Cocoa Puffs, my wisdom for the ages crashed back down to earth. I wasn't going to save humanity, but I had a reason for my walk and some questions to take with me.

Inside the circle of sage, through dreams and other urgings, I heard again and again that I am no different from anyone else living in this hothouse-flower dispensation we call modernity. That I am imbalanced and coarse in my relationships to people, to nature, and to community, and in the end not much better than the goons I ridicule for ripping across the land on ATVs or "camping" in air-conditioned motorhomes. Voting Green, eating local foods, and knowing the names of things is not going to be enough to answer the questions that hound my entry into the last decades of life: what do I do with all this desire, what is the meaning of a man and a woman coming together in life, and how do I finally grow up in my relationships?

The worst part was having to admit that any spiritual faculties I had once possessed seemed to be dormant, as though the ear of the heart that develops so naturally in childhood had gone deaf, perhaps because I never made use of it to reach adulthood. By the time the fast was over, I'd seen enough of my soul and its ways of listening and speaking to know that I needed to stop wandering in mid-life adolescence, awaken those sleeping senses, and use them to walk purposefully toward whatever comes next.

I didn't have a clue where I would walk, but this was

beginning to feel like some kind of pilgrimage. Whether you choose a road through cropland or a pasture, the northern Great Plains is an intimidating land to walk. Your body receives no enfolding embrace. Anything reckless enough to try standing upright is likely shorter than you. Almost everything is below your waist, if not below ground. When a swale or coulee appears on the horizon, you go there without need of conscious thought. The body wants to be held. The wayfarer in you wants a break from all the exposure.

It was not the prairie as much as its birds that made me a walker. Once you learn their sounds, walking becomes a passage from one note to another along a ligature that ties the world together aurally. The older I get, though, the more my listening shifts inward, and the more I walk just to get my head and heart to talk to one another. A couple of hours tromping through buckbrush and slough bottoms is usually enough to sort through the emotional residue that comes with facing things I cannot change: a friend dying, a daughter moving away, the government abandoning science and sanity. After the first miles go by, the clenching in my chest begins to ease off and my loudest delusions of entitlement fade enough for me to hear the hiss of a savannah sparrow.

This time, though, a short walk wasn't going to be enough. Instead of coming to terms with changes outside of me, I'd have to look inside to things that needed changing.

I knew I wanted to do it at the end of summer, and that I would have to leave my binoculars behind, but where to walk? There are not a lot of sacred paths and ancient temples in my part of the world, not even a holy mountain, or any mountain, come to that. All I've got is the wide open plain running off in all directions from the city, and almost no one calls it holy.

No one, that is, except some of the people who have been here the longest. Several years ago I sat on a panel of artists and writers gathered to talk about the spiritual importance of the Qu'Appelle Valley, a landform that I had celebrated and lamented in my first book. Taking our turns, we did what was expected, singing with reverence from the same hymnal about the great valley's sacred land. The lone Aboriginal artist in the circle, the late Bob Boyer, was batting cleanup. It was a position he relished, and he was scowling, so I knew it was going to be good.

"I don't know what all this crap is about the valley. It's just a trench in the prairie. What's the big deal? It's no holier than any other place." He looked up at the rest of us. "It's all sacred ground. All of it," he said, sweeping his arm out toward the window. Some nervous laughter rippled through the crowd, but we all knew Bob was right. Land doesn't become holy because it appeals to our landscape aesthetic and makes us feel good, any more than it becomes holy when we cover it with temples and shrines.

When friends tells me they are going to Nepal to fill their creative well, or to Machu Picchu to do a prayer walk, my first response has always been a generous twinge of envy, but my second thought is, *Can you restore your soul by taking it to places where it won't know the other souls?* Where the way the creeks turn, the quality of the sunlight, the conversation of the birds will all be unfamiliar?

Maybe you can get your life in order by going for a walk

someplace exotic where the road is long steeped in human striving toward the divine. Maybe some of the humility and gratitude of the indigenous people who have walked there for hundreds of years will rub off and you can take it back with you. But I worry about what happens when we separate spirituality from bodily life and culture, both of which are profoundly connected to soil, climate, and the other givens of place. We are the first generations who have had the means to take that separation to the extremes of spiritual tourism. In the past, some pilgrims always travelled to reach the pilgrimage or holy walk, but not into entirely different biomes and continents. The majority, the people whose repeated visits gave the path and its shrines a soulful patina, were always from that culture and region. Something of the land they walked through was in them, and in turn something of them was in the land.

Like any other creature, we thrive and develop in place. The deepest part of our spiritual selves is formed within a matrix of nature and culture, a *terroir* of the soul. Several years before building his cabin at Walden Pond, Thoreau scribbled into his journal the following simple prescription for spiritual health: "You must converse much with the field and woods if you would imbibe such health into your mind and spirit as you covet for your body." Now that we are making the connection between eating locally and bringing health into our bodies, communities, and ecosystems, why not apply the same ethos for our spiritual healing? If it's good to eat locally, isn't it just as good to heal and feed our souls locally?

No one needs spiritual locavores who harry dinner guests

with figures on the greenhouse gas emissions embedded in a pilgrimage to Lhasa, but maybe we can "imbibe such health" in our spirits as we do for our bodies, by doing the local thing and walking the countryside to "converse with the fields and woods" for a few days.

Undoubtedly, one can have a profound religious experience on a trek that requires travel agents, a 747, and hotels, but when you are as cheap as I am, you claim the high road any way you can. I decided I would follow the simple pattern laid down by every spiritual seeker from the Aborigine walkabout to the travels of the Buddha, Moses, and Jesus, to Saint Francis of Assisi and Gandhi: pack lightly, get my best walking sandals on, and head out the door. I had no desire to get any more religion than I already had, but I wanted to walk out into the country and place my questions before the humbler revelation written into a creek, a roadside lily, or a stand of aspen.

I dug out my large colour satellite map covering the Regina Plains. Almost immediately, I saw that I was most familiar with places within forty miles of the city: small bits of grassland, large wetlands, a coulee here and there, a piece of the valley itself, and a lot of roads. I know which ones to take to find owl nests and how the lady's slippers fill certain ditches. Along most of them, I can recognize the exact contours of hills barely worth noticing, and predict the grasses growing in a neglected cemetery. You could blindfold me and drop me off anywhere within forty miles of the city and if the sun were out I'd be able to wander home along those roads in a couple of days. Beyond that, things get a little fuzzy.

I made a string to scale for forty miles and swung it in a circle centring on the city. When it hit the eastern extremity of the arc, the forty-mile mark passed right through the edge of our land at Cherry Lake. Somehow I had never realized that the south end of the city and our land were sitting on precisely the same latitude. In the next moment I saw that a road I had been taking from the city to watch birds since the early 1980s followed the first fourteen miles of that line. Tracing my finger along its road allowance farther east, I arrived at the northern boundary of our property, but from the satellite map I could see that the actual road was interrupted for miles at two different sections in the middle. That explained it. Travelling the back roads by car, I had always turned south or north where the road gave way to a T-junction and then gone the rest of the way on other roads.

This will work, I thought. A road that is both familiar and new, but will serve well enough as an average transect slicing with Euclidian precision through the circle of my home landscape. There is no way to walk this land without a road. This isn't the Yorkshire dales, criss-crossed with easements and stiles over fences to encourage tweed-clad ramblers. On most of the northern Great Plains, municipal roads and railbeds provide the only public traverse through farmland. I've done my share of trespassing through farmers' fields—and will do some this time—but a few paces swimming through a stand of canola or high-stepping over swathed wheat usually sends me quickly back to the gravel. As for shrines and temples, I would have to look to the living things along the way, which, if the old scriptures are to be believed, hold more of the Holy Spirit than anything we might mortar together or chisel out of stone.

Forty miles. I liked the sound of the number, the Biblical associations of time spent in wilderness where souls are palpated in the hands of God. A lot of pilgrims ahead of me have let that number guide them to renewal. In Spain, it is *Cuaresma*, in Ireland, *Carghas*—a time of being tested, of grace, of searching for some action or sign from the One who will make the pasque flower bloom after the winter, whether we pass the test or not.

PART ONE

Outdoor Complaints

Mature as he was, she might yet be able to help him to the building of the rainbow bridge that should connect the prose in us with the passion. Without it we are meaningless fragments, half monks, half beasts, unconnected arches that have never joined into a man. With it love is born, and alights on the highest curve, glowing against the grey, sober against the fire.

—E.M. Forster, Howards End

1 On the Road Allowance

IT IS JUST AFTER EIGHT IN THE MORNING on a Wednesday in early September. I walked out the front door at seven, made my way south through middle-class subdivisions built fifty years ago, crossed the freeway, and turned left onto the road.

In the city, our tomatoes are in from the garden and our new pullets are growing fat on the remains of our peas and lettuce. At the place we share with two other families out on the prairie, there are still potatoes and squash to be brought in and honey to be gathered from the hives. In wilder places, ducks and other water birds are filling every slough and lake at the end of one of the best breeding seasons in decades for the northern plains. On a trip I made to Grasslands National Park in mid-summer, though, the prairie that greeted my ears was far too quiet. Grassland birds had struggled through another cold and wet spring, trying to hold on to declining populations. The April count of greater sage grouse had located fewer than thirty birds in the province as the oil and gas industry went on shredding the remaining native grassland in the southwest. As always, there were consolations from our little patch of prairie. We burned our southern hills in April, picked wild asparagus in May, braided sweetgrass in June, and counted hundreds of prairie lilies in July. Only the saskatoon berries failed us.

Eating out of your garden and what nature herself offers, minding the birds and flowers that pass through the summer, and joining with others to defend the wild things around you—these are the daily practices that are supposed to keep us connected, grounded to our home landscapes, heal our communities, bond us to one another and to the land.

"Why do those words make me so uncomfortable—'bonding,' 'healing,' 'connecting'?" To say goodbye, I'd followed Karen out into the yard, bringing the remnants of our breakfast discussion with me. She had caught one of the chickens and wanted me to clip a few of its primary feathers—enough to ensure *free-range* doesn't include our neighbours' gardens too.

"They're not bad words," Karen said, "just worn smooth from too much use and abuse. It's like someone talking about 'grace' or 'salvation'—you can't hear the words for all the noise from people using them to sell something. They still have meaning—you've just got to listen harder."

In the kitchen, she had been reading me a passage from a favourite book. It was a definition of "soul" as the fire that animates everything, the organizing principle that holds a living body together, and that humans experience as longing, whether it is desire, nostalgia, lust, or hope. All connecting bonds in nature, it said, from the molecular level to the ties in human relationships, reflect this fire or eros in a certain polarity, an intersection of anima and animus, yin and yang.

We'd had this talk before. Karen says the divine energies of creation are plunged into, immersed in the flesh of living things via the Mother, the vehicle of that incarnation. "It's in your DNA," she says. "The only way science can trace your deep ancestry is through the maternal side, using your mitochondrial DNA."

Okay, I thought, but how is it the yin side of things always gets the earthy moral grounding and yang is left somewhere in the heavens hovering above the plain of longing? And how come women seem to know this stuff, carry it more comfortably than those of us with all the yang?

I thought again about my unease when people talk about connection and healing. Women have it; men want it but don't know it. Is our obsession with the female body a masked desire for a bit of that connection, healing stuff?

"You're leery about those words," Karen said as she placed the hen back down with a pat, "but how else do we talk about what the world needs? Here's another one we've worn threadbare: 'love.' You're looking for connection and healing, but you can't even say the words out loud."

She walked back into the chicken coop, leaving a trace of all I had been ruminating over for much of the summer, the bitter soup of fear and longing that simmers within me now as I stand in this ditch with a phalanx of commuters rolling past in forty-thousand-dollar vehicles. No one walks this kind of prairie road unless they are in trouble. Someone standing in a ditch wearing a backpack is clearly beyond help.

Roads and ditches are all we have left for public land on the most fertile parts of the prairie. Taken together, a road and its margins is what we call "the road allowance," because the sixty-six feet left for it to pass through private farmland is all that the land survey system allowed. Most of this allowance I am walking along actually has a road—a "grid road," which means it follows the lines imposed by the survey's grid pattern—but there are two stretches I will traverse tomorrow and the next day where the allowance is roadless through a couple of miles of bush and slough.

What we in the west "allow" in the east they "concede," but whether it is a concession road or a road allowance, the commons has been reduced to a paltry, linear remnant. Falling out from that decision made in a city far east of here in the late nineteenth century is the other truth dominating the land encircling me: in a fertile landscape, giving up 99 percent of the commons has meant giving up 99 percent of the land's native cover. If there is a sprig of native sage or grass growing anywhere here, it is likely in the ditch, in a cemetery, or along the weedy railway easements. All else is given over to agriculture. The ecological district known as the Regina Plains is estimated to have less than 1 percent of its native cover remaining. Undaunted by anything like truth, the city named its newest shopping zone "Grasslands: the Natural Place to Shop."

I stand in the ditch astounded at the traffic passing by—a road allowance rush hour. Several minutes pass before I can water the brome grass in peace. I look up to a little power station and three sets of transmission lines that come from it, including those double poles that look like giants. All of it serving Regina, home of the On-to-Ottawa Trek, the Regina

Riot, the Regina Manifesto—erstwhile hotbed of radicals and social reform.

Once upon a time, I was a latter-day Regina radical myself, sitting around smoky rooms with assorted Marxists, Trotskyites, students, and union members, all of us imagining we could fix the world if we freed Mandela, stopped mining uranium, and got the Americans out of Nicaragua. I knew what I believed back then; knew even more once I discovered that, compared with the unwashed and suffering hordes of humanity, nature was always beautiful, virtuous, and worthy of defence. Sooner or later, though, you get tired of the see-saw of desire and aversion driving your opinions. That hit me like a tire wrench to the head, somewhere in the middle of my time fasting on the hill, but right now, here on this road, I am supposed to be thinking about connection, looking deeper, seeing if there is anything left to love in a land we have handed over to herbicide-resistant crops.

In the weedy ditch there are mosquitoes biting. Probably the *Culex* variety that carries West Nile, but odds are I've been inoculated with the virus by a previous encounter with these bugs. I would have to check my antibodies to prove it, but I'm not really worried about it anymore. I head up onto the road, where another battalion of SUVs pours into the city, taking a shortcut past the Agriculture and Agri-Food Canada research station crops here in the first mile of my walk due east. This federal government land is one of the only pieces of publicly owned property on the entire forty-mile transect I will follow. Just a tiny piece of the commons, but a sign at the corner says "Authorized Personnel Only."

No one told the bobolinks. Earlier this summer, I stopped to listen at this same spot, not really expecting to find anything on the research station property. Immediately, the burbling chatter of a male bobolink came to the road. There they were: two males singing in flight, wings whirring, heads arched up to the sky. Common yellowthroats and savannah sparrows sang from the same half acre of wet grass, thistle, and dock weeds.

It was an evening in mid-July and I was out with a friend I know from cutting vegetables a couple of times at the soup kitchen in Regina's Marian Centre. Doreen works there, living in community with other lay people who, under the Madonna House Apostolate, make a promise to live in poverty, chastity, and obedience. She had asked me if I would take her and Charlie, a visiting member of their apostolate, for a bird outing some time.

Doreen is a sweet, open-hearted woman, so I knew it would be fun to show her some birds. Her friend Charlie was from Maryland originally and wanted to see some of our landscape and birds before he left. I took them for a slow drive east along the road. Just an average mid-summer evening: warm light coming from behind us, the scent of hay down in windrows, and a good mix of farmland birds.

"Oh my, how beautiful," Doreen would say as each bird showed up in her binoculars. Sometimes it was just a small sound of delight. Both she and Charlie received the birds that came our way with a fresh welcome and complete gratitude for the gift manifest in flight and song.

I found myself relaxing and happier than I am sometimes

when I am alone and grumbling in lament for all that I know is missing from the landscape. An upland sandpiper whistled and I settled into the goodness of the moment. Looking up, we found it flying with rapid, stiff wingbeats before landing on a power pole. Down the road, we watched a solitary sandpiper and a group of six American avocets foraging in Wascana Creek. They lifted into the air and flew back and forth in front of us, up and down the channel, in slow, circling flights.

As the evening passed, I told Charlie and Doreen about the moult of the avocets, the sexual behaviour of the bobolinks, and the natural history of cowbirds. Charlie had not heard "slough" used to describe a wetland and asked me to spell it for him.

Later, we all watched in awe as a vesper sparrow sang to the setting sun from its ditch-side dock plant.

"So many birds," Doreen said as we followed cowbirds moving among some cattle. "I can't believe how many birds there are here!"

I saw all that was missing and they saw all that was there. And instead of complaining, they were utterly grateful, part of them bowing inwardly to each creature, each field of cut hay, or barn, or row of fence. I don't know if I have ever felt that deep receiving thankfulness, but in that moment it seemed like a faculty I had lost and wanted dearly to have back again.

Tim Hortons bags along the roadside from the commuters. Here comes another SUV, the roar of tires on gravel, harried driver at the wheel. Yesterday, I too was heading off to work to pay my loans, but now I am afoot, with walking stave, hoping for some of that Whitman spirit: "Henceforth I whimper no more, postpone no more, need nothing,/Done with indoor complaints, libraries, querulous criticisms,/Strong and content I travel the open road."

That's why I am here. What else, Walt, what else? "The earth, that is sufficient,/I do not want the constellations any nearer,/I know they are very well where they are,/I know they suffice for those who belong to them." And even though he carries his "old delicious burdens" and is "fill'd with them," he declares that he will "fill them in return."

Yes, that's exactly it, but old Walt does not say how he got so happy about his burdens. There's nothing I am carrying I would call even remotely delicious, though I am looking forward to the cookies I brought.

A sharp twinge in my shoulder interrupts the "Song of the Open Road" with an outdoor complaint. First damn mile and it hurts. It has been three months since I fell off the roof and I still can't lift that arm above my head, or reach into my back pocket.

I adjust the strap on my left shoulder as a meadowlark sings from somewhere out on the Agri-Food Canada hayfields where our tax dollars have discovered a new way of jacking up the ecological footprint of hay bales simply by wrapping them in snazzy green plastic. A wind from the northeast miraculously blows the dust away from me and off the road as each truck or car passes. Every so often along the road I see a dead butterfly—the sulphurs and cabbage whites that have been so abundant this year with all the canola in crop. I see a couple of clouded sulphurs with their wings emerging out of the gravel, looking as though they might still be alive.

Holding one in the palm of my hand, I hear a hawk call from the top of one of the double power poles. I can't see it yet, but it sounded like a red-tail. There it is on one of the lower cross-arms, right above a little piece of pasture—the first along the road so far, but mostly non-native grass. I walk over to visit with some heifers, a couple of calves, and three ponies standing in the corner of the pasture. The ponies are sorrels with white socks. There's a bull in there too. He's shamelessly trying to mount one of the heifers. Karen claims never to have seen this happen. I, however, seem to have a knack for coming upon amorous critters. I see animals, wild and domestic, copulating wherever I go: cattle, sparrows, dragonflies, frogs. It happens all the time in pastures as we drive down a highway, and I try to point it out to Karen, but she always seems to look the wrong way or miss it somehow. "It's all about what you're looking for," she says. "You see cattle humping and I'm the one who sees discarded condoms in the gutter." True enough, she finds condoms whenever we walk in the city, but I'd be just as happy if she kept those sightings to herself.

We walked a lot after the surgery that removed the lump in her left breast and the lymph nodes on that side. Some days the chemotherapy and radiation made her too weak to leave the house. Four years later, she is strong and teaching ten yoga classes a week, but I am still having trouble letting her out of my sight. It has been good to pull her closer, but there are times now when I know my grip is too tight.

The hawk is still calling and I see it clearly now; it is a red-tail. He stirs as I draw near, lets himself fall from the perch, and then opens his wings and catches the rising air.

Trust like that, faith in life to bear you up—that was part of what I was hoping I might find by sitting on a hilltop for a while.

The morning after Daniel and his brother left I spent cutting sage and making my circle. At noon I ate a last meal and walked up the hill with a small tent, a sleeping bag, and some water. It was early July and daytime highs were reaching thirty-four degrees. Going without water seemed like the kind of man-up thing I was trying to get away from in life.

I opened the door to the circle on its western edge, walked in, and closed it behind me. I stood to face north, as Daniel had told me to, but my eye went to something glistening amid the tufts of spear grass at my feet. I bent to pick it up. A piece of crinkly plastic candy wrapper balled up. The residue of sugar had welded bits of sand to it, making a little galaxy of quartzite-grit sparkle on the one side. Turning it over, I found some writing in felt pen: *GIVE AWAY!* I looked around me. Neither Daniel nor Karen had been up to the circle or knew its exact location.

Okay, I thought, *so this is how it works*. For the hard cases, we have messages scrawled on candy wrappers. There are probably a few things I should give away, but the one that came to mind when I sat down for the first time in the fasting circle was my lifetime supply of fear and distrust.

Road Conditions: Walking with Walt

Down from the gardens of Asia, descending, radiating,
Adam and Eve appear, then their myriad progeny after them,
Wandering, yearning, curious—with restless explorations,
With questionings, baffled, formless, feverish—
with never-happy hearts, With that sad, incessant refrain,
Wherefore, unsatisfied Soul? and Whither,
O mocking Life?
—Walt Whitman, "Passage to India"

At the age of fifty-four, not quite twenty years after publishing
the great walking verse of his *Leaves of Grass*, Walt Whitman
had a stroke. It was February and he had to learn to walk all
over again. With the help of loving friends and a cane, he had
begun to walk short distances by spring. Fired from his job,
down to his last six hundred dollars, and depressed, he moved
in with his brother and sister-in-law in Camden, New Jersey.
Then he had another stroke. During this dark period he created a new edition of *Leaves*, adding "Passage to India." The
writing helped, but he would say later that what saved his life
was meeting a farm family, Susan and Harry Stafford.

The Staffords invited him to stay with them on their farm
for weeks at a time. Fuelled by farm eggs, chicken, and pork,
Whitman would often go for walks along a wooded stream
nearby, Timber Creek. Using his cane, he dragged his lame
left foot behind him, revelling in landscapes that reminded
him of his childhood rambles on Long Island. He stripped
and swam in the stream, took mud baths, wrestled with saplings, sat on stumps, and watched dragonflies. Between the
creek, the walking, and the creatures he found on his way,
Walt Whitman restored his soul.

2 By Fire

THE SWATHS OF GRAIN IN THE FIELDS I am passing look heavy. Torrential spring rains that made the muddy footing for my ladder back in June were a mixed blessing for the farmers. Some have harvested record-breaking yields—those who were able to get into their fields to seed in May. In early June, while I was listening to the radio and insulating the floor of our chicken coop, I heard Barbara Budd say that 8 million acres of prairie farmland was under water. The Ministry of Agriculture estimates that in an average year Saskatchewan seeds 32 million acres.

Bad news for farmers was tremendous news for ducks. By August, the annual breeding waterfowl surveys were in, estimating 45.6 million breeding ducks in the North American population this year—35 percent above the long-term average. In fifty-six years, the estimate has exceeded 40 million only five times. Aerial pond counts in the United States and Canada showed 8.1 million ponds, a 22 percent increase from last year's estimate and 62 percent above the long-term average. Only one other time in the history of the survey has the figure gone beyond 8 million.

When nature reasserts herself in the storms of a single springtime, how can we not feel emboldened? The flood water that flowed over public and private boundaries, confounding our efforts at assigning blame and responsibility, taught us many things this year, among them, that even in a land so utterly under the thrall of high-yield agriculture, change is possible. Good things come from prairie soil when someone shows us how not to be afraid of stormy waters.

These power lines I am walking past came from the leadership of a man who liked to say it is never too late to build a better world. It was the courage of Tommy Douglas that brought electrical power to the province's farms in the early fifties. A skinny Baptist preacher with revolutionary gospel-driven ideas in the pockets of his baggy pants, Douglas had shocked the world a few years earlier in sweeping to power with the continent's first socialist government. Rural people had elected him because in those days farmers were the natural communitarian progressives. They knew that there was more to be gained from helping one another and sharing costs than from out-competing their neighbours and taking over their land. Electricity, brought in by the Douglas government working with local farm communities, was but one of the many changes that began to alter the way rural people behaved and voted. It certainly eased the burden of farm women, with electric appliances, and for a while it fostered community, bringing light to rinks and town halls in the dark northern winters, but like the farm machinery that took hold after World War II, it also contributed to a scale of farm industrialization that has made neighbours and community all but superfluous.

Today, the remnant population living in rural areas routinely elects politicians who promise more wealth, lower taxes, and the freedom to sell their produce wherever and however they like. Political leaders of all stripes regularly invoke the memory of Tommy Douglas, hoping to borrow some of his integrity and populist appeal. It doesn't seem to matter that party policies are diametrically opposed to every value Douglas stood for. When there are no other examples of honest leaders at hand, it only makes sense to point to the last politician with the maturity to serve his community well.

Now that we have voted on CBC television to make Douglas our "Greatest Canadian," more than ever prairie people are inclined to face political and economic realities by asking, "What would Tommy do?" When this oil and potash boom we are experiencing turns to bust, that question will be asked even more. It's not fair, of course, to use a dead man to stand in for the leader of honour and truth we wish we had, but like everyone else, I ask that question too.

If Tommy were around today, would he be moving beyond issues of economic growth and the public health care system we remember him for? Would he see that the very sources of health and wealth—the human and natural communities—we have always relied upon are being laid waste? The courage we need now is in facing the truth that there is not going to be a publicly funded medicine to heal the mess we have made. If there is medicine that will work, it will come from the human heart in contact with the earth and the Spirit that joins the two.

~

There are meadowlarks sitting on top of hay bales everywhere I look. Not as many as there were before we industrialized farming, but there are a lot here today in front of me, and I am glad of it. The fall migration is on. Meadowlarks flit here and there, jumping on and off the bales, stopping briefly to sing scraps of their song. The angle of light must be just right for them, reminding them of spring. A woolly grey haze is now turning blue as it thins and peels back to the east. The sun poking through rides above the yardarm of each steel power pole as I walk past.

"Autumnal recrudescence," biologists call it. A crocus blooming in September, a barn swallow building a nest that will never be used, or meadowlarks singing when the breeding season is over. Some uses of the word refer to illness, as when an infection that had been quiescent returns, but when I hear birds singing in the fall I think of a good friend who likes to say that recrudescence means becoming crude again.

Again? How about all the time? Somehow the human male doesn't have a breeding season. We are always on. Mindlessly following the ebb and flow of your gonadal longings is fine if you are a fruit fly or a bonobo, but if you are a twenty-first-century man, it is bad for the biosphere.

"That is the Great Unfairness," Joseph used to say. He was the sort of friend my mother might have thought was a bad influence, but she kept her silence, probably happy that I had any friends at all during my university years. He was studying a strange mix of theology and physics, alienating all of his professors, and wasting a lot of time playing kaiser. When I graduated, he was starting a master's degree that he would never finish. "They were threatened by me. What's the point of the academy if they won't let you try tearing it down?"

I never figured out how Joseph paid his heating and food bills once he moved to Whitehorse, but until a year or two ago I would still get long dispatches from him by mail. He liked to say he didn't believe in email or the Internet, though to me much of what he wrote had the feel of ideas gleaned from esoteric blogs and websites. Still, Joseph was my last regular correspondent by mail—another letter-writing friend died three years ago—and so his thick packages were a welcome sight in the mailbox. They often arrived in a manila envelope to accommodate an article from a magazine he wanted me to read, but always the letter was in his pinched script sloping downward to the right and spinning elaborate theories on the demise of civilization, ecological disarray, or something he called "the Nestbuilder Principle." I knew I was in trouble when some of his ideas started to make sense to me, but I tried not to encourage him and instead responded with family news and bird observations. He collected beetles and paid some attention to birds, and that more than anything sustained our correspondence until he stopped writing the winter before last.

Joseph would have loved the movie poster I saw a couple of weeks ago. On my walk downtown to the office, I often glance at the poster for the film playing at the main library's repertory theatre. Who can resist movie posters? This one caught my eye with a standard trick: lots of lovely flesh bathed in morning light. It was a collage of beautiful bodies with tousled hair, the warm tones of shoulders and arms, the lucky young man with three days' beard growth. Somewhere along the way the illusion industry has discovered that the only thing more alluring than perfectly coiffed and mascaraed bed-bound models is *im*perfectly coiffed and mascaraed bed-bound models, because they look all the more post-coitally erotic. Amid the half-dozen images of the flesh on offer in this film was the title, all in caps, *KABOOM*. That seems refreshingly honest, I thought. The creators of this particular illusion seemed to realize that sex is explosive. The vulgarity of "banging" hides a truth: sexual energy can go kaboom and people, women and men, get hurt.

"Sex is part of everything explosive and everything creative, sometimes both at once." Some of the stuff Joseph wrote in his missives contained pieces of truth lacquered over in bombast. "The Big Bang is the primal archetype here, the first 'sexual' act, though the actor was the Creator." Then he said something about wondering what God was doing right up to the moment of that cosmic orgasm, which I thought stepped over a line and did a disservice to a hypothesis that after all had come through the mind and heart of a celibate Belgian priest and astronomer, Monsignor Lemaître.

Adapting freely from old mystics and new prophets, he would make pronouncements that I wanted to disagree with because they sounded pretentious: "The force that creates and expands infinitely throughout the cosmos is its greatest singularity. But it seems to have seeded the whole mess with this energy that manifests itself in both 'the force that through the green fuse drives the flower'—the creative urges that fuel the evolving generations and sometimes destroy us—and, in its purest form, what the Greeks called *agape*, selfless love."

Selfless love? What does a fifty-year-old bachelor living like a remittance man in the Yukon know about selfless love? Even those of us who have been well polished in the tumbler of marriage struggle with it. Women seem to have a physical advantage here, their bodies conscripting them into service once they find a second heart beating beneath their ribs.

The chortle of a meadowlark calls me back to the road as I pass tickle grass and foxtail in the ditch. There is a haze preventing the sun from becoming too hot, and casting a softer light. The wind has dropped to a gentle breeze. Up ahead I think I can see another buteo hawk, again on one of the highest cross-arms, perhaps a hundred and fifty feet above the field. I can't tell what it is, backlit by the sun. The height of the tower puts enough distance between us that it isn't flushing. There she goes, not a buteo at all. It's a peregrine falcon, big enough to be a female. Her leap is more purposeful and urgent, and in a moment her crescent form is borne away on powerful wingbeats, leaving a trace of her, a dark sliver on the sky fading from my retina.

"Sexual dimorphism" is the phrase for this kind of physical difference in the genders of a given species. Like most raptors, a female peregrine falcon is larger than her mate so she can hunt for larger prey and defend herself from males, who are often aggressive and reckless in courtship. Not a bad strategy. I was thinking about the differences between men and women a few weeks ago when I was sitting with a bunch of my closest male friends around a fire.

We usually call a fire every second month or so, and though our gatherings may not be the council fires of the Mohicans, we do a good job of celebrating when someone wins an award, gets a new job, gets rid of a bad job, gets married, has a child. This time, it was just late summer and time for a fire.

The woods were strange and familiar, as they are whenever we come. We never arrive in daylight, but that night the moon, spilling a blue luminescence between darker strokes of tree shadow, made it stranger than usual. Four of us were first to head in, feeling the rise in spirits that comes with renewing our tradition of getting lost in sixty acres of wooded bottomland ten miles from the city. We were happy, but quieter than we are when we come in knowing others are already at the site. My usual strategy of delaying our arrival long enough for the younger men to have the fire going had failed. One of the pleasures of the entry into the woods and getting a bit lost is hearing the crackle of fire, looking up to see an orange glow flicker through the screen of trees, and then hollering out, "Hail, good men of the burning sausage!" or something that suitably recapitulates in irony our descent from men and myths that once circled round other fires.

As we arrived at the opening in the woods, through a thicket of hazel and old nettles, over a ridge and into a swale with three very large green ash trees leaning inward from the circumference, we threw down our gear and headed into the bush to look for deadfall. After nine years, our walks to find firewood are taking us farther from the hearth. Each of us in his piece of the forest, we snapped twigs and branches, bundling them to carry back. I have mastered the art of finding hollow tree limbs. Easy to break and too punky to offer a lot of heat, they make for impressive loads when you return.

I stood back in the woods as I often do at such moments and watched the other men as they worked in their own solitudes gathering wood. Rick, a philosopher-king with a deceiving resemblance to John Denver, was across the clearing past the largest ash tree. His guest, a theatre technician visiting from Edmonton, was south of me somewhere snapping branches invisibly, and Matt, my oldest friend among the fire men, was crouched on the ground before a small pile of twigs, trying to coax it into flame.

Walking back with my arms around what looked to be half a cord of wood, I dumped it next to the hearth with a grunt. Matt made approving sounds and went back to blowing on the notebook paper I'd found in the car, which I was pretty sure this time was not Karen's yoga journal.

"Well, maybe the others will have some more paper," I said, hearing Ron's voice off by the road and then laughter. Moments later a large man-shadow appeared out of the moonlit gloom.

"'Oh, Elcid Barrett cried the town . . .'" It was Nathan, loaded with gear and food, in his best Stan Rogers baritone.

At the fire and at various spots in the woods around us, the reply rang out: "'How I wish I was in Sherbrooke now!'"

Stan, an honorary presence at every fire, usually isn't invoked until the wee hours, when our voices are tuned up from loud storytelling, but Nathan, timing impeccable as always, got us started early.

With more paper from the reinforcements, the fire was

suddenly aroar, casting a circle of light around us as we made space to sit as long as the food, drink, and bullshit would hold out. In the warm radiance I saw faces I had not seen in a few months, together with others I'd seen more recently: Andy, Rick, Ron, the other Ron, Nathan, Tom, Lorne, John, Fraser, and Matt. Only Jasper was missing, but since he moved to the west coast he only makes it to a couple of fires each year.

Bottles were pulled out (anything goes except for industrial brews), backpacks unzipped, and jars and packages opened. Everyone brings some food to share. This time we had lamb shishliki, sour cherries pickled in a herbal liqueur, deer sausage, several loaves of crusty bread, some good chocolate, olives, and brie. Over the years we have eaten everything from the backstrap of a mule deer to clay-fired roast chicken to Gruyère aged far beyond perfection in a broomball bag. From time to time one of the group will bring a dessert infused with extracurricular flavours that usually lead to early napping and sometimes a late bout of dirt-angel making when snow is unavailable. This seems to happen during the fires I miss, perhaps because I am the quiet, responsible one who stays more or less sober and eschews the herbal supplements.

Ron, a big-hearted engineer and mountaineer who comes decked out in Dan'l Boone garb, is our den mother, the one who makes sure no one is left behind. There is always something Ron needs to explain, and this time it was how he managed to get approval from his wife.

"I just made sure Melissa was listening when I talked to Trevor and Matt about having a fire. I told her we needed to have a fire because Trevor was going on this walk. She's not too sure about some of you guys, but if it's for Trevor, then it's okay."

Matt and I are the greybeards of the group and the younger men's wives perhaps imagine we lend a certain *gravitas* to the gatherings. All of us are hooked up with accomplished and creative women: dancers, artists, biologists, healers, yoga teachers, and the like. All are mothers and most do what they can to nurture community in a culture bent on killing it. If they were to gather at a fire, they would have a topic for discussion and a ritual for creating "sacred space." They would start off by "going around the circle for a bit of a check-in." They would not get drunk and they would take precautions, such as bringing a fire extinguisher.

Of course, we have our informal rituals. One is to install a set of handcrafted fire irons Nathan smithed in his shop—twisted iron stakes with hooks and a horizontal loop to support a cast-iron frying pan. As Ron explained his strategy, he was idly jabbing a stake into the ground beneath the fire, but it wouldn't yield. Someone speculated he could be probing the now-congealed stomach contents one of the group tossed on the coals after too much dessert at the last fire. Tom grabbed the iron from Ron and put his whole weight on it. When the stake broke through, it took Tom into the flames for a second. Lots of hollering from the rest of us as we pulled him out before his clothes could ignite.

This sounds bad, I realize, but no one has ever been hurt at a fire unless hangovers count. Our wives know the fires are an outlet for some behaviour they'd just as soon not see in the city anyway; and they know they could do worse. We aren't golfing every spare moment or watching a lot of NFL on TV. Most of us help with the cooking, keep our own homes in repair, share in the tasks of child-rearing, and bite our tongues when our wives take off for a child-free weekend.

Lesser men make their wives handle the birth control, offloading all the risks and discomfort that attend female contraception. Not us. After years of gloving up in bed produces the desired number of children, we head for the vasectomy table—not without some urging from our women, but we go bravely nonetheless. And we come to the fire afterward with our version of what Rick, the one single member of our group, refers to as "the Vasectomy Monologues."

"Oh my God. Here you go again, moanin' about your friggin' sacks." It starts with Jasper's cautionary tale of failing the sperm test afterward and, not without some pride, having to come back for seconds. Nathan turning to one side in his anaesthetic haze and seeing two little bits of snipped "tubing" on a tray. Me passing out after the doctor said, "Can you feel this?" as he gave a brisk little tug on something I did not know I had inside me but which seemed to be attached to my lungs. And someone, can't remember who, had swelling that he describes with reference to Texas grapefruit.

But we are more than reproductively responsible. We can do a lot of stuff. Here is a list of the things in our group portfolio: we sail boats, grow gardens, monitor ecosystems, host radio and television shows, write and perform folk songs, climb mountains of ice and rock, kayak over miles of open ocean, canoe through river rapids, hunt, fish, and trap, survey plant and bird populations, run stage crews for rock concerts and folk festivals, make dinnerware on a potter's wheel, create beautiful and useful things out of steel, stone, paper, and wood, flint-knap obsidian points, start fires with a bow drill, manage prescribed burns in forest and grassland, teach art to children, manage the retooling of an oil refinery, construct theatre sets, find and prepare edible wild plants, and predict the severity of the coming winter by reading the spleen of a pig.

Two of us work professionally as carpenters and the rest of us build things that we hope those two will never see. Someone is building a gypsy wagon, two others are just starting to build passive solar, super-insulated dwellings, and two more of us are planning to do likewise in the next few years. Some of us try to feed our families by hunting and growing our own food. Most of us get our food and beer locally if we can. We like living on the prairie that forms the marginal centre of the continent. We partake in its music, art, and politics, and are duly outraged at the things that destroy its ecology and community.

We are all of that, and yet I imagine every one of us would admit that our wives are better people and more mature than we are. And if we have trouble in our relationships, it is usually because our wives, not without reason, are disappointed with us.

I scanned the faces around the fire. What is it that brings us into the woods on an August night? In the eighties and nineties, men of our age and education were forming circles that looked something like this so that they could do the "men's work" of the mythopoetic movement made famous by poet Robert Bly. Though some of us have actually read *Iron John* and perhaps Sam Keen's *Fire in the Belly* too, these books and the male spirituality efforts they launched are never mentioned at our fires. No drumming, chanting, or dancing bare-chested before the council fire. No heart-to-hearts about our fathers and asshole basketball coaches. Any attempt at serious conversation is subsumed in the next joke. There is reason for our discomfort. When male efforts at "bonding" and soul work made it into the popular consciousness through television and print media, they were received with a mix of suspicion, derision, and dismissal. Men meeting in the woods at a fire became a caricature of the pitiful and ineffectual male following a fad in hopes of recovering his powers in a world supposedly transformed by feminism.

All of us at the fire can remember how it feels to be ridiculed. It was a part of boyhood we did not like, the shrinking between the legs that comes with being the one who is mocked and excluded. But there were many parts of being a boy that we did like, and coming to sit by a fire every couple of months lets us revisit them beyond the scrutiny of wives and other keepers of moral authority. That is exactly the difference between our fires and the ones lit by Robert Bly. The men's movement may have had its hubris and silliness, but it was at least attempting to bring men from boyhood to manhood, to help them pass that threshold in ways that bar mitzvahs and Christian confirmation never really managed to achieve and had in fact displaced.

Our fires, if we are honest with ourselves, are about trying to revive a carefree innocence we still cherish. For a time, we are boys camping in the woods again, among fire-lit shadows with the coyote-howled heavens overhead. There is wildness here and we feel it run through us and among us, leaping from voice to voice in every jibe and laugh, connecting us, making us for the time being a tribe worth belonging to. Anything wild has its dangers. Given the right moment, the fire could burn the woods and us too. The weather alone can kill you here, and our mid-winter fires are warmer for our knowing that. The pathways to our clearing in the woods let us feel lost as we come and go, lost enough to remember why we need each other.

Hard to say how much is the alcohol and how much is our own capacity to draw the fire into our bodies, but that unbridled spirit we feel as we stoke the flames and talk past midnight brings on something that gets us a little closer to feelings that could be called ecstatic. There are times when I think that bonds of a greater intimacy wait for us just outside the circle of light, somewhere in the shadows. If we have so far not made it there, it may be that we are not yet ready to give up the compensations that we feel we have coming to us when we gather.

In the incandescent light of our indoor lives as husbands, fathers, and employees, we set aside plans and dreams, rein in our sexual energies, and sacrifice our needs to the needs of our families. Can you blame us for wanting to pretend for a few hours that we have no one depending on us, for going to a place where we can let out some goofy boy energy and talk in ways that are unacceptable almost anywhere other than a steel mill, an oil well, or a construction site?

I remember wondering about my own father—a good man, faithful to wife and family—when I first heard him using the kind of language he must have lived with every day at the potash mine. It started to happen when I was twelve or thirteen. We were always alone, just the two of us in the garage or backyard, and I remember feeling a revulsion at the ugliness of the words—the way they sounded coming from his mouth raging at a skinned knuckle or dropped tool. The innocence remaining in me felt the injury too. A boy's heart open to everything, to the possibility that that anger might turn on him. (And it did, of course, from time to time.) A father trapped in his own wounds, the failures of his father and older brothers, no space to breathe in and out the disappointment of a father–son moment in the garage that did not go the way he wanted it to. And the boy thinking, *Is this how men talk to other men? Is this what you need to do to become a man?*

Boys wishing they were men; men wishing they were boys. In the face of ridicule from juveniles disguised as adults, the men's movement went more or less into hiding. Or perhaps it was too organized and facilitated, too denatured and afraid to use the stories we carry in our blood memory, the ones that, misapplied, failed us and that we might yet find useful were we able to hear them anew.

Like all men who think and care about the world we will leave to our children, the men who gather round our fires know that something needs to change. We might have theories about what the problem is, might even all agree that our gender of the human species is the most dangerous creature on the planet, but we are suspicious of grand solutions and "save the earth" agendas. Rightly so, because we know in the end it comes down to people living well in their families and communities. But we are afraid of what that might entail and so we stay where we are, afraid of the dark inside ourselves, afraid of falling into it, of even speaking about it.

I never got the knack of my father's cussing, but the bootless anger and nasty tone got into my tool belt of survival skills, and, along with the rest of my demons, they plague me yet. I keep going to the fires because what we have is a bond of sorts and maybe it helps keep me sane.

Sometimes on the drive back to the city, when things are quiet and someone is snoozing in the back seat, the dark enclosure of the car draws us into the kind of space where two or three of us can manage an honest conversation about intimate matters. Often the talk will turn to women: why our wives are so tense, why they are not more willing in bed, or why they demand so much from us. And that is about as far as we get. I drop the others off, drive home, and slip under the bedcovers next to Karen, smelling of woodsmoke and whisky. I go to sleep wondering if any of us would tell the others if our marriage was falling apart, or if we would hear the news of divorce from our wives.

Road Conditions: Before the Horse

A true walk changes the walker.
—Henry D. Thoreau, "Walking"

The first European man to walk across a big stretch of the continent and live to write about it was Cabeza de Vaca. Walking naked for most of the six thousand miles from Florida to Mexico City from 1527 to 1536, he found the forests interlaced with pathways made by people on foot. It was a land of walkers, and, travelling in their company, he was transformed from Spanish soldier to slave to trader to shaman before arriving at his destination. Soon, the horse would begin to change human movement on the continent, but de Vaca's journey, taking him back down through his own human ancestry, was shaped by walking in step with his indigenous hosts. It may be a long time before the land sees such walkers again.

3 Every Road

THINGS HAVE QUIETENED, now that I am past the shortcut for commuters. The odd plane drifts overhead, but finally the sound of the crickets is louder than the thrum of the city behind me. A flock of freshly minted cowbirds flies by. I am passing an acreage where there is a broad shelterbelt of trees around the yard. Earlier this summer I heard an orchard oriole singing from a maple here. A sign by the road says "Evergreen Energy Solutions" and there's a small wind turbine that is not turning in today's light wind. Hard to say what kind of energy solutions they offer—likely geothermal and solar.

One of the original reasons I wanted to make this walk was my worry that if things ever go sideways in the city— food shortages, climate change, pandemic, fuel scarcity, eco- nomic collapse, pick your apocalypse—we may have to come out to our cabin to live. To some people that will sound like survivalist paranoia, but it's a subject that comes up for dis- cussion with some regularity around our fires. Whether it will happen in our lifetimes is anyone's guess, but sooner or later we are going to run out of natural gas to heat our homes here in the hinterland. Sooner or later the agriculture systems we are addicted to are going to collapse, and those who outlast the famine will be growing a lot more of their own food. I doubled our garden last year and started keeping bees again. Next year we hope to double the garden again and plant some fruit trees.

I cross a rail line that's heading northeast. The tall weeds and introduced grasses in the railway easement all along it form the only high vegetation for a couple of miles in every direction other than shelterbelts around farmyards. Everything else has been shorn off: the hay meadows mowed, the oats, wheat, and canola down in swath or already in the bin, with just inches of stubble remaining. To the south I can see darker clouds, a little purple hue in the grey starting to gather now. The weather report predicted some rain today and it looks as though that might happen soon.

On my left now, Wascana Creek is coming near the road. Like most prairie streams at this time of year, it is barely flowing. A couple of teal dabble in one part of the oxbow and farther east a large shorebird stabs at the shallows. Likely an avocet, but it's too far away for me to make out without binoculars. Every so often large fish surface and flip in the water. Unfortunately, there is a good chance they are the introduced carp. Not sure what else that size can make a go of it in this polluted stream.

A story in yesterday's paper said that the concentrations of nitrogen in Wascana Creek are well above the World Health Organization's maximum. Pasqua Lake, the first large body of water downstream of this creek's confluence with the

Qu'Appelle River, collects much of the nutrient load contributed by the city. A limnologist at the University of Regina says it has ten times more nutrients than the Great Lakes had when they were pronounced dead in the 1960s and 1970s.

As well, a newly released paper shows alarming concentrations of compounds from antidepressants, antibiotics, and birth control pills. Undoubtedly, residues from the anti-inflammatories I have been taking for three months have made their way untreated into the watershed too.

Joseph always chalked this sort of thing up to the blindness he said goes with living in a "chronically addicted civilization." His letters were more diatribe than beatitude, but in one of them he was using "blessed are the pure of heart for they shall see God" to argue that when your heart is polluted, you cannot see your role in polluting the world around you. If you are living in a house that makes crystal meth, Joseph said, you're not likely to see what it's doing to the walls.

Fair enough. A civilization of people dependent on pharmaceuticals, bad processed food, and everything from TV to fossil fuels to loveless sex will not recognize God in a muddy little prairie stream, especially in its death throes. With hearts as polluted as our waterways, what chance have we of seeing the holy in this world?

Most galling of all, though, is the thought that the very faith that began with a man who said things like "blessed are the pure of heart for they shall see God" eventually helped produce the ethos that disenchanted the natural world, stripping it of spiritual meaning and handing it over to misbegotten human agency.

The Catholicism I grew up with had almost nothing to say about our responsibilities to nature, to the creatures in the river and the valley, or to the soil that grew crops above on the Plains. It didn't really seem to care what we do to get our daily bread as long as we are given it, and sex only came up as a cause of sin and condemnation. No one ever said we could meet God in a meadow, out fishing on the lake, or even sitting in a lonely place, a hilltop or a garden. Sure, the Gospels had Jesus baptized in a river, fasting in a desert, preaching on mountains, appearing to fishermen in a storm, sweating blood in a garden, but that was just a lot of poetic set location, nothing we should take seriously. And all that talk about trees, grass, wolves, sheep, sparrows, doves, foxes, serpents, mustard seeds, rain, yeast, salt, and light—Jesus didn't really expect us to care about those things. They were just handy metaphors, a bit of colour to liven up the grey oatmeal of a Sunday sermon.

By the time we met in university, Joseph had already shaken the dust of the old faith off his feet. He blamed Saint Augustine for most of the miscarriages of Christendom, including its failure to turn young people into adults. I can't recall why Augustine in particular got all the blame—something to do with body–soul dualism and Plato—but his argument was that the old initiatory processes vanished as Christians wiped out indigenous rituals that had once channelled youthful energies toward right relationship with family, community, and ecology.

I doubt Augustine or any one man can take all the credit, but one way or another, Christianity became a religion that set humanity at odds with the rest of creation. Instead of following Jesus's example and looking for healing and spirit in field, hilltop, and seaside, the faithful took the narrative indoors, built grand idols of brick and stone inside of which the approved rites and liturgies could be conducted by an elite of male priests while everyone else looked on from the pews.

Is there a better way to seed the world with people who don't know what their soul is for or how to open it up to the holiness all around them? Is there a better way to prepare the soil of our cultures to produce a declining patriarchy where confused fifty-two-year-old men sit on hilltops and wander out onto the back roads to see if they can finally wake up from the long snooze of adolescence?

Christianity and its spoiled child, "Western civilization," come in for a boatload of blame these days, almost all of it well deserved. The wreckage is all along this road: over here, we have the great prairie commons emptied of its native people, and on your right, a farmstead on land stripped bare by industrial agriculture, the depleted soils crying out the shame of our Church-ordained right to plunder the earth. There is a nice little purgative hit that comes with blaming. It feels good for a while. You draw your line in the sand, declare what it is you don't believe, and then do whatever it takes to dissociate yourself from any nagging residue of ancestral guilt for obliterating indigenous cultures and wilderness in the New World. If you read the right books and watch the right documentaries, you might be able to trade in any negative feelings for the comforts of joining the smart people who have figured out exactly what is behind our self-destructive myth of progress.

I like consolation as much as the next person, but in the end, blaming religion for cultural and ecological destruction is about as satisfying as blaming the state for the modern market economy and climate change. Justifiable, true, and easily demonstrated, but only a subset of a larger narrative that is much harder to disown, particularly if you are male.

A while ago, Karen gave up on converting me to her eco-feminist perspective on patriarchy and civilization. You know the one: everything destroying the earth, from tar sands to the World Bank, has been hatched by men in positions of power. She used to start off with a sweeping generalization about men in charge of military spending or pesticide regula-tion or the Vatican, and then support it with a few brickbats about male dominance of politics, commerce, science, and reli-gion, as though the mere fact that men hold all the power-ful positions means that they are responsible. By now you'd think she'd know that men are irresponsible. After she was finished, I'd make a lot of sophisticated scoffing noises to buy some time, and then carefully mount my counter-argument: women have to take their share of the blame too. Surely she can see that women are the ones filling the shopping malls and redecorating monster homes in the suburbs, rapaciously fuel-ling the consumerism that erodes community and destroys our waterways and wildness. Of course, every good feminist has an answer for that.

"You're just describing a distortion of womanhood suffering under the testosterone agenda," she would say, or something like that, because I can't actually recall her exact words. "Before agriculture"—oh yeah, here it comes—"in more matriarchal cultures, women were valued for their spiritual wisdom, intuition, and abilities to co-operate, make connections, and form community. And, of course, their sacred capacity to bring forth and nurture life."

Wait a minute, I'd say, so men are responsible not merely for patriarchy but for the collusion of women too? Isn't that just another way of denying women their own power of action and accountability? Huh? Isn't it? Huh? Besides, show me your proof that there ever was a matriarchal golden age when people treated one another and the rest of creation with tenderness. Most respected archaeologists and anthropologists say that was just a lot of New Age hooey.

Faced with my scintillating argument-closer, Karen would inevitably retreat, not because my superior reasoning was male, of course, but just because it was superior. In the years since we first had those discussions, though, my arguments have begun to sound a little less convincing. And I hate that, because all the fun of being right evaporates like spit in a hot wind when you start doubting yourself.

Just for argument's sake, let's say the eco-feminists have it right. Christian patriarchy destroyed religious understanding of our co-belonging with other creatures, and Christian men were minding the store when Western civilization gave birth to science, the Enlightenment, colonialism, economic determinism, the modern nation-state, the multinational corporation, and nearly every other human influence blamed for the state of the world today. What's more, Christian orthodoxy silenced humanity's long-standing dialogue with other creatures, freeing us up to exploit nature beneath an umbrella of indifference to the other-than-human souls around us.

That's all helpful if you want to publish a dissertation to explain the mess we are in. It may even lead to a few big ideas about rediscovering the sacred feminine, deepening our ecological consciousness, re-enchanting the world, and transforming to an earth-centric instead of anthropocentric world view. All of which sounds hopeful enough, but a half century of this kind of palaver hasn't taken us very far. Some would say we've just gone in circles back to a familiar juncture—that place where we once again face the puzzle of our holy longings, and their capacity to break or make bonds to community and nature.

One of the dangers of walking on a prairie road is that you find yourself believing your own grand imaginings. It's the height that does it. The road is elevated for drainage, which means even the soles of my sandals travel a foot or two above the flat plain encircling me. When your head is nearer the clouds than to sea level and looking at any terrestrial thing means you have to cast your eyes downward, a kind of mountaintop mania can take hold of your brain. Once, when I was walking on a trail across fescue prairie benchlands in the Cypress Hills, the whole thing about religion and our broken bonds with the rest of creation was fresh in my mind from having just finished Thomas Berry's *The Dream of the Earth* the night before.

As the trail wove through patches of shrubby cinquefoil and past lupine flowers, my feet fell into a plodding rhythm and a peculiar light-headed, trancelike feeling came over me. I could see in my mind a fork in the trail. I never got there, but I felt sure it was up ahead, and just as sure that the same fork was there on every other trail and road on the prairie, on the continent, on every continent. This is hard to explain, but it was as though every footstep on every road was heading, beyond the failure of all science and philosophy, to a choice where we either relinquish our spiritual monopoly in favour of a democracy of all creaturely souls or we die out clinging to delusions of our monarchic rights above a kingdom of dispirited objects.

Wise men have said that the outer world we have made, of landscapes denuded and denatured, dead zones in the oceans, and thawing ice caps, and the inner world we suffer, of addiction and depression, come from the same break or shattering of relationship. The religious ties that bound us to the earth, that had us talking to rivers and forests, have been broken and we can no longer hear or speak to anyone but ourselves. In that "spiritual autism," to use Thomas Berry's phrase, we have become the loneliest of souls on a small planet crowded by too many of our kind.

Sitting here by the creek, surrounded by many-flowered aster and sow thistle in exuberant bloom, I realize that each blossom has one or more skinny native wasps. There is some scentless camomile here, one introduced species that even the farmers hate. Something is giving off a sweet hay smell. It must be the asters. No. The camomile is scentless, so I try the thistle. Yes, sow thistle smells sweet, which explains the wasps. Scent is one of this life's most intimate ways of communicating. You have to be in proximity to the one giving off the scent, and if it appeals, you draw near to breathe the essence into your own body. What other exchanges would be possible if I could set aside everything that closes me against such intimacy?

As I inhale the aroma of a thistle that came with my Christian ancestors out onto the prairie, I think again about our addicted civilization. Even those of us free of the torment of drugs or alcohol suffer from dependency on lifeways and processes that destroy the beings we no longer communicate with. At the same time, indigenous people, the ones most recently extracted from deeper relationship with grass, and river, and stone, seem tragically vulnerable to the empty promises of intoxication. I wonder if our very susceptibility to both kinds of addiction may owe something to the fact that we stopped recognizing and communicating with spirits in the creatures around us. Physically distanced from wild nature, and cut off from the voices and healing influence of the more-than-human world, are we so starved for real spirit that we look for a surrogate in chemical spirits, whether they come in a bottle or in our brains—making ourselves slaves to the false religion of the dopamine rush?

How curious to think that the human longing at the roots of the crisis may also offer the only way out of it. Whether we call it "religion" or something less troubled with bad memories, a homeopathic prescription may be in order. Is there a spiritual tincture that would lift my relationship with the avocet, the carp, the teal, or the chickens in my garden beyond the cataloguing and binaries of a world view dominated by scientism: this one wild, that one domestic, this one native, that one introduced? If the creek speaks to me, how do I become receptive enough to hear it? I don't know if my ancestors ever spoke to the rivers and trees or listened to the stars, and I don't know exactly what silenced that loquacious universe, but I am prepared to do some talking and listening now.

It's all here with me, as I walk past ditch grass, slough, and abandoned farmstead, the wind running over abused fields and pastures. I strain to hear other voices, but the same old narrative about what we had and what we lost is roaring in my ears again.

Road Conditions: Walking to Free Land

The interior West was not a place but a way, a trail to
the Promised Land, an adventurous, dangerous rite of passage.
—Wallace Stegner, *The American West as Living Space*

When settlers first came west to begin farming the prairie, you could get a homestead of 160 acres of free land, though there was a ten-dollar registration fee. The earliest and poorest of them walked from wherever the railway came nearest the area in which they hoped to stake a claim, carrying a few simple tools and supplies. After choosing an "unclaimed" quarter, they would have to trek to the nearest land-titles office to register their homestead, often travelling fifty or one hundred miles on foot. Less about soul than keeping body and soul together, these long walks became founding myths for families when that first walker succeeded in rooting himself and his descendants in a particular parcel of the prairie.

4 Shadows

BACK ON THE ROAD, I pass by a place I have known for years as Monica Farm. A big white barn faces the road, with "Monica. 1928" painted in a large classic typeface above the door. Across the yard, a small house with several outbuildings, all white. Occupied, but no one appears to be home.

I reach down to the road in front of me and retrieve the breast feather of an owl, a softness my hands are too coarse to feel. Tawny with grey vermiculation on the tip—perhaps a great horned owl. I wonder if it lost the feather while hunting waterfowl. Monica Farm contains a slough where I first learned how to identify ducks. This year the water comes right to the roadside. At the near end I can make out twenty ducks in the shallows, small, unidentifiable shorebirds with them. I did not want the weight of binoculars and knew this would be one spot I would miss them.

A flock of fifteen killdeer lift and move off east. There is something else crouched there, though—a pair of lesser yellowlegs on the mud flats. I can't make out the smaller birds, but they are likely semi-palmated or least sandpipers, the little guys no larger than a sparrow. Blue-winged teal are flying up now in groups of five or six. Then more killdeer. A flight of gadwall, a greater yellowlegs. Then an avocet comes sailing in on arced wings, all white and black, with the burnt orange of spring gone for the winter. A total of four or five lesser yellowlegs, maybe twenty killdeer. And here and there the leasts and semis creeping along in the mud, hidden by the background hues behind them. There are yellow-headed blackbirds moulting in the cattails and bulrushes. A bigger flight of teal lift off the mud flats where they were loafing. I see two, four, six avocets now on a muddy patch that I have been coming to look at for thirty years. One of them still has a bit of orange on its head. The avocets circle around with their necks dipping down below breast level, heads arced forward. They make a two-sided bowed cross because the wings are held in an arc, but the body is arcing too, from the head to the hump of the back and then down again to the dangling feet as they fly over the wetland.

I sit in the roadside grass at the broadest part of the slough, eighty paces across, three hundred long. Water comes right to the road edge and I can see a scattering of dead fish no more than an inch and a half long—sticklebacks, perhaps. In the middle of them floats an addled duck egg. Off-white with little dark brown speckles peppering it, a leftover from the summer's short frenzy of nesting. Even a bad egg looks complete and perfect.

A few things have disappeared along this road since I first started birding here in the early eighties—mostly scraps of native grass and the grassland birds that hung on for a while. A lot has changed, but Monica Slough remains. Robert took me here first to learn the ducks. Much of what I know about birds came along this road on outings with Robert, a prairie naturalist obsessed with birds and mushrooms but well versed in everything from stars to stones, orchids to snakes. He haunted this place spring, summer, and fall. It was in a field beside the slough thirty years ago that he saw one of the last Eskimo curlews ever recorded on the Great Plains. Robert wasn't a trifler—he knew the whimbrel, the long-billed curlew, all the other possibilities. And he bravely made his single-observer report: Eskimo curlew. Monica Slough.

As I sit still, the teal are getting more comfortable with my presence and are starting to float back in. Two of them are paddling over toward me, not realizing I'm here. These may be green-winged teal. I'll see when they get closer.

I doze in the warmth. The torn ligaments in my shoulder have been making it hard to sleep. Most nights I get a few hours in bits and pieces, but I can nod off at the drop of a hat during the day. In front of me here, six feet off into the pond, there are five sticks from last year's bulrushes amidst this year's growth and some new cattails emerging. The dried-up stems from last year, broken off and yellow with dark brown stains where they each touch the surface, make such graceful, simple patterns in the water. Dead sticks jutting out of a slough, but, arranged just so, their reflections form a visual haiku as elegant as egret plumes. A wind passes over and the dark lines on the water wiggle hypnotically.

Between consciousness and sleep, there are those unfamiliar places where you can sometimes slip into other ways of being present to things passing through. A whisper on waking, a moment where you could swear another body has pressed against yours with a warm embrace, and then, as you stir to that thought, the sense of it fades. A region is opened up, you enter briefly, leave again, but get no map to find your way back. It happens too rarely in my life, because I have been faint-hearted in the face of things I cannot explain. Rilke wrote of the courage required to stay open to existence in all its possibilities:

> We must assume our existence as broadly as we in any way can; everything, even the unheard-of, must be possible in it. That is at bottom the only courage that is demanded of us: to have courage for the most strange, the most singular and the most inexplicable that we may encounter. That mankind has in this sense been cowardly has done life endless harm; the experiences that are called "visions," the whole so-called "spirit-world," death, all those things that are so closely akin to us, have by daily parrying been so crowded out of life that the senses with which we could have grasped them are atrophied. To say nothing of God.

The days I fasted and prayed on the hilltop in my circle of buffalo sage, I had a few brilliant moments when my whining managed to get beyond the pain in my shoulder, the growling in my belly, and the ticks and ants biting my arse, so that I could plunge into the deeper ponds of despond where my self-pity likes to wallow. Day one, I convinced myself for the thousandth time that I deserve a better life, one where having five dependants does not require me to keep a nine-to-five job. Day two, with hunger vying with heatstroke to be the main theme occupying my moaning, I eventually located another favourite slough of confused entitlement: desire—for sex, enlightenment, greatness, a restored grassland wilderness, peace on earth, and everything else that is supposed to come my way. The first two nights there was plenty to complain about—mosquitoes taking up where the ants and ticks had left off, hard ground, shoulder, and a deer that kept me awake with all its huffing and stamping noises. I'd sit up and look around in the moonlight, but could never see it, then fall back to my sleeping bag, with a refrain going through my head: what the hell am I doing here? I starve myself, pray my ass off, suffer through heat, bug bites, and boredom, and get nothing. Nothing but a cryptic candy-wrapper message, and Lord knows where that came from anyway.

Each morning, when the rising sun made it impossible to sleep any longer, I'd sit up and resolve to do better. Mornings were good. The heat and wind were down, the valley was bathed in the warm tones of sunrise, and there were birds. I watched flights of black-crowned night herons make their way back to the bottomland marsh after the dawn hunt for frogs. Redstarts and vireos sang in the coulee north of me. Ring-necked ducks whizzed overhead on wings that sang in the air. My favourite, though, was the daily visit of a Say's phoebe, a small, unassuming flycatcher with a wash of burnt orange on its lower belly. He had been singing all spring down by our cabin, apparently unable to attract a mate. I was surprised to see him all the way up on top of the hill but liked watching him sally out to snap at a fly with an audible *snick*.

While I watched the birds each morning, I would see a small figure walking out on the road a half mile away in the valley bottom. Too far to see the face, but I recognized the light step. Karen would stop and turn to look up at the hill I was sitting on. I would wave and she would lift an arm in reply, then sit for a few minutes before heading back toward the cabin.

Karen knows every bit of my self-absorbed, neurotic indulgences without me having to say a word. Probably knew I was up there whining and what I was whining about. When I got back from the hospital and was icing my shoulder in bed with a bag of frozen peas, we talked. She suggested some alternative therapies I might try: acupuncture, homeopathy, reiki, ayurvedic medicine, chakra work, and a few others I cannot remember.

I gave my usual response. "You know I don't feel comfortable doing that stuff. I'd like to, but I don't know what it is. I guess my heart's just not in it."

"Your heart? It's your head that's not into it. Okay, you're the one with the injury, not me."

She was right, of course. I didn't have a clue about my heart, the things it was supposed to do or be. Around that time I was reading in Bill Plotkin's *Soulcraft* about the "initiatory journey," the discovery of soul that is needed if we are to fully mature and receive the gifts of our own distinct nature. Plotkin says we spend from puberty into early adulthood building a house made of our world view and personality. We just get it built, move in to get comfortable, and there comes a knock at the door. Someone comes in—an angel, a spirit, in the form of loss, depression, crisis, some challenge to identity—and says it's time to go. It feels like an eviction, but it's an invitation. Plotkin, a depth psychologist and wilderness guide, says it is actually a "call to adventure."

"Adventure." *I can do that*, I thought. I already know a bit about spirituality. Done some yoga, some meditating. I've read Thomas Merton, Jack Kornfield, Thich Nhat Hanh, Eknath Easwaran, and the other two Eck-men: Meister Eckhart and Eckhart Tolle. This should be familiar turf.

Twenty-three pages into the book, though, it was clear Plotkin was talking about an adventure and a spiritual path I had absolutely no experience with. He described the direction in which most spiritual traditions head in the West—even our attempts at Buddhism—as "upward." Heading for the light of heaven or inner enlightenment, we apply mindfulness, contemplation, prayer, and meditation to transcend the ego and find peace and unity with all that is. Any longings or visions that well up inside us are a distraction we are simply to observe and let pass.

This upward orientation and detachment is important in our spiritual lives, Plotkin explains, but it is only one half of the whole. The part we seem to have abandoned in modern efforts at spirituality is the descent into the murky caverns of soul, where we search for our particular place in the world and learn what it will take to embody our soul's service to community and creation. That sounded a lot like the way Daniel talks, the journey he's been gently nudging me toward for a few years now. What makes us avoid the downward journey? Even asking this question, Plotkin says, puts us "in a position similar to women raised in Western religions who have long suspected that half the story—the divine feminine—has been left out. But this similarity is not coincidental. . . . The wild, earthy, sensual half of the spiritual journey is the half that the uninitiated masculine mind experiences as feminine and therefore as non-essential and perhaps undesirable or even harmful."

I read that passage to Karen, hoping she would appreciate all I was learning while I lived on the bed with my soggy bag of peas, analgesic rubs, and anti-inflammatories. "That's wonderful, dear," she said, and went downstairs to make supper. That got me. She thinks I am afraid even to try one of those voodoo therapies she and her friends always use, so how could I ever expect to dive down into the darkness of soul?

Making a promise to myself that I would be as open, uncritical, and receptive as possible, I got up and looked for a business card I had seen earlier in our house. It was for a massage therapist named Holly who also does "energy work." Booking the appointment took some energy work, but after that, I was surprised at my own ease with the whole thing. I walked into Holly's office a few days later, looking forward to it, even curious about the process.

"Yes, but there is something you are afraid of. Do you feel that—right there?"

Holly, who had removed her sandals to get grounded, was not talking about a place in my shoulder but some region of my "subtle body," I think. She was distractingly pretty, vibrant with health. After a deep breath, she put her chin down and glared with an intensity that had me backing away.

"You fell on your left side. Do you know what that means?" She smiled while I answered with a no. "That is the feminine side. You have injured the feminine in yourself, in your life. Are you suppressing feminine energies in yourself, or in the world around you? Does that sound possible?"

"Maybe. I don't know." It took a minute, but I started to think about the women in my life. With a wife and three daughters, I live in a house awash in estrogen, but that seems to have made me all the more resistant. I thought of the times I have yelled in anger at each of them, and of a good friend who last year suggested I am too controlling and pushy with Karen. That's crazy, I said at the time. And I thought of those years early in our marriage when I was threatening to quit my job as a writer at a provincial Crown corporation. We had a new baby at home, our third, and Karen was home-schooling the first two. I became convinced I would lose my mind if I had to stay another year in my corporate writing job, but I couldn't see then how vulnerable my little family was, how important my role as the one who makes an income, and how near I came to making a desperate and possibly disastrous move. Faced with my craziness, Karen began a course to certify as a childbirth education instructor. She'd spend the day teaching the children on the kitchen table while nursing a newborn, keeping house, paying the bills, and cooking meals. When we were all in bed, she'd be up with a lamp on in the otherwise dark living room studying from binders and textbooks that came in the mail: a beautiful young mother, just wanting to raise her babies at home, but so afraid her mercurial husband was going to either quit his job or go nuts. I eventually pulled back and saw what I was doing, but it took me years to wake up and recognize what a stable force my employment has been in our lives.

I looked at Holly and gave her my best blank doofus stare.

"Let me ask it this way: do you think you may be too aggressive, forcing things, not listening to subtler messages and energies, just pushing through? Is that the way you've been approaching life? Is that how you're going to heal from this fall? You have fallen for a reason, fallen into something— what could that be?"

That was when I came clean and admitted that I have some trouble with this kind of "energy work" or any talk about ch'i or chakras. I'm divided. I can accept that there may be an energetic body, subtle energies that hold together the more observable cellular, biochemical life understood by science. But I have no idea how to experience it, how to feel my heart and such energies, how to use awareness of them to make decisions. I have never been any good at reading even the messages my body yells loudly at me, never mind whispering. I used to injure myself in the weight room regularly. Even with yoga, I am always going too far and irritating the places where tendons connect to bone. And now I am having trouble telling when I should pull back on a physiotherapy exercise because it's hurting my shoulder.

Holly listened and told me it may be that I just need more balance in my life. I fell because I lost my balance, she said, living too strongly on the masculine yang energies, neglecting my heart, and ultimately doing damage to the yin side of things. "What are you afraid of?" she asked.

I thought of the pigeons. "Well, I'm pretty afraid of getting up on the roof again."

I thanked her and left the office knowing exactly what I was afraid of, though I was not going to admit it to her: "The wild, earthy, sensual half of the spiritual journey," that's what. "The half that the uninitiated masculine mind experiences as feminine and therefore as non-essential." A man would be a fool not to be afraid, for that half holds all the shadows, all the demons.

Road Conditions: Women Walking Generously

Attention is the rarest and purest form of generosity.
—Simone Weil, *Waiting for God*

Most of the long walkers we hear about in myth and historic record seem to be men walking toward a goal: hunters or pastoralists seeking new terrain, explorers mapping coastlines, or poets making their lines across country. Leigh Ann Craig, a professor of history at Virginia Commonwealth University, sifted through the miracle accounts at European pilgrimage shrines to show that, despite discouragement from clerics and other men, the pilgrim trails of the late Middle Ages were flush with women walking for the revival of body and soul. While few historic sources say anything about women pilgrims, or record their thoughts or experiences, about half of the miracle stories are about women and girls. The same data show that while 75 percent of men went on pilgrimage to pray for themselves, almost 50 percent of the women walked for the healing of a child, friend, or relative. Craig believes that pilgrimage offered women a form of unsupervised freedom and self-directed devotion in an era when they were constrained by law and social norm at every turn.

5 Pathways

LEAVING MONICA SLOUGH, I continue east toward the bridge where the creek crosses under the road. In addition to the legions of clouded sulphurs and cabbage whites fluttering over the fields, I am beginning to see a lot more dragonflies. A friend who studies them told me recently that these mid-sized ones with red bodies are cherry-faced meadowhawks. I pick a dead one up from the gravel and dust off its cellophane wings to look at the veining there, a pattern with many other echoes in living things: the branching of a tree, a network of capillaries, or game trails over the land.

As I walk, my brain is leaping blithely from cortex to cortex following the nodes of its own networks, making pathways to connect my wandering thoughts. This kind of mindless introspection is our default mode, and in fact neuroscientists call it that: "the default mode network," or DMN. They think of it as a kind of dark energy in the mind's inner universe, a pattern of brain activity that is always on in the background. Early research concluded that the DMN develops during childhood, but now it is thought to be there almost from birth.

I was a gifted daydreamer in school and have the report

cards to prove it. Some of my earliest memories are of zoning out as I lay on our lawn, drew cartoon characters on our front step, or dawdled on detour to school over a spongy fen littered with snails. I still associate the feelings from those reveries with a kind of boundless contentment, a dissolving into the world around me. Any capacity I have to be imaginative and reflective comes from the boy who learned the trick of dreaming with his eyes open, but I'd barely reached adulthood when I discovered that living mindlessly in the brain's default mode has its costs over time.

Brain researchers now believe that a wandering mind is often a worrying mind. Gathering real-time data from volunteers who reported on their thought patterns throughout the day using an application on their smart phones, one study found a strong correlation between adult daydreaming and unhappiness. That made sense to me, as did another study that associates an overactive DMN with anxiety and depression.

By the age of nineteen, the wandering paths in my brain had worn some deep grooves, and the shadowy side of the DMN's dark energy was becoming apparent. Networks once used for reverie became flooded with fear, but at the time the only thing I knew about my mind was that I was very likely losing it. It seemed to happen overnight, and in fact I remember the date: December 16. Dreams replaced by sleepless terror at night and anxiety and nausea during the day—the winter became an endless nightmare of angst narrated by the unhappy souls I was studying in university, from Kierkegaard to Eliot to Sartre. I lost weight, saw doctors and therapists, and tried their advice and drugs. By spring it was gone, more or less, but I lived in fear of it coming back, and though it did—twice over the next decade—I had developed a daily practice that, these many years later, I find out was exactly what my undisciplined mind needed to weather its storms.

Right from the beginning, meditation was for me a kind of prayer, a way to tap on the window between the seen and the unseen. I began with the concentration practice advocated by John Main, a Benedictine monk who adapted Hindu meditation methods, bringing them to the West in the 1970s. As a young Englishman working in Kuala Lumpur in the foreign service, Main met a Hindu monk, the Swami Satyananda. For a year and a half he came to Satyananda for weekly sessions to learn about meditation. Back in England, he joined the Benedictines and, not without encountering some resistance, eventually convinced his order that meditation is a legitimate form of prayer with roots in their own history that run back to John Cassian and the fourth-century Desert Fathers.

Though my practice has changed over the years, incorporating what is called "insight meditation" in the Buddhist tradition, I still open up Main's slender book *Word into Silence* from time to time. Its spare and elegant prose has a soothing effect on me even now, but the older I get, the harder it is to recall the agitation that brought me to Main and the practice.

Recent work at the Yale Therapeutic Neuroscience Clinic using magnetic resonance imaging showed that meditation practice of all kinds allows people to enter a new relationship with their default mode networks. Even in beginners, the DMN monkey-mind becomes less dominant, less of a default mode, and other networks—those in charge of self-awareness and cognition—become more active.

None of which would have been news to Main or anyone else who has sat within the three thousand years of tradition long enough and still enough to let the muddy waters of the mind settle out. Even so, I am enough of a science junkie to appreciate the validation.

The surprise for me after thirty years of sitting each morning is that I still have a distracted, undisciplined mind. As I walk the road, I can manage about three or four steps, staring down at my sandals, staying for the most part in the present moment, and then I am bounding after my daydreams, following a well-worn path toward one cherished narrative or another: Cargill and Monsanto are inheriting the earth; it's a shame we killed the local dairy industry; why don't we tax luxuries like tropical vacations and use the revenue to start young farmers off growing food for a local market?

The difference now is that I know my mind is a monkey, and whether I choose to let it run loose or tether it awhile, I am less inclined to take it seriously. And from time to time the practice, whether it is in sitting or in walking, lets me rest in the natural great peace between my thoughts. That space of nothingness is where the heart makes room for grace. Animals live full-time in that room, which is why their movements are always grace-full.

As I near the bridge, I see a hawk, a northern harrier, wheel and pounce into the half-acre meadow on the far side of the creek. A brief tussle, the barred tail angling up from the grass. It regains its composure, pausing to get a better grip on whatever life it has found, and then launches in a single spring from its long legs, shroud-grey wings sweeping to bear it aloft again. A small body dangles from the shadow flapping off to the east. A scene I have witnessed dozens of times on the prairie, often with a shudder of awe and pity, overlapped by a longing to be or have some of that dance from sky to grass and back again.

The hawk, with its speed and joy and perfect grace, moves in a kind of prayer. Its truth is older than the Rig-Veda and every scripture since, and lies beneath the words that came to the generations through the Buddha and Jesus, told again and refined in the writings of contemplatives from Thomas Merton to Jon Kabat-Zinn to Simone Weil: *prayer is attention.*

Mary Oliver wrote a short and stirring poem that describes a similar encounter with a hawk. She titled it "The Real Prayers Are Not the Words, but the Attention that Comes First." Dark, inattentive energies may swirl in our brains, but they are formed from the same mysteries that spawned our consciousness, our capacity to pay attention, and our religious longings. Being here and awake enough to see the hawk is our real prayer, a way to widen that space for heart, room enough to grow out of our self-absorption, addictions, and neuroses.

Road Conditions: Barefoot Mindfulness and Walking in the Pure Land

"Take off your shoes!" Realize that the ground on which
we stand is holy ground. The act of taking off our shoes is a
gesture of thanksgiving, and it is through thanksgiving
that we enter sacramental life.
—Brother David Steindl-Rast, OSB

Benedictine monk Brother David Steindl-Rast, a leader in Christian–Buddhist dialogue, believes that there is no better way to gratitude and sacrament than walking barefoot. Going barefoot, he says, is a way to encounter grace in your body by getting directly in touch with the earth, feeling the stones and grass beneath your feet. His Buddhist counterpart Thich Nhat Hanh says that mindful walking awakens us to the truth that the "pure land" of Buddhist longing and the "Kingdom of Heaven" of Christian longing are not merely celestial realms but present realities available to us in every step we take upon the earth. "To be making steps on this beautiful planet is a miracle. Master Lin Chi said that the miracle is not to walk on water or in thin air, but the miracle is to walk on the Earth. . . . With the energy of mindfulness, our feet become the Buddha's feet."

6 Of Stones and Rivers

REACHING THE BRIDGE, I walk down the bank for another look at the Wascana. It will be the last time I see any flowing water for the rest of the walk. In the city, it's visible from our bedroom window, a muddy brown shadow sliding through willow trees. Walking its margins, I have shown our children pelicans and kingfishers, muskrats and mink. A pair of beavers raise a family each year in a bank lodge a short walk from our house. At the onset of winter we have found hundreds of small fish frozen in the top three inches of ice. This past spring, snowmelt turned it into a torrent, pushing the creek up over its banks. We had a small lake for a while, kept at bay by sandbags at the end of our block. For once, everyone noticed the creek, gave some attention to the living mystery at the heart of the Regina Plains, the creature that bears away the full spectrum of our virtue and vice. That quiet and mostly forgotten service, receiving unquestioningly everything we wash, dissolve, flush, rinse, and eliminate, deserves, if nothing else, our admiration and respect.

A few minutes ago, a helicopter tracked north along the eastern horizon, a sinister and alien thing rupturing the holy air. Helicopters are almost always bad news for prairie. Only the resource industry can afford the hourly rates. Until recently, a helicopter meant oil and gas, but this one is prospecting for a multinational mining giant from Brazil. Vale S.A., infamous for its contempt for unions and human rights and its destruction of rainforest and rivers, has come north in search of a new form of wealth in a world that is running out of the fertility it needs to feed its seven billion.

Potash, like arable land, has become one of the hottest commodities for international venture capital, and this part of the prairie has more of it in the basement than any other place on the planet. Vale wants to build a solution potash mine four or five miles south of this road, which means it will need a lot of water—as much as 40 million litres every day. That is about fifteen Olympic-sized swimming pools. Although Wascana Creek itself could not meet that demand, the company says it might build a seventy-kilometre pipeline to take water out of the Qu'Appelle River at Katepwa Lake. A watershed that is already stressed from all sides, the Qu'Appelle can ill afford to surrender that much water to extract potash for export only to have it converted into toxic brine. To know the Qu'Appelle and its tributaries, the neglect and abuse they suffer year by year, is to know just how far we are from the bioregional ideal that would have us renew human connection to place by discovering our bonds with rivers and streams.

Once I am under the bridge, the water looks more inviting than I thought it would. I've swum in creeks where cattle stood upstream of me, and in the Milk, the Missouri, and the Saskatchewan, where the waters are too muddy to see your hand just below the surface, but the reports of Wascana's chemical contamination have me spooked. I decide to keep my clothes on and just soak my feet.

I kick off my hiking sandals and stand on the grass above a muddy patch sloping down to the water. I can just make out a current now, with a little back eddy on my side of the creek. It is the unceasing motion of a river that always makes me want to jump in. Like for like, the restlessness within is drawn toward the greater power moving by. Roderick Haig-Brown must have known the feeling. Perhaps Canada's first bioregionalist writer, Haig-Brown penned twenty-five books with titles such as *A River Never Sleeps*, at a desk that looked out on his beloved Campbell River, a stone's throw away. Fishing and wading its shallows year-round, in his last decade of life Haig-Brown finally gave in to the pull, setting aside his waders and fly rod and putting on a wetsuit and snorkelling gear. On Vancouver Island, I met a man named David who often went snorkelling with Haig-Brown in the river. The two of them would spend hours together in the shallows quietly following the Coho salmon and cutthroat trout between boulders as they came in from the sea a mile or two downstream. In a letter to a daughter a few years before he died, Haig-Brown said that he had managed to swim the entire length of the Campbell River in his wetsuit. He was sixty-four at the time.

There is no accounting for the effect of one man's love for a river. When people asked Haig-Brown about his accomplishments as a conservationist, he always said that he had none, that all he had accomplished was a reputation as a conservationist and that the fish, birds, rivers, and forests he had tried to defend were still losing ground. In spite of his opposition, a hydro dam was built on the Campbell River, but today on Vancouver Island some of the world's best stream and estuary restoration work has been done by people inspired by Haig-Brown. Salmon streams all over the Pacific Northwest are being defended and restored by small local groups established by his followers. A fisheries biologist told me that if it had not been for the testimony of Haig-Brown, there would be a dam on the Fraser River today. The Pacific salmon populations are still declining and under attack on all sides, but if there had not been a Haig-Brown to swim in the Campbell River, the battle to save these iconic creatures of sea, river, and forest would have been given up long ago.

I roll my pant legs higher and take a step onto the muddy slope. That foot goes straight for the creek, pulling me along with it, sliding me on my arse toward an unplanned swim. A brief thought flashes through my mind, telling me I might as well go in for the full immersion now, but I'm not sure I'll be able to get back up the slope, which is steeper and slicker than I'd realized. Grabbing on to a rock, I heave myself out onto the mud and then onto the grass, where I can wring my pants out. Yes, there is something about flowing water. The Baptists have it right: when people need to be sanctified, take them down to the river and plunge them in. Moving it indoors denatured the rite to ensure control over anything that wants to flow or pull us in.

The prissy sprinkling I got as an infant would have been

forgettable even if I had been old enough to remember it. Sacrament is worthy of the energies we feel out in the open air, where there are rivers, dirt, wind, sun, and stars. Even my first Eucharist or Communion has faded away, though I was seven or eight at the time. I have a photograph where I am standing with a friend in front of our Esterhazy house, wearing a white shirt and tie, with a red arm band and some dress pants my father sewed for me out of the remains of his wedding suit. The boys in the photo had no chance to understand the meaning of that early rite of faith they had just undergone, not only because they were too young but because it was held inside a church. In the dimly lit chapel, the priest's words echoed from brick walls and fell to the floor, and I was left unstirred by the earthy, bread-to-body, wine-to-blood truth that goes with being a living, enfleshed soul bound to every other particle of creation.

Strangely, there are no churches on this road. In fact, I am walking in a landscape that bears almost no monuments to human spiritual longing: no standing stones, totem poles, medicine wheels, or anything else tilting toward the holy. The closest thing to a religious mark on the land will show up a few miles down the road: a sign directing travellers south to a shrine where a statue of the Virgin Mary overlooks a creek not far from the proposed potash mine.

Prairie people seem to have a particular bond with Mary, whom we sometimes call "Our Lady of the Prairies" or "Mother of Earth and Sky." Among Canadian provinces, only Quebec has more Marian shrines than Saskatchewan. Stones are a primary crop here, abundantly available for shrine construction or sweat lodge, bringing prairie people down to earth in their work and prayer. Spend a day bending over to gather the round boulders from a till-plain field and if you are the least bit attentive you might sense something of their long dreams within the earth. Buffalo hunters and even a few farm people have felt it, the wisdom of creatures formed in the fiery heart of the planet, then shaped, ground down, and reshaped again and again over millions of years by the rising of mountains, the fall of rivers, and the advance of seas. In the sweat lodge, people call the boulders they use "grand-fathers," but the spiritual weight of stone, with its stories of birth and rebirth, has always seemed maternal to me.

In 1916, a boy named Jack Leier watched his mother gather stones to build her own shrine to Mary on their homestead. Whether she told him stories of Mary or of miracles claimed in her name, or whether he simply saw how the hardship and isolation of his mother was assuaged by the spirit of another mother believed to be blessed and holy, Leier was moved forty years later to establish a charitable foundation called Our Lady of the Prairies. The fund has donated millions of dollars to social, environmental, cultural, and spiritual programs in Saskatchewan, including a shelter for abused women, a First Nations heritage park, a spiritual retreat centre in the Qu'Appelle Valley, and a nature centre at an internationally important shorebird reserve.

My earliest memory of religious ritual did not originate in a church either, and that is likely why it stuck. On a road much like this one, a couple of miles south of the town of Esterhazy where we lived, there stands on a low hill a large

stone church, all that remains of a Hungarian colony established in 1886 by a man who claimed to be a Hungarian count.
He named the settlement Kaposvar, after the Hungarian city.
A creek valley of the same name flows east of the site and
down to the Qu'Appelle Valley through the farm where my
Scottish grandparents, the McRaes, lived from 1913 into
the 1950s, raising a passel of children including my mother.
Many of their neighbours were Catholic Hungarians, and
one of them married a McRae girl.

The story of the Kaposvar stone church begins with farmers from the original thirty-five Kaposvar families collecting
the glacial boulders on their land as they broke the prairie
to seed their first crops. By 1906 they had enough to begin
building a church, an ambitious monument to Mary, who
had guided them safely to fertile plains in the New World.
Completing the church the next year, they named it for Mary's
entry into heaven, calling it Our Lady of Assumption. In the
early 1940s the second generation gathered enough stones to
make an outdoor shrine to Mary. It was to honour events in
France sixty years earlier, when a twelve-year-old peasant girl
reported that a young woman about her size had appeared to
her at the mouth of a cave to show her the location of a spring
in the Pyrenees foothills, the spring now known as Lourdes.

By the 1960s, local Catholics from surrounding parishes
would gather annually for a pilgrimage to Kaposvar's Our
Lady of Lourdes shrine in August, near the anniversary of
Mary's death and Assumption. Those pilgrimages, my family
among hundreds of the faithful walking in a procession from
the church to the shrine, let me know, even as a small boy,

that we were on to something. Something that drew us to the luminous ivory-white figure set high in a massive pile of stones, like a jewel inlaid in pewter, or a rose blooming from a cleft of the earth.

"That's Jesus's mother." My mother with her hat, Sunday dress, and purse. Heels puncturing the churchyard lawn.

Jesus—he was the shadowy, anguished figure hanging in the darkened nave of the old Hungarian church. But here was *his* mother outside in the prairie sun, nestled into a wild-looking cave in the rocks. And we were parading around the grass singing her praises. There were spirits out there with us and they liked what we were doing.

This was surely a pagan rite, as Protestants have pointed out, and I am grateful for it. Grateful for the wild truth surviving in Mary, the mother we like to venerate on hilltops and in beautiful places, reminding us that at least some of God remains out in the open air where the swallows are flying and the wind is in charge.

Still damp from my dunking, the creek a mile or two behind me now, I look out across the utterly flat glacial lake bed, the one prairie landscape that is short on stones and rivers. Both are used in rites meant to foster surrender, renewal, and purification. Our bodies may know what the rivers and stones know: that the earth, like our mothers, can revive us, make us clean. Christians took the rites to indoor fonts and altars, but first there was a wild man standing in a river baptizing people, including one born of that mother settlers have venerated all over the prairie.

Mary, more so than her son, was invoked as a spiritual

guide among the mixed-blood people who briefly established a river-based culture on the northern plains before the land was drawn and quartered for white farmers to possess. The Metis had the prairie wisdom to keep faith with rivers, sharing land in communities along the Red, the Assiniboine, the Qu'Appelle, and the Saskatchewan. At some of these places they erected small shrines to Mary, where the people would pray, leaving beads or tobacco as offerings.

One of these shrines, at St. Laurent near Duck Lake along the Saskatchewan River, is still there. Each summer fewer and fewer descendants of the people who stood with Riel and Dumont hold a pilgrimage, recalling their devotion to Mary. In the silence of their thoughts, the old people remember too the stories of their parents and grandparents, and the events of 1885 when prayers were not enough to hold on to their dream of a prairie nation.

As Batoche smouldered above the banks of the Saskatchewan on the final May afternoon of the battle, and General Middleton's troops rounded up any remaining Metis resisters, Gabriel Dumont and his companion Michel Dumas slipped away through the poplars and chokecherries to head south over the prairie. They took a circuitous route across the Missouri Coteau, forded the Saskatchewan River, and then rode through the Cypress Hills to Montana, where they would be safe from prosecution. Some explain their successful escape by saying the police and army patrols, afraid of Dumont's marksmanship, chose not to pursue him. Dumont himself would say later that he was protected by Mary on his passage. Through the eleven days of his journey, travelling a winding six hundred miles, he continually prayed, "You are my mother! Guide me!" And once they made it across the border, the two riders dismounted, knelt, and said a rosary to give thanks to the Virgin.

Every escape needs a holy guide, even my own brief, illusory departure from the less beautiful urban world to one where a patina of the picturesque and natural hides much of the sin and decay. In a couple of days I will be back in the city I left behind, at my desk trying to make a bit more truth out of half-truth, struggling to hold on to my soul in the corporation. And when the clock says it is time, I will pack up my backpack, head for the elevator, and then go out onto streets where many people do not have what is needed to get any job, morally compromising or not. And I will walk through a pedestrian mall named after the man whose family owned a good portion of the real estate the city was built upon when the last buffalo bones were settled onto the heap amid the bones of smallpox victims, the erstwhile buffalo hunters. And in that outdoor mall, if it is reasonably warm, the descendants of those hunters and their mixed-blood kin will be there asking for cigarettes or money to buy coffee, many of them spectral, tattooed, and beleaguered, the human detritus left in the backwash of our progress upon these plains. Their suffering is confluent with the pain held by this prairie I walk through, flows within the same continuum of history won by a misapplied faith alloyed to myths of righteousness and technological triumphalism.

If I were to kneel here on the mud of the Wascana, old Pile of Bones, I would ask Our Lady of Rivers and Stones to help us all gather once again at the riverside, where prairie life still seems wise and gracious and possible. Help us to see that the water flowing through a dry land is not there to make us rich irrigating crops, flushing the effluent of feedlots, or sluicing into potash mines; that its power to draw us together, all cultures, all beings who dwell here, is far more precious than our own short lives, petty differences, and grasping ambitions.

Road Conditions: Walking Home

I remember a July walk of a few summers ago.
—Roderick Haig-Brown, *Measure of the Year*

One July in the 1940s, Roderick Haig-Brown took a float plane ride into a small lake in the wild montane heart of Vancouver Island west of his home in Campbell River. He had promised his daughter Mary that he would finish his work and fly back in time for her First Communion at nine-thirty on Sunday morning. On Saturday, though, rain clouds closed the valley in, grounding the plane. There were thirty miles of bush and mountainside, and the Campbell River (which in his books he called the Elk), between him and his spot in the pew. Religion had been the purview of his wife, Anne, and he generally avoided church, but he had made a promise and Mary would be waiting. When it became obvious that the weather was not going to clear, he started to walk home in driving rain at eight in the evening along an abandoned logging grade. As darkness fell, he forded the river, running high from all the rain. Arriving at a friend's remote cabin at midnight, he slept for a few hours, rose at dawn, and started walking again. At seven-thirty, he walked into a logging camp and cranked up their phone to call a taxi from town. Time was short, so he resumed his walk, hoping to meet the taxi. An hour and a half later, the cab arrived and drove him straight to the church. "At nine-thirty-two I was inside," he wrote in *Measure of the Year*, "watching the back of Mary's white veil in the front pew, still wearing Elk River water in my clothes."

7 Joining the Dance

REACHING THE SPOT WHERE the road cuts across a paved highway, I stand on the shoulder watching trucks heading southeast to the villages of Kronau, Francis, Kendal, Vibank, and Odessa, and on to the headwaters of Wascana Creek. The region bisected by the road I am walking was settled by German Catholics fleeing their colonies on the Volga River in southern Russia. In the late 1700s Catherine the Great had invited them to settle in the Volga region, but after her death the autonomy she had promised them began to disappear. They came to the Great Plains of North America early in the twentieth century, establishing what they called *dorf*s, small villages gathered round a church.

Despite their work ethic, religious cohesion, and a common language, these *dorf*s long ago lost the community life that distinguished them, their bonds of economy and faith dissolved in the corrosive solution of the larger industrial economy. Those that remain have become commuter outposts, shuttling office and blue-collar workers back and forth on this highway to the city.

That topic—the roots of community disintegration—was one that Joseph knew he could always use to get a response from me. "Religious bonds are the only ones that have ever held a community together," he would say. He was willing to allow that religion is often more about division and distinction than it is about the "tie that binds," but he believed that in giving up on all religion we are throwing out the only cultural system that has ever fostered people capable of an ecologically sound interchange between ourselves and the rest of nature.

Once, I made the mistake of writing back saying I didn't believe in golden ages. A week later the phone rang at midnight. "I'm not talking about golden ages," he said. "It's simple. History does not contain long-term models of community and ecological sustainability that leave the spiritual realm out of the picture."

Then he listed current examples among the Amish, the Blang communities in China's Yunnan province, and some contemporary intentional communities. "Are you talking about the polygamists or the free love ones?" I asked, trying to deflect him or at least push the discussion toward the forces I think are eroding community.

"Not everything is about sex," he said.

"Well, your corny Nestbuilder Principle would say otherwise."

Then he corrected me, saying it is about desire, not sex. In his ample spare time Joseph had developed his own Theory of Everything That Is Wrong with the World. His nestbuilder blather always sounded misogynist to my ears, so I would usually stop him before he got wound up, but in giving him the address for a new house we were buying, I'd foolishly mentioned that I thought it was too expensive but Karen really wanted it.

"Of course she does. It belonged to her old girlfriend, right? A girlfriend whose husband makes more money than you, who has provided his wife with a big fancy house. Nestbuilder, my friend, and you can throw in some Girardian mimetic rivalry to boot."

René Girard was one thinker we agreed on, but I took the bait, argued back, and tried to explain that we needed the house because the kids couldn't share rooms anymore. That was all it took. I got what was coming—a long harangue about men being led around by their desire for women, who in turn are led by their desire for physical comforts, all of it driving the out-of-control consumer frenzy that is using up all of the planet's resources and destroying ecosystems. And no, I'm not blaming women, he'd always say. They are just following their biological program to use sex to find the man who will give them the most creature comforts for raising their offspring.

When I said men like comforts too, he pulled out his supporting material: bachelor farmers—surely I remember the Wilbur brothers? Lots of money but they lived like swine, saved every penny, and probably had a smaller ecological footprint than the average urban chihuahua because they never bothered with women. Then it was on to trophy wives, advertising strategies, and the love stories in movies and novels typically set on grand estates, narratives he believed were the equivalent of porn for women. His favourite proof was a build-it-and-she-will-come story of a friend in Whitehorse. The fellow lacked confidence, had never dated a woman, and lived with his mother, but for ten years he used every free moment to work on restoring a three-storey mansion at the end of their street. When it was near completion and he was finishing the bird's-eye maple hardwood on the main floor, an attractive young woman showed up at the front door. She was on the wrong block, looking for another address, but began talking to him about his lovely house. Before leaving, she invited him to a craft show where she was selling some of her pottery. He went, one thing led to another, and they were married and living in the house within the year.

In his more reasonable moments, Joseph's analysis of female failure was more nuanced, painted in finer strokes, and I felt myself drawn in to his argument: "You think I'm blaming women for the mess we're in, but that's not it. I'm just saying they aren't blameless. Sure, men are destroying family, community, and land in obvious ways—domestic and state-sponsored violence, abandoning relationships and moral codes in favour of sex and corporate greed—but women are the other side of this equation. Their participation isn't as spectacular, because instead of being driven by a lust for sex, it is a lust for comfort that leads to restless consuming and a lot of transactions that hurt themselves and the rest of the world."

He had a cousin whose life fit the bill. Janet married a failed junior hockey player who had one of those weird nicknames; I think it was Pinky. Pinky sold hot tubs and liked Janet's legs when she wore high heels. Janet liked beautiful things. Came back from shopping trips to Montana and Vegas with new gold jewellery and interior design ideas. Pinky was good at renovation work and redecorated their split-level on a three-year cycle to suit the latest design scheme in local show homes. Janet's service rep job at the power utility allowed her a year of maternity leave, but she returned to the job three weeks after each of her boys was born. Her mother, a matriarch who looked after the grandchildren around the clock and made all of Janet's decisions on her behalf, shooed her out of the house.

Two years after her mother died, Janet took long-term stress leave from work. She lost touch with the world, because the world no longer had a mother. Buying beautiful things did not help. The Church of the Nazarene was welcoming and told her if she accepted Jesus as her personal saviour, all would be well. That worked for a while, but Pinky, who was confused by Janet's grief, eventually took up with the girl who worked at the front desk for one of his suppliers. Janet started talking funny, so Pinky had her hospitalized to protect her from herself. After the divorce went through, Joseph's sister began to see Janet downtown, at bus stops and in the park, sometimes sitting in front of the Mental Health Association building. Makeup a little too intense, and her hair wilder than it used to be. She'd lost the split-level, but every finger had a gold ring.

What do we do with all this desire? Joseph's nestbuilder theory has been on my mind since the day I fell off the roof. Some days, a piece or two of it makes sense. Our addictions to sex might keep men from growing up, but women can be held back too, and distort or lose the mother in themselves,

by indulging their more socially acceptable desires to build
and decorate the nest. There is something alluring about a
theory that accounts for climate change, monster homes,
Charmin toilet paper, and everything in between. But any
shred of plausibility in it ultimately seems lost in a rearguard
response to the eco-feminist critique of patriarchy, as though
we might be able to deflect blame away from our gender by
pointing at female shopping habits.

Once across the highway, I enter what will be the most deso-
late stretch of the walk. The fields have been harvested, and
the ditches, shallower here, have been mowed. Not a stick to
represent nature and not a bird in sight.

    This is the flattest of plains. Any mountains here were
laid low hundreds of millions of years ago, the valleys filled
in. The landscape of repentance, of *metanoia*, is a plain where
the very emptiness is the fullness of God. The path ahead of
me runs straight as a die to the east. No wild honey, but a few
grasshoppers to stand in for locusts.

    Lots to be repented, though. The most lifeless places on
the prairie today once had the richest ecologies and most
fertile soils: the deep black chernozems of glacial lake beds.
Glacial Lake Regina laid down clay in layers here year after
year as the rich sediments of glacial meltwater settled to the
bottom, forming over a few centuries the fertile peneplain that
settlers converted into cropland in a single generation. The loss
was so rapid, we never had a chance to catalogue what would

have been a distinctive and abundant grassland ecosystem.
The organic matter, carbon, and nutrients stored in the soil
over the millennia are now all but gone, replaced by annual
infusions of fertilizers designed to grow canola or grain.

These fields are among the last places near the city where
we could find McCown's longspurs, one native grassland bird
that somehow made a life here until the early 1990s. When
birder friends visiting from the east came looking for prairie species, I would often take them to these fields to see the
butterfly flight–song displays of the longspurs. In early morning, the birds rose up from summerfallow like undersized
angels, spreading their wings and tails to hang on the wind
once they reached fifteen feet or so off the ground, and then
singing as they fluttered back down. They must have been
nesting in stubble or summerfallow, the closest thing to their
preferred habitat, burnt and barren short-grass prairie. When
local farmers all changed to continuous-cropping practices
and stopped summerfallowing, the longspurs rapidly vanished.

Looking out on the fields hammered down by the passage of monstrous harvesters, it is hard to imagine any nest
ever brooded over, any egg ever hatched. The sterility in
this kind of abused landscape, its utter disenchantment,
its fruitfulness and meaning abducted into industry, has
its analogue in the way we have colonized and debased the
goodness of our own eros. There is a sadness that comes of
misappropriating sexual energy, a kind of functional despair
that hums away in the background for most men if they stop
long enough to listen for it.

The Great Unfairness of having to govern and direct a

powerful longing in our bodies is easier to put up with if we are willing to grant it a story of spiritual origin. A story that says we come from wholeness, a communion with the Spirit that joins all to all, but we are plunked down into a world where everything seems to be disconnected. In such a world, all longing and restlessness is the desire to reconnect, and it arises from that severance we feel in every cell of our bodies. The word *sex* has origins that suggest an understanding of this duality of disconnection and connection. From the Latin *secare*, "to disconnect from the whole," sex is both about feeling cut off and about trying to connect.

Of course, it's the quality of trying that gets you in trouble. Spiritual writers from John of the Cross to Ron Rolheiser have said that eros, the fire inside us that includes sexual energy, is ultimately spiritual energy. How we end up using it determines the nature of our spiritual lives. If most of our eros is channelled toward self-gratification, growing up is going to be a struggle.

It would follow that a certain purity of heart is an important part of the maturing process, not by becoming prudish, but by making sure that your sexual energy is applied within the bounds of fidelity and that other much-maligned virtue, chastity. In our libidinous culture, where most forms of sexual discipline have been declared repressive, and men are offered amped-up erotic stimulation whenever and wherever they desire, purity of heart is getting harder than ever to come by.

Sometimes when Joseph and I got on the topic of community disintegration, I would pull out the latest story of sexual abuse in the news, whether it was in the Church or in the sporting world, and use that to argue that male erotic energies have to take responsibility for the lion's share of the erosion taking place in our communities and ecosystems.

If Joseph were here, I would remind him about that football coach charged with sexual abuse at Pennsylvania State University, one of America's most revered university sports programs. Evidence from a grand jury report shows that the president of the university, the head coach of the team who is a legendary father figure in college sports, the university athletic director, and a handful of other men knew about the abuse for nine years or more. Instead of suspending him until they could investigate, they looked the other way. Several incidents were reported, including one by a young man who says he saw the coach raping a ten-year-old boy in the shower, but they never made it past the president's desk.

None of the men who knew of the abuse applied the kind of power or courage expected of their gender in such moments. The young man, a former quarterback we must assume was strong and healthy, did not intervene when he saw a fifty-eight-year-old man raping a ten-year-old boy. He did report it to the head coach, who in turn reported it to university authorities. No one thought to take the matter any further—not the witness, not the coach, not the athletic director, nor any of the other university officials. Their "remedial actions" were to take away the coach's key to the locker room and tell him that he could no longer bring to campus boys from the Second Mile, an organization for at-risk boys that he had helped to found.

Finally, and not surprisingly, it fell to a woman to take

action. In 2009, the mother of another abused boy filed charges. Eventually, the coach was indicted on forty-five counts related to the sexual abuse of nine boys over a fifteen-year period.

A story such as this is inextricably bound up with our North American obsession with sports, and the undue power athletics has on many campuses, but the collective public outrage that rises to a pitch when these things come to air rarely draws a step or two further back to consider what else is amiss. If the privacy we accord sexual encounters becomes a matter of public interest merely when a certain boundary of behaviour has been breached, and we are depending entirely on institutions, corporations, courts, and governments to handle that public interest and protect the innocent, should we be surprised when the hand-offs and lines of reporting fail us?

To make sense of such horrors and do better than express our disgust in retrospect, we have to get beyond the false duality of public and private and intervene with a third set of interests: the community. There are many forces militating against actual place-based community, but perhaps none is more destructive than the commercial interchange between public and private we see enacted in the marketplace and popular media every minute of every day. By hooking up the corporate profit imperative to the human capacity for addiction and cupidity, the industrial economy has found ten thousand ways to prostitute the collective eros at the very core of community.

I am no longer sure I know what the positive eros connecting soul to soul in a healthy community might feel or look like. I imagine I catch a glimpse of it at the local farmers' market or when my friends show up with tool belts and beer to help rebuild my deck because I fell off the roof and wrecked my shoulder.

Then there is square dancing.

Last summer, Karen and I took our youngest daughter, Maia, to something called the Kenosee Lake Kitchen Party. It was a week-long music camp next to a popular lake in the Moose Mountain uplands. During the day, Karen and Maia took beginner fiddle and I honed my guitar-holding skills while the nine-year-olds in my class learned some basic chording. Each night, after an outdoor concert where we got to hear our teachers play tunes from Celtic, country, bluegrass, and Metis traditions, we'd gather in the mess hall. Pushing all the tables and chairs aside, we'd assemble into circles of eight and wait for the fiddles to begin. Within minutes, the caller, a gifted teacher and musician from the Maritimes, had us all laughing and sweaty, our hearts tripping faster as we swirled and do-si-doed. I would look around the room now and then just to marvel at the spectrum of who we were: sixty prairie people of all ages and colours, some rural, some urban, holding hands and dancing in a church camp mess hall. The August breeze coming in through window screens could not touch the heat we generated, but it joined the spirit running from body to body. Something in us recognized that we were dancing near the mysteries that attach us most intimately to one another, and perhaps further, that the goodness of community resides in our capacity for mutual respect for those mysteries. The respect is everything, because the energies that make us beautiful, that bring us to fertility, that help us bond with one another, are not inherently safe or benign. There is no such thing as "safe sex." There is only this power that can drive us apart or toward one another, that can scatter us to the edges of madness or bring us together in a dance that has the capacity to unite us to one another and to the places we live.

Whether we are religious or not, married or single, straight or gay, sexually obsessed or celibate, I think most of us want to be part of that dance, to restore community, rejoin it to place, and take back our local well-being from the public and private interests now claiming to manage it on our behalf.

Those interests are not run by machines, though it may seem that way. There are souls involved, and mostly male ones, running governments, churches, universities, and corporations on erotic energies they neither understand nor respect.

Road Conditions: Walking Whole

Inciting the movement of nerve impulses across the brain hemispheres helps people to come to terms with their past. They stop being frightened by their imagined futures and feel comfortable and empowered in the present. Walking while holding a traumatic memory in mind in a particular way can produce this result in a very short time.
—Thom Hartmann, *Walking Your Blues Away*

The First Peoples of the Plains traditionally used long walks through the prairie or ritualized back-and-forth dancing to heal themselves in body and mind. Psychotherapists who apply modern bilateral therapies to treat emotional disturbance understand the power of the Siouan and Blackfoot peoples' thirst dance, in which participants dance for long hours around the sacred lodge, holding their transgressions and weaknesses in their hearts and chanting prayers for the creator's grace. Thom Hartmann, an American psychotherapist, argues that walking long distances is how nature intended us to recover from stress or trauma. It may also help people get over their impulses toward addiction. Aboriginal people in recovery from substance abuse often break free from their habits by returning to the sacred thirst dance. Alcoholics or porn addicts who go for long solo walks to cope with their cravings find the same results. One man writing on his website about walking away from addiction said, "There is something about that rhythmic drumming of my feet against the ground and the swinging of my arms in harmony with my legs that grounds me to my surroundings and puts my world back in order."

8 Little Queens

IN THE LAST MILE I have found fewer dead animals on the road, which makes sense given the impoverished landscape: a meadow vole, a wood frog, and the usual large insects, dragonflies, and butterflies. I also found a bumblebee.

I have been placing the larger bodies in the ditch as I go. Karen says she feels something zing through her chest whenever we drive past something dead on the road. All I know is, taking them off the road and muttering a short prayer makes me feel better.

I read in the paper that officials recorded thirteen thousand collisions with animals on the province's roads last year. Four people died from encounters with moose. Almost all of the thirteen thousand animals would have died, and if you added the smaller critters, from snakes to bumblebees, the total would be in the millions. Saskatchewan has been called the roadkill capital of the world. When I was a teenager living through the tail end of hippie culture's idealism and back-to-the-land dreams reaching the prairie hinterland via TV and radio broadcast, I got hold of a *Whole Earth Catalog*, something of a bible for the movement in its latter days. I pored over it looking for references to my part of the world and found only one: in a segment on how to live off roadkill, southern Saskatchewan was highlighted as the best place to find it owing to an abundance of both roads and wildlife. The south of France has its truffles, but the south of Saskatchewan has roadkill porcupines.

Taking the bumblebee in my hand, I see an orange band across its yellow belly. I don't know the native bees well, but this one may be the orange-belted bumblebee. I wonder if it is a queen. If it is, she would have founded her colony by emerging from her winter den in spring and looking for a mouse hole or some other cavity in the ground where she could raise her brood and store a small amount of honey for herself and her offspring. Secreting platelets of wax from her body, she would have formed a little honey pot the size of a man's thumb tip to hold the nectar she gathered from flowers. As she filled the pot, she would have decorated the floor around it with the pollen she picked up at each blossom.

Beneath these battered fields, there could be a secret chamber with a small pot of gold bestowing the sweetness of the land and made by a little queen whose comings and goings are critical to the sex lives of the flowering plants that so many other creatures depend on. Nature, even here, continues to offer these lavish little gestures of hope. The honey she makes is a distillate of the eros in clover, dandelion, and goldenrod bloom, and if I could taste it, smell its earthy fragrance, it would, like all honey, bear that suggestive, musky tang that placed it beneath the tongue and on the lips of the bedchambered bride in the Song of Songs. In Greek mythology, Eros was said to have dipped his arrows in honey.

The alarming decline in numbers of all pollinators is one of the surest signs that we may finally be wearing out the very eros that makes life possible. The spring before last my family decided to start keeping honeybees out at our weekend farm, mostly because we like honey and wanted to make some mead, but also because we knew our land would be a healthy place for bees to forage.

A week or so after my fall—pathetic that I seem to be marking time by it, but I am—my twelve-year-old daughter, Maia, and I were having breakfast at the land with a guest, a young man named Brian who was going to camp for the week while we went back to the city. The three of us were chatting as we looked out over the yard and lake. Maia asked me what the bees do in their hives all day.

Now, the day before, when Brian arrived and set up his tent on the grass, Karen had suggested I take him for a walk.

"What for?" I said.

"I just think it might be a good idea, that's all."

It has taken me nearly thirty years to recognize when Karen is following up on some feeling she gets in her belly—partly because she never actually says, "I have a feeling in my belly," but mostly because I am not that good at reading the signs. This time I did. I set aside my resistance and walked over to Brian where he sat by the firepit reading a book.

"I'm going for a little walk. Would you like to come?"

Brian is a tall, serious-looking young man, in his mid-twenties I would guess. Short hair, glasses, sensible clothing. As we made our way through the lower aspen woods and up onto the grassy hills, we talked about plants we were passing and the prescribed burn Karen and I did in spring. Later, we got around to his philosophy classes, and the teachers he liked best, and then, just as we made the turn back and the descent into the valley along the old road to the yard, he told me, with a note of apology in his voice, that his studies were his way of preparing to enter the Catholic seminary if indeed he decided to make that commitment.

"This week of camping is part of my process of figuring out if it is the right choice for me."

My mind went to thoughts of myself at his age and the things I was doing, or at least wanted to be doing. I could not imagine having to make such a decision no matter how long I camped alone. My hilltop fast was still a week or two into the future, and it was good to meet a young man whose spiritual longings had led him to a quiet place where nature is still in charge so that he could look into his own heart and find his path in life. I felt some admiration for his mettle at being willing to consider choosing celibacy, mixed with my standard irritation at knowing that it need not be this way, that celibacy and priesthood should not be indelibly hitched.

"Oh, good for you," I said, and then I tried to throw in something suitably supportive, but it came out sounding like "Some of my best friends are celibate." I did register my concerns about the Church only ordaining celibate men as priests and then undercut that assertion with something vague about the spiritual validity of choosing a celibate path. I quickly veered toward things I have read on the topic to see if I could find safer ground. I didn't.

Back at the cabin, I went to tell Karen what I had learned.

"You know what that guy is doing here?"

She was stringing yarn up a cedar post to encourage scarlet runner beans.

"So, it's some kind of discernment process," she said, not looking up. "You should loan him your copy of *The Holy Longing*."

"Uh, yeah. I should. . . . But, well, I just think it's so unfair. It's hard enough to make a decision to become a priest. But it gets all mixed up with having to decide whether you want to give up on sexual intimacy for your lifetime! Hell, at his age I was an atheist one week and a believer the next, and I broke into a sweat every time I talked to a girl."

The next morning, as Maia and I ate breakfast with Brian, everything that issued from my mouth seemed to be a metaphor for sexual abstinence. I was Basil in that episode of *Fawlty Towers* where he has German guests at his inn and tells all his staff, "Whatever you do, don't mention the war," and then of course does nothing but that himself.

Maia was no help. If anything, she was my guileless side-kick, feeding me lines. First we were talking about our chickens and the problem of having to give the young males away before they started crowing. Maia said she wished there was a way to prevent the males from becoming roosters.

"Yeah," I said, "too bad you can't neuter them, give them a cockledoodlectomy. Ha ha."

A bird hovered over the gravel driveway for a second and then pounced.

"There it is again," I said, happy to share my knowledge of local birdlife, "the Say's phoebe. He's been here all spring, but I'm pretty sure he's alone. No females anywhere around. He doesn't sing at all anymore. For the first week or two he was pretty vocal, trying to attract a female, but he's been silent for a month now."

"Maybe he's clinically depressed," Brian said.

"Well, who wouldn't be? There's not much point in singing if there are no females around to hear you."

And that was when, right out of the blue, Maia asked about the bees. "What do they do in their hives all day?"

I love it when one of my children shows the slightest interest in nature, so I settled in for a short dissertation. I talked about some of the workers, who are all female, going out to forage, while others remained behind to guard the hive, make brood comb, and feed the developing larvae.

"What about the males, the drones? What do they do?"

"The drones? Lots of people think they do nothing much, but I think they must have some purpose besides trying to mate with the queen. Even then it's only a few that actually get to have sex with her. When she wants to be impregnated, she heads for the sun. All the drones chase her into the sky and the few that stick with her to the end of her flight get to join her in one moment of airborne ecstasy. But that's it. There's a whole lot of drones who don't even get to have that one experience with the queen before they . . . die."

That was when I looked at Brian and realized what was going on. I stopped and did my best to ignore the catbird building its nest and the male hummingbird scrolling U-shaped courtship manoeuvres above his mate in the lilac hedge.

Later that day, as we drove away leaving Brian for his week

of discernment, I wondered if perhaps Maia and I could be contracted by seminaries to test the will of more young men considering a life of celibacy. When we came back the next week, we found his tent collapsed on the ground in a sodden pile and no sign of Brian. We heard later that a wild storm one night flattened his tent with him inside. Cutting his way out with a pocketknife, he jumped in his car and drove away.

In the end, it is nature that will test the ways we apply our desire in life, but if I ever have another chance to talk to a young man considering the celibate life, here is what I would like to say:

I would say celibacy is like any other chosen orientation of our sexual energies: you can do it well or you can do it badly. We've all heard of religious people whose celibacy was at best optional, at worst a cloak disguising unspeakable evil—but I have met a few celibate men and women who I believe are doing it well. Many seem to have a different light, a gently held flame whose radiance is refracted into their own way of making love in the world.

And I would advise him to get a copy of Rilke's *The Book of Hours*, and read the poems in the section entitled "The Book of a Monastic Life"—not because they praise celibacy, but because they were written by a twenty-three-year-old poet who was no monk and yet knew that the stirrings in himself were more than physical urges to be indulged. Rilke felt every desire a young man feels, but he carried them in a way that transformed them into a ripening, a ferment for the holy.

Not long ago, I opened our copy of *The Book of Hours* and a small folded slip of paper fell to the floor. Unfolding it, I read the text printed at the top, "Daily Abbey Weather Report," and smiled, remembering that James often used his weather-reporting forms as bookmarks. He'd given the book to Karen about five years before he died.

A Benedictine monk who lived in a small aspen wood as a hermit, Father James Gray wrote and published a book review every week, and recorded weather data for the government twice a day. The pathway to his cabin door was worn by the feet of people who came to him for his unconditional love and wise counsel. We found in him that rare soul who made it across the rainbow bridge joining monk to beast, fully a man in whom "love is born, and alights on the highest curve, glowing against the grey, sober against the fire."

Whenever I showed up for a dose of that fire, he would clap his great hands on me, squeezing my arms and pounding my back. That very physical welcome let me know I was there in the flesh after all the letters back and forth and that he was there too, muscle, sinew, and bone formed by his labours in the bush and his beloved flower garden. James was strong, with a healthy, fully incarnated eros he received directly from the aspen woods and the surrounding prairie, informed always by Scripture and reflected in the sacraments of his faith, but also by his delight in great literature and Eastern mysticism. He meditated, practised yoga, and read widely in the sacred texts of all traditions. On his wall was an image of Bede Griffiths, a fellow Benedictine. Griffiths, a lifelong model for James, was an Englishman who trained under C.S. Lewis at Oxford before becoming a monk and then moving to India, where he eventually received the title Swami Dayananda. Griffiths followed mystical yogic traditions that included a form of what is called Brahmacharya, or restraining of erotic energies. James never spoke of it, but I have wondered if his celibacy drew life from the mindful practice of Brahmacharya as he encountered it in Griffiths's writings.

I saw him three days before he died. It was Good Friday, 2009. An aorta had burst in his heart and he could barely speak as he lay in his hospital bed. We hugged and held on to each other. He gave me his blessing and I blessed him back. He spoke slowly, in weak whispers, and though I could not hear much of it, I caught the words "Karen" and "children." By the way he squeezed my arm hard for emphasis, I knew he was trying to encourage me, to tell me to be strong and courageous, to do well by my wife and family, to always love and cherish them. That life and strength in him were still there, now for a last time passing on to me his deepest love and letting me know that despite my doubts I am a good man.

From our long talks and letters, James knew all my weaknesses and vanity—the things that tormented me, the confusion I felt as a father and a husband, my longing to do something good for the prairie and its human and natural communities. I went home that day realizing I was still suffering from old storylines, feeling sorry for myself and resenting Karen and our children for holding me back from a life I believed I had coming to me.

When I left the hospital ward, a woman who had been James's neighbour for thirty-four years stopped in to see him. As long as he had lived as a hermit, she was there across the field, a single mother living on a piece of land just south of the abbey grounds. An attractive woman, she looked to be a few years younger than him, and bore herself with a feminine elegance I knew James would enjoy as she sat holding his hand and reading from one of Thomas Merton's books. I never doubted that James liked women. He connected with Karen instantly, and when she came for visits they would sit knee to knee, laughing at each other's stories until I eventually had to break things up so we could get back to more substantial topics. Many women sought him out in his cabin in the bush. Was the smile of a woman, her mere presence, radiating that lovely feminine otherness, somehow enough? Was it the same joy he breathed in when he watched the hummingbirds among his lupines and delphiniums, or fed the chickadees and nuthatches in the palm of his hand?

In the abbey weather report that had fallen from the book of Rilke poems, James's pencil marks showed a high of ten degrees and a low of one degree Celsius. Partly cloudy with a moderate wind. It was 8:15 in the morning on April 13, 2004. Next to the date, in his tight cursive, it said, "St. Martin. The last martyr pope, 655." Every day, James believed, was a day to remember a saint, not for the sake of piety or even tradition, but because we must be ready to give an account of the hope that is within us, and the saints in our midst are, like a bee's underground honey chamber, great wellsprings of hope. I looked at the date again. April 13, 2004. It was five years later to the day that James died. Saint Martin will have to make room for another one whose witness was a wellspring for so many.

~

Something in the light has shifted, granting more contrast to the edges of the fields where one type of crop gives way to the next. In another breath the surface, sectioned into the patches that make the prairie a checkerboard, softens or becomes translucent and I imagine I can see to the layers below, to the unifying soil that flows in gradients from clay through loam to sand, holding on to a forgotten community that is real and foundational. Though we pay them little mind, the life-nurturing bonds kept in soil and remembered in the honey stored underground by little queens will be here long after the last crops are harvested or left to wither in the sun.

Road Conditions: Walking Sutra

*When walking in the awareness of the highest reality
(brahmacharya) is firmly established, then a great
strength, capacity, or vitality (virya) is acquired.*
—Sutra 2:38

The Brahmacharya sutra of yogic tradition is said to be about "walking with God" or "prayerful conduct." Brahma is the Hindu deity of creation. *Charya* means "to walk actively." Yoga recognizes that there is something holy and grounding about mindful motion of the body. Traditional interpretations of Brahmacharya have focused on celibacy as a spiritual ideal to be cultivated in one's life, either permanently, as in the discipline of a monastic, or during a phase of life as a single person awaiting the bonds of marriage, or as a ritual practice of temporary abstinence to be followed even by married people. Contemporary yoga teacher Donna Farhi says, "*Brahmacharya* means that we use our sexual energy to regenerate our connection to our spiritual self." The general tenor of most teachings on Brahmacharya, traditional or modern, seems to recognize that by choosing restraint and continence in the face of life's many temptations, by mindfully husbanding the creative energies in our flesh, we align ourselves with the motion of the creator—we walk with God.

9 Monk or Beast

JUST OFF THE ROAD there is a little slough twenty by forty feet, a low-lying area too wet to be seeded this spring. In it there are three lesser yellowlegs rocking up and down, teeter, pick, teeter, pick—their perfect reflections in the water copying the motion. I decide to copy too, recalling Plotkin's advice to look for ways to communicate with the wild ones. As I bow at the waist, a raven flies by.

Ahead are two matching yellow combine harvesters and three grain trucks bringing in the crop, with Swainson's hawks overhead hunting in the ware of the machines. On the edge of the field is a sign that says, "Pest Control Experimental Site. Do not enter without authorization. For information contact Syngenta, Syngenta Crop Protection Canada." The phone number is in Alberta. On the next two power poles I can see three more hawks, the local purveyors of unauthorized pest control.

Here come two grain trucks off the field, each carrying several tons of wheat. They head up the road and straight for a farmyard at the centre of a vast field. Above its trees the peaks of many large grain silos reflect light back to the sky.

I've seen four different trucks come and go out of there. This man owns a lot of land, harvests a lot of wheat.

These days, we watch truckloads of grain pass by and sense that something in us and in the earth is harmed when food is grown and consumed with little intimacy, care, and respect. The local and slow food movements are showing us that the way we grow, distribute, prepare, and eat food is important for the health of our body-to-earth exchanges. The next step may be to realize that the energy that brings pollen to ovary and grows the grain, once it enters our bodies, also needs to be husbanded. The way we respond to our desire to merge, connect, and be fruitful—stirrings felt so deeply but often so shallowly expressed—determines the quality of our body-to-body exchanges. Partly because we have the freedom to choose our response, and partly because we live so high on the trophic pyramid, our expressions of fruitfulness have more powerful consequences than those in the plants and animals we eat.

In a world bathed in industrial and impersonal sex, where real connection and tenderness are rare, will we sense also that something in us and in the earth is being harmed from the same absence of intimacy, care, and respect? Will we learn that any given expression of our erotic energies either connects us to or divides us from the world around us and our souls? We are discovering that we must steward the energies captured by nature in hydrocarbons or in living plants and animals, and thereby improve the ways we receive the fruits of the earth, but we still struggle to see the primary responsibility we each bear for the small but cumulatively significant explosions of energy we access and transmit as we respond to our own longings to connect, merge, and be fruitful. Learning how to steward the way we bear fruit ourselves as spiritual/sexual beings with a full set of animal desires and angelic ambitions may be more important to the human journey than we can fully understand.

Not long ago, I was sitting in the Calgary airport waiting for an early connecting flight. There were flight attendants, all with Starbucks in hand, chatting in a circle. An attractive woman, a passenger about my age, sat down near me and set up her laptop. Fashionable high-heel cowboy boots with buckles and straps, black leather jacket, dyed hair long over her shoulders: I had her pegged as an Alberta trophy wife. With her laptop facing me only a few feet away, I had a full look at the photo she used for her desktop background. It was an aerial shot of an elaborate farmyard in grain-growing country. There was a barn, T-shaped, and nearby a stately hip-roof house made of red brick, with a widow's walk and trimmed with white shutters and columns. All of it surrounded by several acres of lawn, it was the picture of prairie farm splendour.

Suddenly, there was a video feed on her screen. She had called home on Skype and we were looking into the dimly lit kitchen of her dream home, facing the man who had most likely built it for her. Wire-rimmed glasses, a moustache, ball cap, and plaid shirt—he was her Mr. Darcy. I did my best to avert my eyes and go back to my book, but Joseph's nonsense about women and the men who build them elaborate houses was making it hard to concentrate.

There is a relationship between the female desire for home

and the male desire for sex, but it is so much more complex and nuanced than a bird building a nest to attract his mate. As the woman began talking to her husband, she smiled and her eyes began to shine, and then she leaned forward and whispered something into the computer. The shadowy figure on the screen gave an aw-shucks kind of laugh and said, "Yeah, well, I miss you too."

In its false reductions, an equation aiming to describe the fires that stir human longing has nothing to say about the creative powers of restraint and forbearance, never mind the possibility of genuine bonds in physical intimacy. The year Karen was diagnosed with breast cancer, I began to learn something about this subtler side of desire. At the end of her chemotherapy and radiation treatments, she went away to attend a forty-day Buddhist retreat. It was to be a silent retreat and they were told they would have to practise Brahmacharya by refraining from any sexual activity—and yes, that includes flying solo. I thought I would do the same at home while she was away. In solidarity. It's not even six weeks—how hard can it be?

Turns out forty days and forty nights can be very hard, but in the weeks where I managed it, I think I felt something shift. I seemed to have more energy and found myself building a sun loft I had been dreaming of making for years. The work on the book I was writing at the time flowed along with less effort and a new clarity. Some nights I wasn't sleeping well, but the hours awake brought on new insights—ideas for the loft, for the book, and for my muddled pondering over what to do with sexual desire.

At the time, I was reading books by Southern novelist

Walker Percy, whom Alfred Kazin once described as "the satiric Dostoyevsky of the bayou." Published in the sixties and seventies, Percy's narratives are the best fiction I have come across for understanding the sad craziness of our soul-corrosive, apocalyptic world. James had suggested Percy as a writer I might enjoy, but I opened up one of his novels, *Love in the Ruins*, not knowing what to expect. As the narrator, a psychiatrist named Tom More, describes the action in the opening pages, he says, "I believe in God and the whole business, but I love women best, music and science next, whiskey next, God fourth, and my fellow man hardly at all."

I was surprised to see how Percy uses birds in the story and that he clearly knew something about the way they move and behave, but I was hooked more by his humour and depictions of male desire. With a deceiving innocence and not a note of crass eroticism, Tom allows us to feel the very pull of desire in his attentions to the curve of a knee or the downy hair on the neck of one of his three girlfriends.

Set in the near future, when the world seems to be facing a meltdown that only our narrator knows about—we wonder about his sanity—the story takes a savage plunge into the absurd, libido-driven, flattened-out cosmos of modernity. Science and religion both come in for some deliciously hilarious kicks, as Tom treats himself, his patients, and friends with a device he has invented for diagnosing and adjusting the soul. By the time I had finished the book, though, I was left with an uneasy feeling I could not name, as though the doctor's caliper had taken the measure of my soul as well, and found it wanting.

Wondering about the soul behind a novel so wise, funny, and disturbing, I looked for biographical information on Percy. His grandfather killed himself the year he was born, and twelve years after that, Percy's father shot himself. His mother died two years later, plunging her car into a stream, an event that haunted Percy as another possible suicide. In the crucible of these painful facts of abandonment, Walker and his brother were raised by an uncle, Will Percy, a poet and significant literary figure in Mississippi. With his uncle's encouragement, he entered medical school, became enamoured of the scientific method, and then as an intern underwent his own crisis of despair after contracting tuberculosis. Later calling it "the best disease I ever had," Percy spoke of his time recovering from TB as a turning point in his life, because in the middle of his despair he decided to abandon his plans to be a psychiatrist, and instead began writing novels.

A character in *Love in the Ruins* speaks for Percy when he says, "I am surrounded by the corpses of souls." The living death I encountered in reading Percy was almost unbearably sad, but no more sad than the culture it caricatures. The current fetish for zombie films and zombie culture among young people suddenly made a bit more sense to me. The adolescent brain seems to be drawn to the ambivalent interplay between the eros in the body and the opposing principle of death, which the Greeks called *thanatos*. The more I read Percy's novels, the more I began to recognize his moral battleground in my own life. To see that I had long been ignoring the fight as the background hum of despair within desire.

The rain has come, so I pull a poncho out of my pack. A

soft drizzle like this falling straight down makes me think of funerals. Death will come on its own, but until then I want to walk and breathe in body and soul as alive as I can be, not deadened by enslavement to desire, to the false promises of the sensuous that would have me believe this is all there is, this flesh, this short life. If we are, as Forster suggested, half beast, half monk in need of a rainbow bridge, then that bridge is a kind of covenant, a bond and promise with spiritual significance regulating all of the ways we connect with the otherness around us. Without such a bond, our mishandled eros anchors us hard to the beast part of being a man. It shuts down our spiritual senses so we cannot hear the spirits around us calling out for mercy; it makes us into the rogue primate that for his own pleasure will flay the earth of her skin.

I have met many bright young men who seem unable to connect with other people except as tools for satisfying their needs. Friends, women, parents are merely objects to service them, bring them food, run their business, give them pleasure. They might label themselves as atheist or Christian or some other orientation to ideas of God and spirit, but they live a functional disenchantment, as though the innocence they lost in puberty brought them into the shallowest of worlds where there is sex and death and nothing else. Even more than my own generation of men, they have come of age in a culture where the female body is presented to them as a source of fantasy and self-gratification. Sexual acts at best are expressions of feelings that might include "love," but much of the time are merely part of bodily function, no more or less meaningful than any other expulsion of fluids. And whether performed alone or by more than one adult consensually involved in the arousal or the act itself, no harm is done.

A friend of mine, a responsible, intelligent man in his thirties who has read widely in philosophy and who loves his wife and children, told me a story once to illustrate his view of sex, a view which I believe many men share. In a university class, his professor posed a scenario to stimulate discussion on the topic of sexuality within the public sphere. You are at a restaurant with your date and you suddenly notice that a couple at another table have stripped off their clothing and begun to copulate on their table amid the flatware and water glasses. Are you or your date being harmed in any way? Whereupon my friend, ever the pragmatist, asked a clarifying question: are they attractive or ugly?

With pornography becoming as mainstream as microwave food, this kind of question does not arise from a rare moral deformity. There is a new utilitarian common sense that says anything goes, even public sex, as long as there is adult consent and reasonably attractive bodies. Only the prude would be shocked, once we have deconstructed desire and determined that the sensuality and longings we feel are nothing more than hormonal responses to stimuli.

The only sounds now are the raindrops hitting my hat and poncho, the swish of my pant legs, the crunch of my sandals on the gravel. And the crickets, the ever-present crickets of early September. I feel completely isolated here in my little rain shadow, grateful for the shelter as I walk.

On the hot mid-summer days I spent on the hilltop, there was no rain. To keep the sun off by day I had a length of polyester material patterned in green and brown camouflage that helped my encampment disappear on the hilltop. It was thin and gauzy enough to let air flow through and I could either suspend it from sticks or cover my body with it, depending on the angle of the sun and the heat. Each night I would try sleeping outside until the mosquitoes chased me into the little tent, a low hemisphere of nylon screen staked to the ground. With the fly off, I lay back and watched the stars wheel past, my mind slowly cooling from the sun-baked obsessions of daytime.

One afternoon, after seeing an unfamiliar vehicle drive down into the valley, I fell under a delusion that another man had come to seduce Karen, who was alone in the cabin. Sweating in the midday heat, I became possessed by an unbearable jealousy feeding on vivid scenarios running through my thoughts. For hours I fought the urge to run down the hill, and then I heard voices wafting up from the valley bottom. That was it: the crude little animal in the basement of my brain took over, dispatching alarms and detailed instructions. It was time to take some action. Blood pounding in my ears, I wrapped myself in my sheet and left the circle, walking a few steps toward the voices. There, as I stood on one of the glacial erratics that cover the hilltop, I saw two figures walking toward the parked car. It was Karen with a good friend, one of the other women from our weekend community. For some reason I had not recognized the car.

As I slunk back to the circle, limbs still awash in adrenalin, the paranoia exploding in my head collapsed down into a black hole of shame. I could have used a hole. I wanted to crawl under the grasses and stones to hide from the merciless sky. The rest of that day, as I stewed in the July heat, a wretched parade of my transgressions passed by. And no matter how I tried, I could not wrestle my way out of the truth of what I have done to Karen and other women, in my possessiveness, anger, jealousy, and lust. What difference did it make that I had never broken my marriage vows, if I had countless times been unfaithful in heart and mind, if I had been pushy, manipulative, controlling, and contemptuous in response to the nurturing and gentle energies of women? Any accomplishment or virtue I might have clung to for consolation was tainted by the desire that dominates my encounter with the feminine in the world, the vanity that drives me to fuss over my reputation and appearance, and the egoism that keeps me trapped in serving myself first and last.

It was one big loathe-fest long into the night. I lay in the tent, shoulder and ribs aching, unable to sleep, staring at the stars, and imagining that the churning in my belly was more than hunger, that a dark, murky something there was breech and trying to turn the other way.

ROAD CONDITIONS: WALKING EXISTENTIALISTS

*Man is more than an organism in an environment, more than
an integrated personality, more even than a mature and creative
individual, as the phrase goes. He is a wayfarer and a pilgrim.*
—Walker Percy, in his reception speech for the
National Book Award, 1962

Walker Percy's transition from medical student to novelist
was in part guided by his reading of existentialist thinkers who understood the pilgrim nature of the human soul.
Gabriel Marcel's description of man as the wayfaring creature
became a central image for Percy, but the core of his thought
on the nature of life in the age of anxiety came from reading
Søren Kierkegaard, the nineteenth-century Danish philosopher. Kierkegaard walked the streets of Copenhagen to work
out the conflict in his soul, along the way discovering insights
that form some of the foundations of modern existentialist
thinking. His most famous statement on walking was written in a letter to a beloved sister-in-law, a kindred spirit
often bedridden by her bouts of melancholy. "Do not on any
account cease to take pleasure in walking: I have walked my

best thoughts into existence, and I know of no thought so heavy that one cannot walk away from it. . . . If anyone denies that health is to be found in motion, then I walk away from all morbid objections. Thus if you go on walking, all will go well enough."

10 Better Signs

CLOUDS TO THE SOUTH look like a full-on thunderstorm brewing. Just ahead on the north side of the road is a gas station, several miles from the city or any other retail business. As I approach, the sign becomes readable: "Cowessess Gas and Grocery. Tobacco Products, Convenience Store, Full Serve." In the middle of wheat and canola crops entirely owned by white farmers sits this property now owned by Cowessess First Nation, a band whose reserve is one hundred and twenty-five miles east of here along the rim of the Qu'Appelle Valley.

Metis, First Nations, and white people have been fighting over the matter of who owns what pieces of the prairie for two hundred years, at least since Cuthbert Grant and his Metis pemmican traders rode out from the Qu'Appelle to try to scare away the first settlers just getting a foothold on its eastern edge, where Winnipeg is today. The twenty colonists killed at Seven Oaks in those events were still on the minds of the juries that convicted Louis Riel and Poundmaker in a Regina courtroom seventy years later. With new treaties signed, the buffalo gone, and most First

Nations on reserves studying to shed their savage ways and become farmers, the powers in Ottawa and Regina believed they had finally snuffed out the Aboriginal claim to the prairie. This anomalous gas station says otherwise.

One hundred and twenty-five years after Riel's hanging, he is a cultural hero praised in legislatures and honoured in the naming of buildings and highways. The Metis struggle to maintain a vexed cultural identity in hybrid form, and do what they can to assert hunting and fishing rights. And while there is scant agreement on what the treaties actually mean, status Indians have fought and won new battles to get the land they are entitled to under treaties, and to be compensated for lands that were stolen from them in the early years of settlement. This "Treaty Land Entitlement" process is part of the reason there is a gas station and convenience store out here in the middle of nowhere.

Oddly placed gas stations like this one are popping up next to urban centres, following a simple business model: undercut the price of gas in the city and even white people will drive out here to buy their fuel and get some cigarettes at the same time.

After buying a chocolate bar and iced tea, I go outside to sit on an old bench seat salvaged out of a truck and leaning against the building next to the door. Above my head a speaker broadcasts Tim McGraw's "Live Like You Were Dying" out to the gophers at the edge of the paved space. A sign across from me asks, "How much did Cowessess save you today?" Today the price is a dollar nineteen per litre, probably five cents cheaper than in the city. A better question is how they sell gas at a lower price than everybody else. I ask the man pumping gas.

"I have no idea—it has something to do with taxes."

"Taxes?"

"If you have a status card, it's ten cents off of this. So it's a buck nine."

"Okay, but even a dollar nineteen is cheaper whether you have a card or not."

"Yup."

A sign in the field next to the station says, "Future Site of Cowessess Urban Housing Development." The gas station attendant does not know much about that either, seems skeptical. Like most Canadian First Nations, Cowessess is looking for new ways to support its people on a limited resource base. The band has thirty-seven hundred souls under its care, but only seven hundred of them live on the reserve. The rest, mostly younger people, live in Regina and other urban centres. When their ancestors signed a treaty in the 1870s, Cowessess First Nation would have been much smaller.

The assumption that Aboriginal cultures would be subsumed by white settler culture has proven spectacularly wrong. Instead, the treaty system and the Indian Act, managed by a bizarre bureaucratic tango between Indian Affairs and Indian leadership, fostered the kind of poverty and disprivilege that inevitably leads to rapid population growth. Throw in some cultural obliteration orchestrated by Church-run residential schools and Aboriginal people are leading the way not only in population growth but in every column of the statistical spreadsheet for human misery—suicide, unemployment, addiction, obesity, illiteracy, and domestic violence. Saskatchewan leads the world in the incarceration of its indigenous people. Seventy percent of the men and women in our jails are of Aboriginal ancestry.

A few weeks ago, I showed Daniel the article in the local paper with that stunning figure. Most of it would be property crimes, I said, but almost all of this kind of crime comes from the structural inequality that keeps Aboriginal people in an underclass that has no property.

"Ahh, that's a lot of baloney white people like to believe," he said. "You give yourselves too much credit. Indians were already heading for trouble long before you got here."

I am slow at coming around to accept many of the controversial things Daniel tells me, which is why this was the third or fourth time he explained to me what has happened in "this place." Nevertheless, whenever he talks to me about these matters, he is patient. His gaze lowers, he becomes quiet, chooses his words with great forethought, and without ever naming the source of his understanding but instead referring simply to "they" or "those ones." A slight lift of his head or movement of a hand lets me know that this is spiritual knowledge from messages received during long hours in the lodge, and not merely someone's theory.

"The people in this place were given sacred things to be honoured—the tipi, the dog, and the buffalo." As I listen, he makes drawings on napkins or moves the salt and pepper shakers to represent what he is saying. "And they were given the Sun Dance and the lodge to help them do those things, to find their walk here on the earth. They were told that a time of suffering and fighting would come. It would come from the east, but even before that happened, they were forgetting to honour those things they were given." He makes a sweeping motion with the side of his hand across the table.

"When other Indians from the east came bringing the first white people, some people here had already stopped honouring the dog, the tipi, and the buffalo. They gave them up for other things, forgot about the lodge and the Sun Dance. That is why the buffalo disappeared. Then the Indians who came from the east started making deals and treaties with the whites as though they had always been here and this was their place. They were hand-picked by the Crown as the ones who would co-operate and sign treaties for land that was not theirs."

Once, I asked Daniel what he thought of a story in the paper about elaborate spending by board members for the Indian gaming authority in charge of casinos. "Yep, at the trough again." Pointing to one of the chiefs in the photo, he said, "This one thinks he is taking the moral high ground by complaining about the others, but it is just a strategy. What better way to get more at the trough yourself than to complain that others are taking too much?

"These guys play the pity, blame, pity, blame game and complain about treaty rights. To negotiate a treaty you have to negotiate from a sovereign position. None of these chiefs are sovereign—the only sovereign Indians are the ones who are not on the take, people who aren't involved in the politics and band councils. They're all playing a game and the rules are made by the Canadian government. They like to talk like they are sovereign, but they have never been sovereign—not from the beginning when they came out west with the British and tracked down the Indians who were here and then started making deals, treaties, as though they had always been here. The people who were here didn't want to give the land away. Look at Sitting Bull and Kicking Horse—they were not going to sell off their land in treaties. Sitting Bull was a spiritual leader, he knew this place. He said, this is my home and I will fight those who want to take it. He knew the earth was his mother—you don't sell your mother even if you are starving.

"The people who lived in this place knew what it was." He opened the newspaper and began drawing. He made three lines radiating from a large triangle into a smaller one on top, with a small circle near the bottom of the large triangle.

"It looks like a tipi," I say.

He nods. "This is the structure at the centre of the earth and the sun. Knowledge passes through this vortex"—he points to the place where the lines all cross—"back and forth from those who sit at the fire to the creator. Nothing is more sacred, but these chiefs have used this structure in building their casinos. It's there in all of the casinos, and it is a desecration to use it in such a place of greed. But all of this is ending—it's falling apart.

"You watch, soon these guys who have squandered everything will have to sell their reserve land to pay their debts. It is happening already, because when they go to get loans, they have to put up collateral and that will be a piece of land on the reserve that is being used by someone whom they don't like."

Last year, Daniel asked me if I could help him and his

brother find a piece of land like ours. I asked why. He said it came in a message during a lodge ceremony.

"They're telling us we have to move the lodge. They said people would try to make it difficult to continue where we are. And that's already happening, so we've got to find some land. They told us in the lodge what kind of place to look for." Once they bring the lodge to a new place, he said, they are to shift it each ceremony to another patch of ground and over time make a specific shape on the land. He drew the pattern for me and it looked like the point of an arrow.

I told Daniel I would ask around, but so far I haven't found any land for sale in our area. I offered to discuss it with our community to see if we could let them set up on a corner of our property, but he said he wants to be sure this time that they have clear title to the place so no one can tell them what to do or not do.

This is what things have come to. Instead of the prairie doing the possessing, people have to possess the prairie. And so banks, real estate agents, and lawyers will be enlisted to help Daniel secure a place where he can follow one of the last remaining spiritual practices that connect people to the land here, that channel the voices of creation through stone, the grandfathers or "ancient ones," by heating them to their origins in fire and then pouring water to release into the air the messages they carry.

Most of this has to do with imposing agricultural models of land tenure on a place where hunting people lived with their own, more fluid form of tenure, but I cannot think of Daniel's search for a place to hold ceremonies without seeing the other devastating displacement that has happened here. First they lose almost their entire ancestral land base in treaties that have been questioned from all sides since the day they were signed. Poverty and hunger come next, but to bring on the levels of violence and misery seen in First Nations communities today, another step was needed: the silencing of the very voices Daniel assents to in the lodge.

Although he shakes his head when he hears me blame Christendom, I know it is partly because he will never accept passing all the blame on to others. "We did it to ourselves," he says. "We stopped honouring what we were given. It's easy to blame the priests. Anyway, I go to church myself now and then. They told us, in the lodge, that the One Who Wears the Crown—he is the real deal."

And then I ask him about all the time and money he has spent trying to help young Aboriginal people stay away from addictions and gangs. What about all the substance abuse—it's more than self-medicating, it's a search for lost spirits, isn't it? The spirits that Daniel and others are finding again by going back to the ritual processes the priests said were superstitious pagan nonsense. They know those rites are needed to carry young people across the threshold to full adult life and spiritual maturity. In tearing indigenous people away from their religious bonds to family and creation, the residential school system prepared them for membership in our culture of chronic addiction and adolescence. Add to that a few generations of poverty and you've got all you need to make statistics and headlines.

Here is a recent one. It was a sunny Saturday afternoon

with hundreds of people in the park surrounding Wascana Creek where it has been formed into a lake in the city. Cyclists, joggers, dog walkers, groups of young people circulated the water on the promenade. An Aboriginal man, looking dishevelled and upset, approached a woman to ask for help. "My friend just died over there! Can you call for help?"

He was so distraught, the woman had trouble getting the details she needed to call 911 on her cellphone. The man said his friend had gone into the lake for a swim but then sank below the surface without coming back up. How long ago? Thirty minutes, he said. All that time he was running around the lake frantically asking people if he could use their phones to call for help. People interviewed later would say they were afraid he might steal their phone. They did not believe him.

The woman who finally made the call said that the man told her he had given up and was on his way to the Legislature to find a phone there, but seeing a group of young Aboriginal people, he decided to give it one more try.

"I'm upset because it took him so long to find someone to help him," she said in the newspaper report. "If he were non-Aboriginal and clean-shaven, would people have listened to him and made that call?"

A civic authority interviewed in the paper reminded everyone that swimming in the lake is forbidden. The bylaw against swimming in the city's only body of water, however, is not to protect people from drowning. It is "mainly for health reasons," she said, mentioning pollution from upstream agricultural runoff. However, the incident may stimulate a review of the park's "signage" needs.

Better signs. That should do it. Maybe a few that say "Aboriginal People Will Not Bite," or "'Love Your Neighbour' Includes Indians," or "What Would It Cost Us If We Started Caring for One Another and This Creek?"

ROAD CONDITIONS: POUNDMAKER'S WALK

*In 1882 at Fort Ellice I saw a young Cree who on foot
had just brought in dispatches from Fort Qu'Appelle 125 miles
away in 25 hours. It created almost no comment.*
—Ernest Thompson Seton, *The Gospel of the Red Man*

Fort Ellice was near the confluence of the Qu'Appelle and
Assiniboine rivers just east of where the boundary between
Saskatchewan and Manitoba is today. During the 1885
resistance by Aboriginal peoples in the northwest, the fort
was an important mustering point for the Canadian army.
After the battles at Batoche, Duck Lake, and Cutknife were
over, and Riel and others had been executed in Regina, the
great Cree chief Poundmaker remained in jail, convicted of
treason despite his efforts to keep his own band from joining
the resistance. When it became clear that he might die of
the tuberculosis he'd contracted in prison, he was released.
After returning to his reserve at Sweetgrass, he decided he
would travel to Blackfoot Crossing to pay his respects to his
adoptive father, Crowfoot, whose intervention had prevented
the prison officials from cutting his hair. There was but one

horse among all of Poundmaker's people, so he would not take it. He walked the two hundred fifty miles slowly with his wife, Stony Woman, who did all she could to relieve his fever and cough. He worsened as he travelled through the rains of May, but rallied when he arrived and enjoyed several weeks of visiting with Crowfoot. However, there are wounds too deep to be healed. Poundmaker died that summer among his adoptive family. It is said that he fell to the earth while taking part in the thirst dance.

11 Retreat

THE RAIN IS ALL THERE IS now. The harvested fields running off to all horizons, straw yellow fading to grey at the edges, and the rain falling on all of it. Without any moral position, without any obligation, without any expectation, simply falling on the prairie world the way the sunlight falls on most days.

This stretch of ditch has not been mowed in a while. There are some millet plants that snuck in when the crop was seeded, but the rest of the margin from field to road is filled with the brome grass that dominates most prairie ditches here. I stop for a moment to watch the rain striking the wide blades arced in perfect loops. Every leaf in the curled canopy is bejewelled with crystal droplets, but it is the dark green depths beneath that draw my eye. How long would it take, staring into brome, to find something good in an invasive species that has displaced millions of acres of native grass?

One good thing leaps from the grass out onto the road. In my hand and unperturbed, the frog would fit on a dollar coin. These are the ones I used to catch in ditches for fishing bait when I was a boy. In any damp place back then, boreal chorus frogs hopped before each step of your rubber boot. We'd stuff them into stubby beer bottles, which rolled around in the bottom of the canoe until we were over the pickerel hole and could begin to troll.

Seeing a large truck coming, I put the frog back into the ditch. I move to the left side of the road to let the truck pass, but it slows to a stop. A semi-trailer pulling a flatbed, with remnants of hay on the bottom. The window comes down on the passenger side where I stand, revealing a teenaged boy. The driver, a man about my age, leans across and says, "You walking to Strawberry Lakes today?" He remembers me. He is the one farmer I spoke to on my scouting trip a month and a half ago.

"Jeff, right?" I say. "It's Cherry Lake, but yeah, Strawberry is close by. I won't get there for a couple days, though."

As we talk about the walk, he says, "You know, if you're interested in this road, you should talk to my mom. She's pretty old, but she still remembers the old stories. She grew up near those lakes."

I ask for her maiden name, but before he says it, I realize I know the name and the place he is talking about. His mother is one of the last surviving members of the Belgian family who ran a market garden and nursery in an isolated little valley just south of our land. Her grandfather, a merchant, sold his store in Belgium and brought his wife and children to settle here in 1903.

"My grandfather—Mom's dad—he had market gardens too. They lived just up the hill from his father's original homestead," Jeff continues. "She said he used to truck his flowers and vegetables into the city along this road. They called it a highway back then, number 16. We still call it 'Old 16,' but it's probably in better shape now than it was back then. Anyway, once a week they'd drive into Regina and deliver stuff to the little corner stores in each neighbourhood."

"When did that end?" I ask.

"Oh, sometime in the fifties, I think she said. After the Safeway stores and that came along."

I thank Jeff and say goodbye after we have agreed to arrange a time when he can take me to visit his mother, now living in a care home in the city.

For several years now, the members of our little community of urban refugees at Cherry Lake have been making regular pilgrimages to the old homestead where Jeff's ancestors grew their market gardens for fifty years. Usually on spring or fall days we will walk south along a settler trail that bisects our land and then up out of our valley and across a short stretch of upland before taking a narrow draw down again into the next valley. At the bottom, a long row of seventy-five-foot-high white spruce trees takes us down the last hundred paces. We step over a spring that undercuts the trail, past a sprawling willow tree, and into the shade of what feels like the remnants of a lost world. Geraniums still grow near the barn, which is the only original structure standing. The rest are down to stone cellars, concrete foundations, and a strange adobe-clay wall that crumbles more with the passing of each year.

I've returned in every season, had campfires there, slept overnight a few times, napped beside the barn. A decaying homestead in a picturesque valley carries the usual dose of prairie nostalgia—the bittersweet despair leftover from vanished lifeways—but I think we keep coming back to this one because of hope.

For us it is a shrine commemorating one of the places where subsistence agriculture and the local food economy were last seen. We wander the flood plain next to the old yard site, looking for any evidence of where the gardens might have been—places that grew carrots, beets, potatoes, and turnips—all the while thinking, *If it worked sixty years ago here, it can work again.* Going there arises from the same longing that sends us out to pick saskatoon berries in July and finds us stalking the wild asparagus in May. The asparagus grows at another lost garden in an orchard leftover from homesteading days. We search the weedy undergrowth until we find the bright green stalks jutting up impudently from the winter-worn earth and trumpeting the fecundity of spring. We snap them off and eat a few as we gather. The taste of a green thing still tender from its sunward leap is as good as dipping your cup in a mountain stream. A draft of courage from wild asparagus lets us know that health and wildness still flow together beneath this belaboured land.

I'm taking a detour to avoid a Rottweiler and a mastiff in farmyards coming up over the next couple of miles. On a side road heading north, I walk past the loveliest field I have seen all day. It's an uncut alfalfa crop, festooned with purple flowers. I make my way north through the edge of it in a mix of tame hay spangled with yellow blossoms of gumweed.

Flocks of Brewer's blackbirds scoot ahead of me as I go. The clumps of alfalfa seem to be lit from within. A savannah sparrow flies in and lands on the barbed-wire fence. And another one ahead of it, and another one on a post. I stop to watch, wondering if these will be the last of them I will see before next May.

Turning east again along the north edge of the alfalfa, I follow what looks to be an abandoned easement of some kind, a space between fencelines that has been planted with scrubby Manchurian elms and ash trees. Halfway along, I come across a hunting roost: a small shed mounted twelve feet up on posts, with a ladder and trap door beneath. Nearby is a patch where someone has put out bait, oats or something to attract deer. And then, attached to a tree, a case that is meant to hold a motion-activated camera. Using the camera's time signature, the hunter who has set this up can find out exactly what time of day the largest bucks come to feed at the bait. With fifteen quarter sections to seed, spray, and harvest and a job in the city, a farmer needs a place where he can hide out, whether the deer are coming or not.

The man-cave impulse is one way to respond when the signal-to-noise ratio of being a husband and father bottoms out at zero to one. It does not have to be a hideout—a garage stocked with beer fridge and big-screen TV, or a hunting roost like this one. Sometimes we just retreat into our own headspace, or out to the green world of fairways, forests, lakes, and mountains. We all do it. Today I am pretending to be *homo viator*, but there are a lot of days when I just want to be *homo troglodytus*. The quest and the cave are both ways to retreat. Writers like John

Gray have said men handle stress by retreating and figuring things out while their brains are occupied doing something else. That may be, but what about the things we are doing while we are escaping? Cave and quest endeavours are not merely incidental; they have something to say about the appeal of the retreat and about the times when retreating may disrupt the very balance men are looking for.

The balance I am talking about is more of a polarity, a flow between the opposite charges of what we sometimes identify as masculine and feminine qualities. Spiritual thinkers from the other side of the planet who have been attempting to understand that flow for twenty-five hundred years would say that all people have an innate bisexual yin/yang reality within which a given person—whether male or female in physical form—expresses his or her self as predominantly feminine or predominantly masculine in nature. However, each person, again, regardless of physical gender or sexual orientation, has also an inner aspect which is the opposite of his or her outer aspect. Okay, fine, but here in the West at least, that Taoist polarity between inner and outer aspects seems to be less than balanced as we overvalue the yang at the expense of the yin. Regardless of the gender identity we choose to put on our driver's licences, the world we see every day in the marketplace or in the news is run on qualities often stereotypically asso-ciated with masculinity—leading, outward-directed, aggres-sive, independent, goal-oriented—while the qualities usually associated with femininity—receptive, inward-directed, passive, interdependent, process-oriented—are suppressed. Discovering that women are persons too has not so much taught us to respect feminine energy as it has fostered a culture where everyone is duly rewarded for acting from the masculine side of his or her nature.

When the people who are expected to be exemplary at all of those prevailing qualities—adult men—go too far and indulge their masculine impulses, leading becomes domineering, outward-directed becomes distracted, aggressive becomes violent, independent becomes selfish, and goal-oriented becomes obsessed.

Just as often, we underperform, failing those expectations. Too much warrior or too much wimp and we are off to the garage or the golf course looking for an escape from the dissonance of living in a time when the women around us are often doing a better job of manning up to the realities of life. And ultimately for men, it is the *doing* that counts. Think of the archetypal caver, Batman. He captures the male imagination not merely because his cave was well equipped with cool stuff (although that doesn't hurt), but because of what he was *doing* from his cave— saving Gotham—and because that activity brought some balance into a life that otherwise was askew from having to dampen down his desire to assert his will on the world. Bruce Wayne's social calendar—the mayor's ball, munching canapés at art openings—required truckloads of yin energy, enough to send any man down the batpole.

But cleaning up Gotham is only one half of a man's retreat. Much of the time we escape to a place where we can stop acting on the world and just sit with a beer and watch someone else do it. If Bruce Wayne had been a father who ran a trucking company or walked steel girders for a living, his cave would have looked more like a sports bar.

Both kinds of retreat, quest and cave, are attempts at restoring balance, at negotiating that polarity of masculine and feminine energies. When I hide out to watch college basketball on TV, I am looking to experience some of the classic outward male qualities, but I am doing it in a way that is stereotypically feminine, by using my capacity to empathize in passively receiving and taking in the motion and drama I see on the screen. On the other hand, if I head out the door instead to be engaged in a dynamic activity—actually playing the sport, hiking through a valley, digging in my garden, or building something for my honeybees—then I am working toward goals and, in the case of a sport, testing myself against others, but the action happens upon or within a field that receives the energy I offer in a way that to men is mysteriously and deeply satisfying. Either way, whether I am watching basketball or playing it, there is a polarity at work that is pleasing, an interplay between giving and receiving that is not unlike the one we hope to experience in our encounters with women.

If I think of the cave and the quest in these terms, then I also know exactly what I am retreating from and why. The real world beyond the basketball game or garage is made complicated by a mismatch between what I expect from others—women in particular—and what I actually encounter. Karen is cranky for two days because the children are not listening to her and she has too much on her schedule. On a good day, when I am able to be more present, I will listen sympathetically. But most days I give her several suggestions about what she might drop from her schedule, about going to bed earlier, getting up earlier, and then I promise to talk to the kids and make supper. Of course, she resists most if not all of what I say. Conventional relationship wisdom here says that the mistake I made was in giving suggestions instead of merely listening empathetically. And that is absolutely correct, but whether I empathize or give advice that is not received, over time the throttling of male energy has me looking out the window.

The trouble comes for men when we lose our courage for the real world of female bosses, girlfriends, wives, and daughters. A woman says no and we either get pushy or we quail in fear. Neither one feels very good, and if it happens often enough we can get stuck in one of the two retreat modes—either spending too much time being that questing, dynamic force working on the world or, perhaps worse and more common for contemporary men, spending too much time in the cave passively receiving the dynamic activity of others. The first imbalance can lead to a kind of inflated or aggravated male dynamism (men obsessed with golf or hunting; professional athletes who bring their violence home with them), and the latter to a deflation or cooling down of a man's capacity to access masculine energies and act with presence and honour in the world (men addicted to gaming or pornography).

Not that great things don't come from men hiding out for a spell. A couple of years after Thoreau received his no from Ellen Sewall, he headed for the woods just outside Concord.

He managed to get a fine book out of his cave story and we are all the better for it.

Like most men, I prefer to think I am fearless, but encountering the feminine in our souls and in others can be scarier than walking past big farm dogs. Most of us don't have the balls to simply listen to and love a woman when she is at her most volatile and fractious, to absorb the blows of relationship and somehow respond out of our strength rather than out of our injury. Walking down a prairie road requires no courage, but it will take some to find the balance that will let me live mindfully with the dissonance and confusion I often feel in the presence of all that is feminine in life.

Tonight, with any luck, my cave will be a bivouac beneath a prairie sky. The detour has taken me farther afield than I thought it would. To get back to Old 16, I follow a rail line I know will intersect in a mile or so. Two Swainson's hawks have been following me for so long I have forgotten they are there until I stop along the train tracks to rest and eat some jerky. This seems to confuse them at first, but then they climb to circle higher, staying overhead and screaming every few seconds.

The rain has stopped, the clouds parting to allow a shaft of light through from the sun dropping in the west. I am seeing more birds on this last stretch, partly because, as I near the edge of the old glacial lake bed, the soil becomes sandier and not as good for growing crops. There are grasses, native and introduced, growing in the ditch and in fenced pastures. Along the rail line I flush a small covey of grey partridge. The soft thwirr of wings, then their voices, *took-took-took* as they glide back into tall grasses. A fall gathering of eighty magpies forms a straggling ribbon in the air as they lift from a hay yard and bank, their white bellies facing my way to follow the wind. And then, along the first stretch of native pasture, I hear a strident scolding sound and, turning toward it, find a pearly grey bird fifteen feet away perched on a sign, staring at me through its black Zorro mask. A loggerhead shrike, the first I have seen all year, sitting on its perch like a small god. After a few seconds it takes off in a flickering blur of the black and white on its wings, fast and straight as a bee to clover, landing right next to another shrike down the fenceline.

I stand still and watch the two of them on the barbed wire, hoping they will stay too. A rare bird, an emissary of the hidden and holy, surfaces in your day as a small joy whose vitality wraps itself around you. Unmerited, undeserved, unbidden, it is a surprise in every way, and though you know it cannot last, you want to pitch a tent right there on the mountaintop and not let the memory of that embrace fade.

These thoughts are soon replaced by others born of worry. Pesticides, habitat destruction, and perhaps shortage of prey are making every pair of shrikes more important these days. I wonder if this pair nested here, but if they succeeded, I should also be seeing some juveniles. The loggerhead, an unusual songbird for its predatory habits, has been a threatened species now for a couple of decades. When I began birding on this road, they were common and nesting in the countryside all around Regina. We are now down to somewhere fewer than seven thousand pairs in the province—a very low number for a songbird.

The two of them begin to preen and I back slowly across the road to the opposite ditch, leaving them to the peace of their pasture. Within days they will be heading south to Texas or Mexico.

A mile ahead of me now are the low hills of the Davin moraine at the edge of the Regina Plains. A pile of sand and gravel melting out of ice from the last glacier to pull out of here, the ridge is the biggest piece of unploughed prairie for miles in any direction. The road cuts through its northern edge and continues east, but this is where I will camp for the night.

Stepping over the fence, I see my first mule deer, two does, bounding lightly over the rump of a hill. The native spear grass has been bleached blond by the sun and it swishes softly as I climb the ninety feet to the top. Once there, I sit down in the shorter grama grass and thread-leaved sedge, facing back west for a look at the road, now sharply outlined in shadows from the low light. The surveyors plotted the lines well. The road runs straight as a pool cue, the mark of some geometry-mad demigod, penetrating the prairie in a kind of perfection, its vanishing point an infinite convergence somewhere along the fourteen miles to the city, a day's walk away.

Enclosing the road on either side, though, are forms of the recumbent earth that put me in mind of contours I know more intimately. The light not so much falling upon it as coming from inside, the way a living body burns with its own inner fire.

The mind cannot hope to follow all of the changes in even this small expanse of the earth's flesh spread before me, cannot hold the hidden shifts from mile to mile and season to season, giving life and receiving death. The surveyed strip of gravel is not part of the blossoming mystery but a clumsy attempt to enter it, an unchanging artifact of our desire to know and possess what ultimately cannot be known or possessed. Snow, rain, wind, and travellers leave their marks, but the road stays the same: a persistent and austere presence, but also, and paradoxically, an icon of movement and desire, a conveyor of all that is powerful and possible. To experience its potency and motion, you drive it at sixty miles an hour. On foot, I felt nothing of that, only the road's contemplative welcome, more monk than beast, looking for that rainbow bridge to join the two, and offering its abiding invitation: read what you find here, meditate, pray, and ponder.

A monk who lived for a time in caves came up with that sequence for spiritual practice more than fourteen hundred years ago. Saint Benedict called it *lectio divina*, and of course the text to be read was Scripture, not life at the roadside. James taught it to me once when I visited him in his hermitage: first read (*lectio*), then meditate (*meditatio*), then pray (*oratio*), and finally contemplate (*contemplatio*). This has been a day of *via divina*, and with the sun losing out to storm clouds, I am already missing the ascetic fraternity of the road.

The light shifts and suddenly this hilltop view offers nothing more than a summary of the nostalgic prairie landscape aesthetic. Take some farmland, add a road, and bathe it all in warm light from a setting sun. It is a paradigm repeated in thousands of prairie landscape paintings, most of them hope-lessly sentimental. The artist I always associate with a scene of this kind is Ernest Luthi. A farm boy who could not stop himself from putting lines and colours to the things he saw around him, Luthi was familiar with every kind of sky. His clouds, represented in oil and watercolour, have been scattered across western Canada with the generations of postwar farm-land refugees who still get misty-eyed at an image of threshing crews and stooks in a field.

A lifetime bachelor, Luthi lived in the town of Punnichy an hour north of here, cloistered with his brother in a small house they built themselves. Some would say his paintings present a prairie Arcadia of agricultural man that glosses over much of the story, but Luthi's images always turn my head. He had an intense understanding of the light, shade, and form at work here and a hand able to get it down in a simple palette and two dimensions.

Yes, this is a Luthi landscape, and I decide I like it after all: road and sky, the pathway of man beneath the wild heav-ens, the land an innocent bystander. All that's missing is a rainbow.

There will be more rain, and a good thunderstorm by the looks of it. I head downhill to find a lower place to camp, out of any wind and lightning that might be heading this way. In a cleft at the south end of the ridge I find two fences running east, parallel to one another, twelve feet apart. There are no trees, and it might not be wise to camp near them anyway, but the spacing of the fencelines will be perfect for mounting my plastic tarp. The bivouac bag will keep some rain off, but this is looking like it'll be more than some.

I tuck a pebble into each corner of the plastic sheet, tying it with cord and then stringing it tight to the fence. My stave propped beneath the top end makes a peak to ensure the water will run off. I tug on the lines to see if they will be able to take some wind. All is well, and with darkness and the first raindrops falling, I retreat beneath the plastic and set up my sleeping bag and bivouac. I open a tin of chicken and dig out my paperback copy of Peter Matthiessen's *The Snow Leopard*. The rain is steady now.

As Matthiessen and George Schaller climb toward the Tibetan plateau, my prairie storm joins the narrative and becomes a Himalayan monsoon. The wind pulls hard on the lines of my shelter, but it is holding—for now. I check for water pooling at the edges of my bivouc. It's getting close, but there's nothing I can do other than curl up into a ball. I shut off my headlamp, cower inside the zippered bag, and try to will myself to sleep. A big gust tosses my stave aside and the whipping sound of the plastic sheet becomes so loud I have difficulty distinguishing it from the approaching thunder. Then the wind picks up to a full-on gale and I start to feel the rain on my bivouac bag. The plastic sheet has torn free and become a lash slapping the wet blue pile between the fence posts.

A high chanting howl of prairie banshees riding the storm brings the lightning right overhead. I bounce from my ground pad with each crack of thunder, either in fear or in vibration from the shock wave splitting the air. I'm getting wetter from the bottom up, but I am busy wondering what electrical charge wet grass and fence posts carry compared with, say, a damp human lump on the ground. There is nowhere to go, nothing I can do to get warmer, drier, braver, safer. After fifty or sixty Hail Marys the centre of the storm passes over, leaving the wind and rain to carry on without the heavy artillery. Wet but not shivering, which means I might make it. A silent grace for the worms that spun the threads in my long johns. Mercifully, after an hour of wondering how the searchers will ever find my body, I slip into the oblivion of sleep.

Road Conditions: Walking Out of the Cave

I think that I cannot preserve my health and spirits, unless I spend
four hours a day at least and it is commonly more than that—
sauntering through the woods and over the hills and fields.
—Henry D. Thoreau, "Walking"

Too much time sitting in the cave may not be good for a man's sex life. A study published in *Urology* suggests that men need to be doing more questing than caving if they want to stay sexually active. Dr. Irwin Goldstein, from Boston University School of Medicine, did a nine-year study of six hundred men who had no impotence problems at the outset of his research. The results showed that a brisk two-mile walk each day can reduce men's risk of impotence. The men who kept exercising or took up exercising in middle age reduced their risk of impotence. Exercise improves blood flow to all parts of the body, and vigorous walking in particular seems to maintain blood flow in all the places men like to keep healthy. The men in Goldstein's study who merely stopped smoking, lost weight, or cut back on drinking, however, did not show a reduced incidence of impotence.

PART TWO

Small Deaths

Nearly all men marry in the most profound ignorance of women and of love.

—Honoré de Balzac, *Physiologie du Mariage*, Meditation VII

Keeping to one woman is a small price for so much as seeing one woman. . . . A man is a fool who complains that he cannot enter Eden by five gates at once.

—G.K. Chesterton, *Orthodoxy*

12 Greater Beings

CAST UP ON THE SHORES OF MORNING, I waken in dumb surprise. Not so much that I am still here, but that the world of grass and hillside is still here too. With the sound of ducks dabbling somewhere behind me, I open the bivouac and look outside expecting to see a lot of water. Nothing, not even a puddle. I search the skies for a rainbow in the sodden clouds receding to the east, but there is none. As a member of the lost tribes of Genesis, I am a sucker for the rainbow's mythic promise.

I warm myself with thoughts of the fires of tribesmen around which the flood tale first took shape. What a poetic and conflicted moment in our narrative descent it was when our spiritual ancestors first spoke the meaning of the rainbow. "I have placed my bow in the heavens as a reminder of our covenant and a promise that I will not destroy the earth in flood again." And from that moment forward, the people celebrated each multicoloured arch in the sky.

There is a tradition in the Jewish Midrash that says, hold on there, don't go chasing rainbows for solace. If the generation is living righteously, they won't need any rainbows.

Right living is its own protection against annihilation. The generation that sees a lot of rainbows is being reminded to look to its own obligations under the covenant. Its people must strive to be worthy of living in a world that does not need the rainbow's protection, by purifying and healing their own hearts, yes, but also by purifying and healing the heart of the world. The obligations of the One who places rainbows in the sky have been met and continue to be met each time the sun rises. It is humanity that must meet its obligations and commit itself to preserving the world and its inhabitants.

A rainbow excludes nothing, includes everything. The same everything held in a mythical ark on the sea now reflected in an arch in the sky shining light in every colour human eyes can see. By the time the story was written down in the book of Genesis, the author knew just how thick-skulled and recalcitrant his audience was. In the eight short verses where God fills Noah in on the details of the covenant, its radically inclusive terms are repeated six times. The phrasing varies only slightly from one iteration to the next, but the message is made abundantly clear: *This deal is not just about you; it's between me and all life on the earth, it's about every living creature on the planet. Did you get that? Everything that lives. Everything.*

After a breakfast of granola, old raisins, and peanuts, and a change into slightly less soggy clothing, I strike my camp, resolving to dry it out in midday sun if the clouds part.

I head northeast across the pasture, walking through the cured spear grass of an ecological refugium that until a few years ago still supported ferruginous hawks, long-billed curlews, Sprague's pipits, and Baird's sparrows. I should hit the road in about a mile, right where its easting trajectory is briefly subsumed by a stretch of Highway 48 before continuing on its own. I can hear cars on the highway ahead of me and the high-pitched vibrato of approaching Swainson's hawks. They have found me. I can't be entirely sure it is the same hawks, but these two have the plumage of yesterday's pair. Their toffee-coloured hoods contrasting with shining white breastplates make them look like winged versions of medieval knights, or at least the Hollywood version that lingers in my memory from Saturday afternoon movies.

The two hawks circle a hundred feet over my head. Where were they all night in that storm? Roosting by the road until they saw the opportunity shape traipsing across the pasture? They accompany me, screaming their high, quavering cries every twenty seconds, as I travel a short stretch of the rail line toward the highway.

My bones are warming up with each stride, heart pumping faster but nothing like the adrenalin-charged cadence in my chest as the storm passed over last night. There's no way to know how near those lightning bolts came to finding me, but a couple of times it felt as though the explosions of electricity were running through the earth without slowing down to worry about boundaries.

Wet pant legs sticking to my calves, feet squelching in my sandals, but I am imperturbable. I have been pummelled by the full-on fury of a prairie storm, chastened by the dark angels of the night into something stronger than I was yesterday. I leave the pasture and square my shoulders to the highway. What is that Rilke poem, where he talks about "being defeated, decisively,/by constantly greater beings"? Something about choosing to fight with tiny things, but if only we could let ourselves be dominated by the things that choose to fight with us—as if by an immense storm—then we would gain their strength and not even need names.

Who wouldn't feel stronger after surviving a night like that one? Here I am, upright and reasonably warm again, carrying on my back everything I need to live for the next couple of days. It's going to be hard to top that storm. Not sure I can find any "constantly greater beings" to wrestle with on a highway where everyone else is rushing into the city to shop at Home Depot and Winners.

Why is this van pulling over right in front of me? It's a woman with lovely dark eyes and she is smiling at me. Shining hair falling in soft waves from under a toque. Those are the lips, nose, and cheeks of the greater being I fell in love with thirty years ago.

"Karen, what are you doing here?"

"Thought you might like some dry clothes and another sleeping bag."

The scent of hot oatmeal porridge beckons from the front seat of the van, but all I can think of just now is that this woman deserves to have more of her genes carried forward. She ignores my gracious offer of assistance in that process.

"Get in and I'll pour you some tea. What's with the hawks?"

"They're my new best friends. Getting on my nerves a bit, actually."

As I climb into the passenger seat, she tells me she's been driving the road since sun-up looking for me.

"How am I ever going to be a great naturalist writer if my wife shows up with hot breakfasts and dry gear after every storm? I mean, Thoreau, Matthiessen—none of those guys had women serving them. . . . Is that toast with peanut butter?"

"Yeah, well," Karen says, passing the toast, "Matthiessen's wife died of cancer right before his trek and he had a dozen porters and Sherpas with him. And everyone knows Thoreau nipped into Concord for a good meal now and then. You're just ignoring the hawks, aren't you?"

I take a swig of tea and look out the window at the one perched on a fence post across the ditch. "What am I supposed to do with them?"

"I don't know—that's for you to figure out, I guess. But you might try talking to them. If I know you, you're ripping along too fast. Try slowing down, listening more."

She didn't say it, but I could hear the maxim she always throws into this kind of conversation: "Connection, it's all about connection."

Karen begins to talk about plans for the weekend honey gathering, the friends who are planning to come, the supplies we need, but I am looking at her and marvelling at my good fortune to be in the daily presence of such a grace-filled creature.

Glancing down at her left arm, I see she is wearing her pressure wrap, which means that she has scratched her finger or hand in the garden or kitchen again. When women have lymph nodes on their underarm removed during breast cancer surgery, that arm can lose its capacity to circulate lymph fluid. The smallest scratch or bruise can bring on swelling and pain as the fluid flows toward the injury and gets stuck. It can take several days or even weeks to recover and for many women it becomes a source of chronic pain and swelling for the rest of their lives. So far Karen has done well, but each time it happens we are both reminded of the anxiety that gripped our lives during her year of therapy.

Right now, the sight of her wrapped arm has me feeling smug for becoming a bit more gentle and attentive in recent years. In part it was learning the light massage methods for coaxing lymph back up Karen's arm that has taught me that healing often requires the lightest of hands. I guffawed when the therapist first showed me how to do it. The most ridiculous little strokes, just barely pressing into the flesh, but carefully, patiently overlapping as you sweep and release in slow, soft touches up the limb. It feels as though I'm trying to roll an ant along Karen's arm without squishing it. Any more pressure can make things worse by blocking the channels. *Channels* is the kind of word people who teach this massage technique use when they describe it. They refer to "watersheds" and work by visualizing the flow of lymph through channels, eddies, and basins. This riverine vocabulary is part of why I have become a lymphatic massage enthusiast, though I will admit it has also given me a new excuse to touch my wife slowly and tenderly.

This way of massaging came as a great revelation to me, for I have lived most of my life thinking that anything worth doing is worth doing with a firm hand. As I make the small

circles with my fingers at lymph nodes above Karen's collar-
bone and under her arm, and then sweep a hand in short, pausing caresses across her upper chest and along her arm, I think
about the cells carried in that flow of lymph fluid, the lympho-
cytes of various kinds that are busy defending our bodies from
tumours, viruses, and bacteria. The effort of paying attention
to my fingers and the pressure they exert has had me wondering about all the times I have pushed too hard in a world where
many things respond only to gentleness and patience. If we
can help restore the flow of healing waters in a body this way,
can we do likewise in the land? Where else are there rivers of
healing that are best moved with a loving caress?

Another discovery that year came from our bedcovers.
Karen has always accused me of taking all the covers, but I
knew she was exaggerating. Sure, there were usually more on
my side, but she was kicking them off or something. During
the weeks of chemotherapy I would often wake in the night
and look at her. One time, as I turned over to go to sleep
again, I looked back over my shoulder and saw that there
was nothing between her and the cold November air of our
bedroom. I realized then it was a mechanical problem made
worse by inattention. If you have two people in a bed, one
small and curvy and the other large and angular, and the large
one is inclined to rotate outward, the covers are going to end
up on his side.

That night, I reached back and threw the quilt and sheet
over her, tucked them in at her shoulders. It has become a
nightly ritual. When I turn over, I look to see if I've exposed
her to the air and then toss the covers back. Karen probably

has not noticed, but I congratulate myself on my largesse every time I do it, happy to have someone to love and care for. One night, after finding Karen coverless again, I was struck by the image of her being exposed for years because I was taking something mindlessly and then denying it when she pointed it out. If I can do this in my sleep, what am I doing in my waking life that is leaving her exposed?

"I've got a change of clothes for you in the back if you need it." I thank her and step out of the van to swap wet gear for dry. With a kiss, Karen puts me back on the road drier of foot and warmer of heart. The two hawks resume their escort.

If I can waive my disbelief long enough to consider the possibility that selfless love is a real force in this universe, then there are other things I can believe too. That I have a responsibility to figure out how to talk to hawks and everything else bound under a covenant between creator and created; that a creature only grows into its beauty when truly loved and received with gratitude; and that this may be our real charism, the unrecognized role and largely unfulfilled purpose of the human: to keep the earth, the soft, alluring, receptive beauty that she has become, by seeing her through souls that we strengthen and awaken by wrestling with constantly greater beings until we can act and touch her with gentleness, wisdom, and patience. Stories of wildlife thriving in Chernobyl and the Korean Demilitarized Zone may argue that the earth would be better off without *Homo sapiens*, but I am dreamer enough to wonder what we do not understand about the role of the human witness and the power of our caress.

Road Conditions: Walking a New Language

*The spotted hawk swoops by and accuses me, he complains
Of my gab and my loitering. I too am not a bit tamed,
I too am untranslatable, I sound my barbaric yawp
over the roofs of the world.*
—Walt Whitman, *Song of Myself*

Until quite recently, human beings looked to nature for insight
and inspiration as well as food. Reading the signs of the
meadow, the river, or the woods was more than a survival skill;
it was a way to develop the self within its nurturing matrix of
creaturely life. Animals advised adolescents on the threshold
of adulthood. Plants whispered of their healing properties.
Bill Plotkin and David Abram say the human spirit does not
develop fully when we undervalue the wildness within and
without and disengage from the "more-than-human-world."
But our resistance, our unflagging confidence in rationality,
keeps us impermeable, closed, and dubious. The language
of nature may remain untranslatable, but walking or sitting
alone in wildness at least places you within earshot. In time,

you become more porous, less obtuse and guarded. Thoughts that leap to mind are not dismissed as mere imagination, as a dragonfly lands on your arm, a robin pounces on a small snake to defend its nest, or a hundred spiders balloon across your path. The untranslatable is still worth listening to, for even with our own speaking, much of the meaning is carried in the sound itself or in the body of the speaker.

13 Lilies, Grubs, and Slough Hockey

THE HAWKS VEER OFF AND LAND a half mile away in a field shortly after I ask them why they are following me. I stare in their direction for a spell, wondering what I am supposed to do next. The rest of the morning passes in a five-mile trudge along pavement to get to the spot where the highway turns off my path and leaves me to the quiet prairie road again.

Once I am off the highway, I enter the least travelled section of road along the route. Perhaps because no farmers use this stretch for their main access, the municipality doesn't gravel the road here or mow the ditches. The bed is low, just a two-track dirt road, with some weeds springing up in the middle in defiance of the last time a grader passed this way. The dirt is the same stuff growing crops in fields to my right and left. Within ten paces I have collected fifteen pounds of it on my sandals, prairie gumbo with just the right character- istics to hold spring runoff long enough for wetland birds to raise their young. No vehicle has passed this way since last night's downpour. The mud surface is utterly unmarked save for the tracks of a coyote and a raccoon seemingly walking side by side and heading east before me.

I move to the grassy edges to keep the sandal load to a minimum. There are periwinkle blossoms of aster there and splashes of goldenrod among the grasses. Within the first mile I arrive at my halfway water cache, where I have stashed three litres in a jug beneath a roadside willow. Twenty miles to go and a day and a half to travel it: this is a good spot for lunch and a nap. After a cold meal of crackers, cheese, and canned chicken, I make a bed in the ditch using my pack and rain poncho. I lean back and brush up against the stems of what look to be two lilies well past bloom, the western red lily or "prairie lily" beloved of farm people in the region.

This past June, the lilies bloomed in profusion on a patch of native grassland we had burned the year before in early spring. What kind of subtle forces would be gathered from the earth into a flower that flourishes after a prairie fire? A medicine woman I met once told me she listens to each plant to learn what it is for. I gather that she is listening with an ear subtler than the ones holding up my glasses and that the plants are communicating with something other than words. Hawks might speak the same way, but right now, looking at these spent lilies, the only voices I can conjure are from two women who wrote a splendid book on the western red lily. In *Prairie Phoenix*, Bonnie Lawrence and Anna Leighton tell many ecological stories, but one of my favourites is about meadow voles. The voles make a bargain with the lily by eating some of the bulbs while at the same time scattering bulb scales far enough from the mother plant to propagate new lilies.

The aboveground love life of the lily is just as fascinating. The lily faces directly upward all the time, holding its anthers up to the sun. These are the dark, rice grain–sized structures perched atop the stamens, the little packets where they make the pollen necessary for fertilization. The astounding thing about the western red lily is its capacity to keep its pollen in optimal condition by opening and closing its anthers in response to the weather. If it rains, the anthers pull on their overcoats and zip up to keep the wet out. On sunny days, good for attracting pollinators, the anthers open wide and expose their pollen grains to all comers.

Science categorizes pollination by the vector, or means, of pollen transfer, using some fancy words concocted by adding syllables before the suffix -*phily*, which comes from one of the Greek words for love. If science could speak entirely in numbers, this remnant of poetry, like so many others, would be expunged from our scholarly attempts to describe nature, leaving us with mechanisms where there is no love of any kind at play. Ornithophily in plants tells us that the hummingbird loves flowers and in that bond ensures more of both hummingbirds and flowers.

Large flowers such as lilies attract large pollinators. In mid-continent, one of the largest is the ruby-throated hummingbird, but like most hummers it prefers to access flowers from the side or bottom. It can't dip its bill into a blossom that points straight up. One of the next-largest pollinators in the aspen parkland prairie is the swallowtail butterfly, a black-and-yellow-striped beauty whose wingspan would fill the palm of my hand. The four curled petals of a lily flower facing up to the sky make a platform perfectly suited to the swallowtail. It lights on the blossom and feeds, picking up grains of pollen as the undersides of its wings brush softly against the open anthers. Some of those pollen grains may land on the stigma of another flower as the swallowtail moves around from plant to plant. Once it reaches another flower's stigma, the pollen grain germinates. From there it becomes one of those microscopic miracles of nature we love to watch in time-lapse nature films. The germinated grain forms a pollen tube, which elongates until it penetrates the style, the female receptacle leading to the lily's ovary. Once it finds its way into this inner chamber, the pollen tube will deposit sperm cells in a precise spot within the embryo sac, accomplishing its task of fertilization.

To manage this tricky bit of navigation down the style into the ovary and then through the embryo sac, the pollen tube is following the siren song of chemicals coming from the ovules, the very source of the flower's maternity. We think of that last step as the sexual moment, but the meeting of sperm and egg that fosters new lily seeds starts with a lot of other call-and-response connections that in the broader sense are expressions of the eros that lives in all creatures.

Something summons the lily up from the ground. In earlier times a hunter wanting to attract buffalo might have lit the prairie on fire, burning off the thatch from previous years and nurturing a sprout from a bulb scale tossed aside by a vole. Sun brings the lily to bloom, bloom brings butterfly, butterfly brings pollen, and little eggs inside the lily bring the pollen tube down into the place where lilies begin. It is a circle of creative, erotic connection that is merely one paradigmatic sample of the generative, evolving life of the planet that continues to unfold because the loveliness of creatures attracts the kinds of exchanges that lead to the making of more lovely things.

Here is another set of exchanges. Surrounding the two lilies at my side are dozens of goldenrod plants. Each one of them has a squash ball–sized expansion in its stem, as though the plant has swallowed something too large for its gullet: galls from the goldenrod gall fly. These "flies" hardly rate the name since they are rarely airborne and spend their entire lives on goldenrod plants. The male fly hangs out on one of the flower buds, looking suave, and waits for a female to happen by. When a female shows up, he does a little nuptial dance to get things going. Once they mate, she goes and looks for the right spot to lay an egg, which she manages by injecting it through her ovipositor into the fleshy stem of the goldenrod plant. After hatching, a chemical in the larva's saliva causes the plant stem to grow a gall, which becomes its home and food. The gall continues to grow until the fall, when the larva excavates an escape route in preparation for its emergence as a fly the following spring.

Taking a year to develop fully, goldenrod fly larvae are hosts to two species of parasitic wasp and food for one species of beetle in summer. In winter I see chickadees and downy woodpeckers whacking away at the galls to get the little nugget of flesh inside. I sometimes cut a gall open to see the grub sleeping its glycol-assisted days away. Once when I did this, I was with Ron, one of my fireside friends. We had taken our seven-year-old girls along with us for a camp-out at the old market-gardening homestead south of our land. Ron had not seen a goldenrod fly grub before, but he took the glossy white little spiral and popped it in his mouth. "Tastes like chicken," he said. After some prompting, his daughter followed suit. When Maia looked up at me hoping for rescue, I told her that I make it a policy to almost never follow Ron's example.

There are enough goldenrod galls in this ditch for me to dig out a few tablespoons' worth of grubs, but I'm not sure how well that would sit on top of my canned chicken. I imagine earlier prairie dwellers would have eaten them when protein was scarce. A book on traditional plant use Ron loaned me mentions nothing about the goldenrod fly as food, but it does say that Anishinabe people employed them to do some tricky woodwork. Taking a short piece of red-osier dogwood branch, they would make a small hole in one end, insert the grub, and then seal it up with pitch. The grub would dig its way to the other end, hollowing out the branch into a perfect pipestem.

Prayers borne on smoke drawn through a stem hollowed out by a fly larva: is there a better way to honour the One whose spirit is the unseen made manifest in the interchanges between fly and goldenrod, and beetle, and wasp, and woodpecker, and hunter?

I awake from my nap in sunlight. In the blue overhead there are clusters of small popcorn clouds interconnected by filaments of spun floss that run across half a mile of sky between the clusters. A dragonfly, another cherry-faced meadowhawk, lands on my knee and I feel a surge of melancholy, a familiar whisper that was there beneath the noise of the storm last night, though I usually feel it on waking from a midday nap. It's mostly disappointment at having surfaced from the blissful dissolution of slumber into the daylight where my self reasserts its standard swindle of separation and everything around me recedes like pond ripples from a tossed pebble. There is nothing to do with such a feeling but to stand and walk on in bewilderment.

The road begins to rise as it passes through gently rolling terrain, the "hummocky moraine" common in aspen parkland prairie. At all points of the compass I can see here and there the small copses of aspen trees we call bluffs. Somewhere in the last few miles I crossed an invisible boundary between what ecologists term the mixed-grass prairie and the aspen parkland eco-regions.

Up ahead, the horizon is a mere half mile away—a knoll over which the road disappears. Beneath it are two sub-horizons, lower hills the path ribbons over in pleasing arcs. I pass an aspen-fringed slough the size of a large putting green. A family of ruddy ducks swims away from me as I walk by, but my thoughts drift to a frozen slough we played hockey on when I was a kid.

An adolescent boy discovers a few bodily pleasures, but some of them are not sexual, or at least not overtly so. I have three specific memories of a kind of euphoria that came into my body between the ages of twelve and fifteen, and all three moments involved playing a sport outdoors with no adults around. One came with a floating hook shot I managed to sink in a playground pickup game of basketball; another happened at sunset on the high tee of the fourteenth hole of Holiday Park Golf Course in Saskatoon as I watched my ball go straight, for once, in a miraculous arc that in that moment was somehow responsible for the gold-tinged green splendour sculpted with blue shadows and rolling away from me to the horizon. But the first, most lasting and intense, was a game of slough hockey on a wetland just outside the city limits. I think I was twelve years old.

It was a blindingly bright day, the air itself alight with frost crystals sparkling around us as we skated over the ice. In my memory I can see the blue vault overhead and feel the presence of the other boys, who had finally invited me to join their shinny game. I have a clear image of the puck sliding into a scalloped bay at the edge where the cattails stuck up through snow, me gliding in after it, digging it out with my Bobby Hull curve, and sending it back to the centre, where everyone else waited. But that wasn't it. The pleasure that overcame me, and which I feel only the merest glimmers of now in recollection, had nothing to do with my performance but everything to do with the slough we played upon. Sliding over that wild ice above the sleeping marsh, within boundaries that turned in lovely contours fringed by bulrushes, I felt a weightlessness, an exhilaration run through me as though I had taken leave of the ground.

For years, whenever I drove by the slough, I would try to invoke something of that feeling, but it became dimmer over time. Eventually the wetland was filled in and paved over with strip malls. I have heard other men describe their childhood memories of slough hockey in similar terms. Once, over beer, a fellow who sells farm machinery told me that it reminded him of the sensation he'd get as a teenager using horses to cut calves out of his father's herd. The horse and pasture became something he felt he was "flowing through or in," he said. Hockey on the right slough felt the same way. As we talked, we came to a place where I think we both realized there was something sexual in the experiences we were describing, and that was where we pulled back.

A boy filled with adolescent energy skates over a slough after a puck, moving and being moved by other bodies within an alluring cosmos. There is something receptive and feminine about the space, as there is in every field, fairway, or court where I have stroked, thrown, or chased a ball. Standing in for the earth herself, the field of our play calls something forth from our bodies the way sun calls lily, lily calls butterfly, and ovule calls pollen tube, all of it bearing echoes of a joy we are privileged to pay homage to in our limbs and loins.

Road Conditions: Walking into Aspen Parkland

To day we pitcht to ye outermost Edge of ye woods
This plain affords Nothing but short Round
Sticky grass & Buffilo & a great sort of a Bear
—from Henry Kelsey's journal, August 20, 1690

Every landscape has its own emotional signature as we walk through it. Aspen parkland resonates deeply with a visual code for home that some say is wound into our chromosomes. Geographers and habitat selection scientists who subscribe to the "prospect refuge theory" say we like the look of open country with wooded copses because our ancestors liked it too. Hunters prefer landscapes where there is enough cover to hide in but also a distant view from there—a refuge with a prospect. When artist C.W. Jefferys came to paint Henry Kelsey, he placed him on the edge of an aspen wood looking out upon a plain filled with bison. Kelsey's journal entry for the date of his emergence from the woods shows that he has seen both bison and another good reason to take shelter: the plains grizzly. Looking like a character from a James Fenimore Cooper novel, Kelsey leans against the bole of an aspen with musket at his side, as his Indian guides (which he called the Naywatame poets, now believed to have been the Hidatsa) take cover in the willows. Jefferys, in depicting Kelsey at that moment in his journey out of the boreal forest and onto the aspen parkland prairie, created a tableau with an emotional charge that hearkens back to our emergence as the upright, bipedal hominids who left the jungle for the savannah.

14 Sirens

IN PLACE OF THE HAWKS, a small, swirling cloud of butter-flies escorts me eastward. Most are the usual whites and sulphurs, though a single Milbert's tortoiseshell adds a dab of dark orange to the fluttering mob. I think it's a Milbert's. If I find a dead one on the road, I'll slip it into my copy of *The Snow Leopard* and identify it at home. The collecting urge often shows up early in a naturalist. A good friend of mine recalls his sister's horror when she discovered his collection of beetles and butterflies pinned and mounted on her menstrual pads. Pressing bugs in books as an eight-year-old was probably the first sign I wanted to know what things were called. Any butterflies and dragonflies I could get my hands on went into the middle of my parents' Reader's Digest Condensed Books, where perhaps the words of *Last of the Mohicans* or *Lorna Doone* would assign names to the squashed forms.

I have yet to see a vehicle on this ungravelled piece of road. I walk in the middle, pretending that foot traffic is all it ever receives. Warm sun on my neck, there is just enough of a breeze to ruffle my pant legs and make the grass whisper in long hisses that rise and fall. The sound shifts to a deeper roar in the aspen leaves of a bluff next to another slough. On my left, a field of uncut wheat shines and sways, in golden calendar-photo glory.

Something has moved onto the road ahead at an intersection. It is a young girl on a black horse with a red dog at its side. Girl, horse, and dog freeze and look at me and then turn back the way they came. Moments later, a large brown horse appears at the intersection with a woman at the reins. The two riders continue toward me and I walk ahead trying to loosen my stride and look like something other than a vagabond of dubious character, which is of course exactly how I look.

Horses are supposed to be the most gentle of brutes, but they have never wasted any of their tenderness on me. Whenever I try riding, the horse and I labour in mutual suspicion—me suspecting the horse has plans to rub me off on the nearest tree and the horse suspecting I am a putz who can be rubbed off on the nearest tree. Horses seem to be at their gentlest in the presence of innocence, which may be why young girls love and understand them better than nervous old men. We have all seen that communion of girl and beast, her backbone flowing easily with the canter of the horse, the flip of her hair echoing the flip of the pony's tail.

I stop to watch the riders approach: the woman, a young mother on an ambling chestnut quarter horse, sitting with ease in the saddle as though she has grown up there. Her nursling, strapped against her belly, likely will grow up with horses. Perhaps four months old, she is facing outward astride the saddle horn with her head nestled between the twin endowments that keep her fat and pink.

Now, I have a certain acquired competency in this area, and not merely because my wife breastfed each of our children until the age of two or three. Karen has for twenty-five years been a leader for her local La Leche League group. LLL at first blush appears to be a bunch of mothers supporting other mothers in nursing and child-rearing, but anyone closely associated with its women soon begins to realize it is in fact a clever front for an organization with a subversive agenda to undermine the power of the state, eroding its grip on health care, social welfare, and education. LLL's apparatchiks operate within tightly knit cell groups, which report to party HQ up a strict line of command. *La leche* means "the milk" in Spanish, the language of choice for radicals.

As a man married to one of these freedom fighters, I often answer the phone to hear the shaky voice of a young mother who wants to join the struggle but is still suffering beneath the hegemony of mothers-in-law or doctors with their propaganda of formula, cribs, and scheduled feedings. If Karen is on call to give breastfeeding counsel but out on an errand when the phone rings, I am sometimes tempted to take a stab at it myself. You learn a few things over the decades of hearing your wife offering advice. I am well acquainted with most of the stock responses to the usual issues: latch problems, engorgement, cracked nipples, babies who seem to nurse all night. Another LLL father I knew, a man with a soft voice and unassuming manner, did just that once or twice: "Mmhmm, yes, well it does sound like nipple confusion, dear. I think you might want to stop using the soother and perhaps set aside the breast pump and bottle until baby's latch improves."

As the mother brings her horse to a halt with an imperceptible command, it is the trained eye of an LLL father fully conversant in the lore that allows me to notice the small dark blotch on her turquoise T-shirt straining to contain things. Indeed, I ascertain, this baby is getting all she needs right from her mother. As we exchange greetings, I make note of the child's rosy complexion, strawberry-blond hair, and glistening eyes, all evincing the health of a prolactin- and oxytocin-filled mother whose practice of on-demand nursing is sustaining optimal milk gland function.

Without the benefit of my years under Karen's LLL influence, I might have been more distracted when a loose tendril of the young woman's hair strayed eastward as she turned to point up the road in answer to my question. The mere sight of a woman of such robust health atop a horse with baby strapped to her like some heraldic emblem, dog faithful at her side and surrounded by fields of grain ready for the harvest, might well have had me thinking of Epona, the Celtic mother goddess and protectress of horses, maternity, fertility, dogs, crops, and health. Epona, who often appeared naked like a water nymph at a spring. Epona, who . . .

". . . you sure you really want to walk through that swamp?"

The protectress of rash travellers is asking a question, which I discern by the rising tone. Something about the road allowance disappearing up ahead into a marsh. I shrug my shoulders in fake bravado. "Should be okay. I've got lots of time."

She wishes me luck, we say goodbye, and I resume my journey, flushed from the effort of trying to hold two conversations at once: one with the woman and the other a loud harangue with my hindbrain. *No, a woman's beauty is not there for your pleasure, and no, this woman is not the least bit stirred by the magnetism you never had even when you were not several years past your best–before date.*

A friend of mine estimates he falls in love four or five times a minute as he walks along a crowded downtown street in Montreal or Vancouver. I think that may well be a fair estimate, but out here on a prairie road, your guard is down. You don't expect to be smote by a fertility goddess on horseback.

There is a direct feed between a man's eye and approximately one pint of sexual desire transmitters sloshing around somewhere past every neuron that ever had a second thought or scruple, and when something stirring enough to stimulate that bypass casts its form upon the retina, the brain tips one way or the other and everything gets a lust bath. That's the science, but to the man walking down rue Ste-Catherine or Robson Street, it can be mightily confusing. The main problem, of course, is that the eye-to-lust hand-off mistakes covetousness for love.

I wasn't even ten years old the first time I confused the two. It was 1967 and I was at a birthday party for a school friend. He took three or four of us into his father's office and pulled a shiny-looking magazine out from under a daybed. It fell open in his hands, releasing into the room a dark-eyed genie with hair the colour of bittersweet chocolate and buttery gold skin running all over the place, making the subtlest forms and shadows. She smiled at us, recumbent in a string hammock, one leg bent, the two peaks of flesh above her arched ribs catching light from the failing sun. The planet lurched to a halt and I wondered if the flashing in my head was maybe a little like the time my sister reached for her lamp and put her hand in the light socket. In a moment of sudden clarity I knew the purpose of the universe: to make women who can lie in hammocks and glow and make your head feel all fuzzy and nice.

That discovery brought new focus to my development as an artist. My daily practice of drawing Snoopy and Charlie Brown soon gave way to studies of the undraped figures sitting in the studio of my imagination. I became quite skilled at drawing naked women and found I could employ my craft at school to ingratiate myself with the boys who were the chieftains in our recess reprise of *Lord of the Flies*. The brief spike in my status ended the day Mrs. Horvath discovered me rendering a lovely odalisque in pencil on the Arborite of my desktop. Seven years later, in the first model-drawing sessions of my university Fine Arts course, my charcoal gesture drawings of live nudes were disastrously tentative. The task of drawing a real, three-dimensional woman, unretouched and pale skinned, unnerved me. I promptly switched my studies to English Literature and Political Science, where lying was harder to detect.

I think it was in watching birds, though, that I began to see how desire makes the eye into an instrument of possession, consumption. One late November morning, Robert called me from a pay phone in a breathless voice. He had found a guillemot on an open patch of water on the otherwise frozen Wascana Lake.

"It's diving a lot, but I've had good looks at it. Pretty sure it's a black guillemot." This is the siren song of an inland bird-lister: an ocean-going alcid appears, sacrificing itself to the gods who send rarities to swell the roster of check marks for any birder who will travel to see them. I threw my spotting scope in the car and raced to the lake, ten minutes away.

"Wow. It's so little," I said, getting my first eye gulps through twenty-times magnification. I had never seen a sea-bird of any kind and this one looked merely an inch or two bigger than a robin. It was all alone in a circle of ice-free water about sixty feet across, diving constantly with wings partly unfolded and ready to use in swimming down to get crayfish and anything else that might keep it alive. There was something about the way it dove, that rapid flip down into the depths, that was endearing. I wondered aloud what its chances were.

"Not good," Robert said. "A seabird this far from the ocean is pretty well doomed."

I had a lot of moments like that with Robert—looking at death-row kittiwakes, eiders, yellow-billed loons, and other birds that had gone far off course in their yearly passages. After we got our looks in, I'd go home to make one more check mark on my life list. Then I'd feel my spirits sag in post-climactic melancholy.

The most obsessed bird-listers are almost always men, and British men have the original franchise on the mania. They have a phrase to describe those moments when they get a really good view of a rare bird. "Crippling look," they say. I imagine their knees buckling in ecstasy as they clap eyes on an oriental turtle dove, but there *is* a crippling effect from the wrong kind of looking. Though I was hobbled as an artist by habits of idealizing the female form in titillating caricature, it was when I returned to art to draw birds that I started to wonder about the quality of my gaze upon beautiful creatures.

To learn the wood warblers that migrate through my portion of the plains, I decided I would paint all twenty-eight of them in gouache and watercolour on a large sheet of poster board. I had some photographs to work from but needed to see more of the plumage details, so I asked Robert to smuggle me some study skins from the museum where he worked. He would bring me two or three species at a time, as I made my way from Tennessee warbler to yellow-breasted chat. I passed the spare hours of an entire winter at a drafting table I bought for the project, holding a cotton-stuffed warbler in one hand and a brush in the other, often feeling some of the same heightened sensations I had once experienced as I drew the contours of a woman.

Nothing but feathers, bill, and feet, the study skin of a small bird is so weightless you have to look at your hand to make sure it is still there. Most of them I knew from life, seeing them zip among the leaves that inspired their shades of green and yellow, and though each hue was there in all the right places on the feathered form in my hand, it was not a bird. Embalming had taken it from subject to object, but as I struggled to bring each warbler back to life on the poster board, it occurred to me that the way I was pursuing and watching birds was doing the same thing. Even the painting I was creating—with the warblers arranged in a grid all facing the same direction in the same posture showing only the front half of each bird—owed more to the dusty old natural history museum drawer that held the study skins than it did to the souls with wings that warblers are in life.

I finished the painting but stowed it away in the basement, embarrassed at what I had wrought. Not long after that I gave up listing and the obsession with rare birds, and started looking for ways to enjoy the common ones breeding or overwintering on the plains. The last time I ran across the warbler painting among my other failed artwork in our crawl space, though, I dusted it off and brought it upstairs.

I had been reading a book by Thomas Berry and come upon his now-famous axiom, "The universe is a communion of subjects, not a collection of objects." I decided to frame the poster and hang it in our living room. Now I look at the warblers arrayed in their awkwardly conscripted eros and innocence and I think about what it takes to shift my gaze from leer to witness. It reminds me that I have at least the capacity to go from collecting objects to communing with subjects, and that my eye can help make it so.

As much as I would love to blame Hugh Hefner for all of this, it is not that simple. Here on this sun-drenched afternoon, with widgeon and teal in every puddle along the road, I walk in full awareness that lust is a very human experience, but that it can get between me and the goodness of this life, turning beauty and mystery into dispirited matter, *matériel* for the most selfish of purposes. Today I met a lovely young woman on this path. As we spoke, I wrestled with the old longings, but something of the spirit and grace in all women, plain or lovely, was there too. It got past my squabbling thoughts and settled

in me like a wordless invitation to change and be washed clean
in the presence of all that is feminine in this creation, all that
has suffered from man's unchaste indulgence of desire. It would
have scared her, but I felt an impulse then and there to make an
apology, to say forgive me for not seeing you as I should have,
as the daughter of another father, no doubt wed to a good man,
the man who cultivates these fields I walk past. I hope he looks
upon you with the gaze you deserve. I hope he treats you well.

Road Conditions: Low-Stimulus Walking

*Nature shows are much more like cities, both entities being elabor-
ate human constructs: fast-paced, multi-storied, and artificially lit.*
—Charles Siebert, "How TV's Nature Shows
Make All the Earth a Stage"

*Television is the flavour enhancer of the audiovisual world,
providing unnatural levels of sensory stimulation.*
—Aric Sigman, "Visual Voodoo:
the Biological Impact of Watching TV"

The sensuous pleasures of walking down an utterly unremarkable road are small and easily overlooked. One's capacity to
experience those pleasures, though, may be dampened by the
sensory stimulation that one encounters in the rest of life.
Most landscapes will look shabby up against the stimulat-
ing imagery packaged and sold as "nature" on our computer
and television screens. In actual life, very few roads have
waterfalls, canyons, or craggy peaks. Even fewer have polar
bears, trumpeting elephants, or great herds of wildebeest. But
our sensitivity to the gifts of creation is being diminished

by stimuli even more arousing than nature documentaries. In *Cupid's Poisoned Arrow*, Marnia Robinson applies brain chemistry research to argue that the prevalence of erotically charged imagery both in the public sphere and online is providing a readily available "super-stimulus" that is overwhelming the pleasure-reward circuitry of our mammalian brains, leading to a cascade of emotional, sexual, relationship, and social issues. Interpreting neurochemical and behavioural work done on other mammals, and combining it with the testimony of recovering porn addicts who contribute to her website (www.reuniting.org), as well as insights from ancient and more recent texts on the spiritual benefits of conserving sexual energies, she makes a strong case for changing from "fertilization-based" sex to "bonding-based" sex, urging readers to recover the sense of well-being, delight, and connectedness that comes with greater continence in one's daily encounters with desire.

15 Tilth

As I reach the intersection of the farm access where the riders turned onto the road, a coyote sixty paces away rises to the crown of the driveway and stops to watch me. I return the favour. We lock eyes and I nod. The coyote turns his head and then flows like river water into the high brome grass of the ditch, a tawny silver shimmering through the swaying green. I stand and strain to listen for anything within me. There is a faint trace of something—a cold embrace of otherness, a sense of being assessed by the wild intelligence of a hunter. Am I not hunted, then, only hunter? The cougars who make fifty-mile circuits through the prairie these days would be happy to answer that question. A few months ago a biologist friend emailed me an unforgettable photograph. It shows a large cougar, caught in the flash of a motion-activated camera fixed to a fence post in the Moose Mountain uplands southeast of here. The big cat fills the frame, walking toward the lens with a coyote clamped in its mouth and limp as a rag doll.

The living coyote moving away, replaced by the image of another one hanging from the jaws of a cougar, becomes a memento mori. Hunted or not, I am entering the dangerous years for men, when our hearts give out, sometimes before we've learned how to use them well. The men on my mother's side died of angina and strokes, my father has struggled with high blood pressure for twenty years. "What does it mean to live with heart?" I asked Holly, the massage therapist who gave me the energetic consultation.

"It's listening to the inner life, not ignoring subtler messages that bubble up." She smiled. I was probably squinting. "It's not magic. Your soul speaks to you through your heart. It's easy for that ear in the heart to go deaf, so it takes some practice to tune in. Some focus."

Tuning in and out is something I understand. The older I get, the more I "watch" birds by ear, often leaving my binoculars at home. Robert always said you have to learn the common bird sounds first. "Learn every sound a robin or a house sparrow makes so you can screen them out and listen for other stuff."

I got good at screening. "How is it," Karen is fond of asking, "that a person who doesn't hear his wife mention a potluck coming up on the weekend can hear a chickadee hiccup on the other side of the woods?"

This seems to be a day made for tuning in. A garter snake crossing the road, perhaps heading for a winter den, stops and tastes the air with its tongue as I stand overhead. Another hunter sizing me up: *Is this thing prey or predator, meal or enemy? Or potential mate?* The tongue flicking in and out of its closed mouth collects molecules of pheromones and other chemicals and then deposits them on an opening in its palate where the receptors of its Jacobson's organ can translate the information and pass it on to its brain. This garter takes its time with the processing, using the two sides of its split tongue to triangulate my position before arriving at "possible danger" and then slithering off the road.

I remember reading once that the human embryo has a similar organ, or at least a vestigial version of one, and that although scientists don't believe it is functional, a remnant of the organ persists until birth and beyond in some people.

The snake may have me at a disadvantage, gathering more information from me than I can gather from her, but the thought of molecules speaking to that small soul passing over the road reminds me that I am awash in the same living flow where we cycle tiny galaxies of stuff made of elements born in the heart of bigger galaxies, in exchanges that are real whether I can detect them or not.

In my better moments with birds, I have felt glimmerings of an intuitive faculty that gives me a sense of a bird being present moments before actually seeing or hearing it. It seems to occur—or perhaps I am able to see it occurring—more when I am in landscapes less familiar to me, because when I am away from home I am less inclined to explain the intuition away as the consequence of knowing which birds are associated with which habitats. Once, it happened as I walked along a river in British Columbia, watching chum salmon a couple of miles inland from the Salish Sea. It was early winter and I was not really expecting to see birds, other than the eagles and gulls that were feeding on the dying fish. I stopped to watch a group of big glaucous-winged gulls loafing on fallen logs over a small set of rapids where a narrow strand of the river was tumbling through boulders toward the head of an island to join the main. As I moved my head to look back at the trail and resume my walk, a precognitive message whispered in my consciousness: *dipper, there's a dipper here.* I turned my head and there it was, a fat dollop of a bird, the colour of the shadow side of a small standing wave, right in the river, plunging headfirst under the flow after bits of life caught between rocks. I was not thinking of dippers—in fact never realized they could be found so near the sea—but something in the place or the bird itself told me that the swimming songbird who dives after caddis fly larvae was there.

Whatever the process, when this happens to me with wild creatures, this kind of intuitive reception of signals I cannot explain, I chalk it up to soul. The organizing principle that makes this snake or coyote or dipper a great deal more than a collection of matter gives each creature a particular wavelength that we can attune ourselves to. I knew a boy who loved snakes of all kinds. He found them wherever he went in the city or countryside. I'd walk in front looking but not seeing so much as a quiver in the grass, while he was a step behind, diving left and right, catching garters and smooth green snakes right at the side of the trail.

These days, the human race seems particularly keen on sending and receiving messages. If I had a smart phone with me here in the middle of nowhere, and perhaps a twelve-year-old to show me how to use it, I could fire off a text message to a friend in Kurdistan, upload a photograph of the road to a chat group for people who like to walk really straight roads, book a backhoe to drain a slough I don't like, or use an app to find the nearest pub selling decent German beer. The environing air that once bore subtler signals to anyone who would listen is suddenly awash with radio waves connecting desire and desired all over the planet in a sphere of instant communication.

That engineers devised a network of networks that can handle all that transmission and transaction is impressive, I suppose, but it is crude and unsophisticated next to the universe of interchanges going on in the first few inches of soil beneath the flax crop I am walking past. One small region of that universe—the hair's-breadth zone known as the "rhizosphere" surrounding each tiny rootlet—fosters and hosts untold associations, exchanges, signalling, messaging, and monitoring related to a range of soil conditions, weather, plant health indicators, nutrient availability, predation, and pathogens that expands every time a grad student takes a closer look.

This impossibly complex network monitoring and maintaining the soil health that feeds a lot of life above and below ground is of course powered by the sun. The network recycles its own waste, and instead of filling the air with electromagnetic frequencies, it moderates a balance of gases in the atmosphere by sequestering carbon. All of this happens through the ministrations of a microscopically thin sheath of fungi wrapped around roots. It is hard to think of a creature less charismatic than a root fungus you can't see, but these organisms, which scientists call arbuscular mycorrhizal fungi, or AMFs, have been evolving for 460 million years and are crucial to life all over the planet.

The AMFs here, in forming the nexus of plant–soil symbiosis in this field, are quietly doing their work, regulating much of what goes on between the flax and the entire complex ecology it supports and draws life from in the soil. Exquisitely attuned to chemical signals in their environment, they monitor and interact with the world around the roots and within the plants, modifying plant growth, inhibiting the growth of pathogens, fostering plant resistance to drought and other nasty conditions, improving soil structure, and preventing soil erosion and nutrient loss through solubility. Even more important for those of us who like to eat plants and animals that eat plants is the role of AMFs in helping crops access phosphorus and nitrogen, as well as vital trace elements such as zinc. The flax growing here is particularly dependent on AMFs for its uptake of phosphorus when it is in low concentrations in the soil.

Soil scientists are constantly uncovering new marvels being managed by AMFs. They have found, for example, that AMFs monitor and regulate root density and patterns to influence the amount of pressure applied by plant roots. The pressure roots exert on soil particles is minuscule but vital in helping to align and bind soil together in ways that prevent water from flushing away nutrients and other materials important for soil health. But root pressure is only part of the story of soil aggregation.

When I first took up growing things in a tiny backyard plot thirty years ago, I discovered the word *tilth* and would sprinkle it liberally into gardening conversations whenever I could, just to let people know I was a man of the soil, someone who could hold a clump of dirt, roll it through his fingers, and make squinty-eyed assessments. I liked the sound of it—*tilth*, an earthy word you might hear in "The Miller's Tale." I could imagine Mr. Michaluk, my grade twelve English teacher, pronouncing it in his recitation of Chaucer's "Prologue." By tilth, we mean the feeling of soil in the hand, the way it sticks together or comes apart. Like a lot of things in gardening, it's a Goldilocks measure: good tilth means not too much and not too little soil aggregation.

Soil scientists were not quite sure what was responsible for tilth until 1996, when an American researcher named Sara F. Wright peered into the universe in some grains of soil and found a new star, a soil constituent she called "glomalin." It is glomalin that gives soil its tilth. This substance, Wright and her colleagues have found, is what keeps together the organic matter in our gardens and farms. It is the stuff we are always trying to support and feed with forkfuls from our compost heaps. No one was surprised when it turned out that AMFs, the overachievers of the soil world, are also the source of glomalin.

The way AMFs produce glomalin is yet another poetic moment in the life and death going on beneath our feet. Mycorrhizae, like most other fungi, have filaments called "hyphae" through which they connect to the soil. In a mushroom, these threadlike structures might look like a plant's roots, but they function differently because the fungus is not getting any of its energy directly from sunlight. In AMFs, the hyphae are constantly dying off and shedding, and when that happens, glomalin is secreted in the soil.

Happily named, glomalin is sticky. Little gobs of it glom on to plant rootlets and living hyphae, forming sticky string nets that hold together the sand, silt, and clay bits that make up soil, along with decaying plant stuff and other carbon-containing organic matter. That carbon-holding capacity is what has everyone excited about glomalin, which itself is 30 to 40 percent carbon. Researchers are hoping that glomalin might be a carbon-sequestering wonder-goo that will help slow down the climate swings that are melting permafrost in the Arctic and freezing the homeless in Europe. Just across the border in North Dakota, Kristine A. Nichols, a colleague of Sara Wright's, uses glomalin measurements to gauge which farming or rangeland practices work best for storing carbon. If we could apply economic instruments to support the right agricultural practices, our soils might do a better job of taking in and retaining carbon for longer periods, keeping it out of the atmosphere.

When I first read the U.S. Agricultural Research Service article declaring that a substance called glomalin holds on to as much as a third of the planet's stored soil carbon, the word sounded like something the folks at Findhorn would have used to name a faerie in their garden. *I spoke to Glomalin this morning by the lettuces and he suggested we amend the soil with some ash from the fireplace.*

Back when I discovered the joy of growing my own carrots and was trying out everything from "square foot gardening" to the lunar sowing advice from *The Old Farmer's Almanac*, I read a little book about the New Age community that had formed in the 1960s near Findhorn, Scotland.

The founders, an English couple and a Canadian woman, said that they talked to plants to learn from them how to improve the stony soil. Each plant had its spirit or faerie. These they called "devas," claiming that it was messages and co-operation from the devas that enabled them to grow their famously gigantic vegetables in abundance.

Like any good rationalist, I set the book aside and immediately reached for more plausible explanations for their monstrous broccoli and marrows. I wasn't about to start looking for garrulous vegetable faeries between my tomato plants, but I did wonder whether it is possible to pay closer attention to one's seedlings and sprouts, seek their guidance in a sense. For Findhorn, the proof has been in their success in converting lifeless, thin soil into rich humus that produces forty-pound cabbages. Today, though two of the founders are gone, Findhorn is one of the most successful intentional communities in the world, with four hundred residents in their eco-village. Their work has won international recognition for sustainable land use and community development. None of this would have happened if there had not been three people foolish and brave enough to announce that they were having conversations with spirits in their garden.

I always say my first three years of gardening produced my best gardens, and while no devas spoke to me, I know I was in my own way listening more closely, as I fussed over the soil and plants with a gentle hand. And with that there came a certain affection, a bond I felt with those few square feet of earth. If there are wispy little fungi embracing the roots of my tomatoes and eggplants in the most intimate of bonds, receiving and sending messages to give each plant what it needs from the soil and the sun, is it possible that my garden might be able to include me in its web of communication and mutual benefit? This stuff is helping to regulate the climate of the planet in its spare time—surely it can sense the difference between a gentle, affectionate gardener and a crude one.

In my life, the prototype of a garden tended with love was my aunt Bea's patch surrounded by a picket fence and perched on the rim of the eastern Qu'Appelle Valley, where she lived out her days until she reached her eighties. Her skin was as brown and wrinkled as the tobacco she rolled in her cigarettes, tanned from hours spent hilling potatoes and beans between waves of lilies and larkspur. On prairie farms, the loveliest gardens have almost always been tended by women, often grandmothers, whose years of birthing babies and feeding husbands and children have burnished their souls enough to reflect back the love that shines forth from a row of peas or the faces of daisies. Men who are able to garden well are almost always older, retired blokes who have set aside the warrior ways of farm and business and settled into an equilibrium between their animus and anima. My father-in-law, Jack, took up gardening after a career as a civil engineer and deputy minister in charge of building roads and highways all over the province. Now he tends his squash, potatoes, beets, carrots, and beans with the same gentle attentiveness that he applies in talking to his grandchildren, who have been raised on his vegetables, and he gets the same good results.

At Findhorn, it was a woman who first sensed the presence of spirits in the garden. Dorothy Maclean, originally from

Ontario, said that each vegetable species has its own "over-lighting being" or consciousness that holds a kind of blueprint or archetype for the ultimate expression of that species. She reported that they were like fields of energy emanating a joy-fulness that made her want to call them angels, but she chose the Sanskrit "deva" for its meaning of "shining one."

There are no instruments to measure or record the expressions of a garden deva, but the attuned soul plays a role in most discoveries, scientific or otherwise, as anyone who has studied the eureka moments of human genius will tell you. It fascinates me that glomalin was there all along, but one hundred years of scientists studying AMFs and soil ecology did not detect it. Maybe we had to wait for women to start looking into the mysteries of soil or for someone whose soul was calibrated just right for the work of discovering the little things that make all the difference.

As it turns out, the glomalin story is not finished. So far this mysterious substance that can hold on to carbon for up to one hundred years is resisting definitive biochemical explanation. No one knows its exact makeup. That seems right to me. A subtle but crucial soil element that avoided detection for so long should resist the calipers of explanation, and hold on to a little bit of its pixie dust.

Common as dirt, hard to explain, and hidden in plain sight: glomalin has a lot in common with spiritual wisdom. Maybe that is why sacred texts are filled with stories of vine-yards, yeast, gardens, seeds, lotus flowers, dirt, and farmers.

In the Bhagavad-Gita, Krishna, the godhead, speaks to the prince Arjuna, and says:

Wise yogis love Me ceaselessly. They know that the love they are experiencing for Me is Me, for I am love, Arjuna. Just as the good farmer puts all his attention on to the soil, concentrating his mind fully on cultivating the land, yogis give their minds and hearts fully to the Divine, knowing that God alone is the source of everything.

The Tao locates wisdom in the soil as well:

Returning to the soil is rest; Returning to the soil is destiny. Returning to one's destiny is finding the eternal law. Knowing the eternal law is wisdom. Not knowing it invites disaster.

Twentieth-century Zen master Shunryu Suzuki said, "Our tendency is to be interested in something that is growing in the garden, not in the bare soil itself. But if you want to have a good harvest, the most important thing is to make the soil rich and cultivate it well."

The earthiest of spiritual talk, though, is contained in the parables of the Synoptic Gospels. "A sower went out to sow . . ." begins the story of a farmer tossing seed on various kinds of soil, some poor, some with thorns, and some rich. After the parable, Jesus provides a rare decoding, which reveals that the story of the sower is about cultivating the soul's deeper consciousness—the very capacity that allows us to hear and understand spiritual wisdom in the Word, revealed both in sacred texts and in the book of nature itself.

We are the shallow, rocky soil, the soil without tilth, when the lure of wealth and fear of persecution render us spiritually blind and deaf. We remain on the outside, unable to see and hear the inner world in ways that feed the soul. That inner world Jesus calls the Kingdom of Heaven, and in the verses that come between the parable and the decoding, he locates the inner kingdom in a farmer's field (as a hidden treasure), in seed (the small seed of the mustard tree, which grows into a bush to shelter the birds of the air), and in yeast, which, appropriately enough, is an airborne counterpart of soil fungi.

If the soul force in creation is hidden in the earth and its smallest powers of growth and regeneration, as well as in our own flesh, then the very exercise of becoming attuned to its subtle reign within nature is the greater share of spiritual practice, of cultivating the soil of our own souls.

If I sit on a hill or walk a road hoping to foster some sensitivity and cross into a life where I am attentive to subtler energies, it is not to sort out the spirit in things from the matter. I want to be able to feel their confluence, the messy incarnation of the divine in the flesh of everything from soil fungi to the grain being harvested in these fields, to the enzymes and proteins that allow my body to transform bread from that grain into the muscle, bone, and sinew that moves me down this road.

In a land where there are probably more seeds planted annually per square mile of soil than in most other places on the planet, we still have a chance to get this right. Our gardening and farming practices on the prairie are a way to bring flesh and spirit together again, to make contact with this earth and find what is still powerful inside it. In the life of grassland soils there is a native gladness that has been here speaking its old truths from beneath the stones and silt and clay since before the glaciers rearranged the furniture. That deep-downness is with us yet, feeding the roots of the wheat and barley and flax planted each spring in furrows alongside this road, making the crickets sing, fattening the vole, and drawing the hawk out across the hayfield.

I haven't gardened the same way since those first years. I am not sure why, but I gradually stopped spending as much time tending my rows of vegetables, and gardening became a chore I took up grudgingly. At my age I should be able to slow down and learn to listen to the shining ones, let them show me the right time to sow my beets or carrots. Next spring I will see what the dirt and I can do together.

Looking out at the flax field again, I genuflect inwardly to the treasure hidden there: the Kingdom of Heaven enclosed within the rhizosphere, in the gentle, clever fungi that send out filaments into the earth and around and within the roots of plants, shedding them in time to provide the tilth that feeds us all.

Road Conditions: Walking Two-Legged Together

This is the body: a witness to creation as a fundamental gift, and so a witness to Love as the source from which this same giving springs. Masculinity-femininity—namely, sex—is the original sign of a creative donation [by God] and of an awareness on the part of man, of a gift lived so to speak in an original way.
—Pope John Paul II, General Audience, January 9, 1980,
"The Nuptial Meaning of the Body"

Before we mouse-clicked our way across the hidden landscapes of soil shown via electron microscope, before we hoed between rows of deva-blessed cabbages, our hunting ancestors were using their hands to bear nuptial gifts to one another, and standing upright to do it. Bipedalism was at the very least a good adaptation for efficient long-distance travel. Daniel Lieberman, a professor of human evolution at Harvard, speculates that our female hunter-gatherer ancestors averaged nine kilometres daily (fifteen for males), much of it running. Freeing up our hands by walking on two feet, however, may have also helped foster stronger pair bonds in early hominids. C. Owen Lovejoy of Kent State University did the anatomical work on both Lucy and her even older ancestor "Ardi" (short for *Ardipithecus*). He believes that bipedalism was an important adaptation that sent our ancestors onto a separate path of sexual behaviour from our knuckle-walking relatives approximately six million years ago. When *Ardipithecus*-like hominids first began to walk on hind limbs alone, it may have been a superior way for males to forage and bring back "good provider" gifts to females—a useful strategy if you were not the dominant male with the biggest canid teeth. Skeptics suggest that freeing the hands was more likely a way to beat up a competitor or fend off predators while on the ground, but the well-named Lovejoy has stood firm on his argument that bipedalism and monogamy go gift-bearing hand in hand.

16 First Dancers

A MUSKRAT IN A DITCH SLOUGH paddles a brief arc and then dives with a splash at seeing me loom over the horizon of the road. Two gadwall drakes take flight to the east. Chorus frogs are trilling from every wet spot at the roadside. One of the farmers around here still summerfallows his fields and the black soil has attracted a fall assembly of horned larks. Their high, tinkling *tee-sip, tee-ee, sip* cries precede them into the air as they fly up in threes and fours, making little flights that seem more urgent than their mid-summer movement, as they rehearse for the day they will leave for other fields to the south.

A flotilla of twenty sulphur butterflies gathered at a wet spot on the road stops me in my tracks. With their lemon-yellow sails held aloft and aligned windward, they make a miniature tall ships regatta on the puddle. Up ahead is another puddle with another regatta just getting under way. Two are drinking and ten more are fluttering, landing one or two at a time until a dozen are gathered and lined up. As I approach, they depart in the same chaotic swirl that brought them there, couples breaking away to circle around one another in the air in tight loops. No flocking in unison like sandpipers. They come together and apart with the apparent random-ness of subatomic particles, bumping into one another and then moving on. If there is a hive mind here, it is not one that I can see.

The day is heating up now in late afternoon, turning the cricket song into one long trill coming in stereo from both ditches like an auditory electric fence. Another, softer, and lower-pitched sound falls through that barrier, but it drifts away on the wind, leaving me to wonder if I imagined it. I stop to silence the crunch of my sandals on gravel. There it is again, a rolling *groo-oo-oa*, a reedy woodwind glissando coming from the sky up ahead where the allowance relin-quishes its road to cut through two miles of bush and wet-lands. The cry of a sandhill crane blowing in on a prairie breeze is for me a touchstone of hope for the survival of wild-ness here in this corner of the aspen parkland.

The first time I saw sandhill cranes, I was with my father hunting them. He called them wild turkeys, which even to my twelve-year-old sensibilities seemed unfair to the slender-necked birds gracefully stepping between swaths of grain. I don't recall either of us ever managing to shoot one, or even getting close enough to point our guns at one. We'd sit in our Dodge Coronet with the windows rolled down, watch-ing and listening from the roadside as, one after another, great waving lines of the cranes rolled across the river breaks and into the fields from their nighttime roost on the South Saskatchewan. A string of thirty or forty would often stray closer to our car, veering just out of shotgun range but near enough for us to see the great wings wider than a man's out-stretched arms, the long neck in front, legs trailing behind, back hunched. Between the silences that kept us staring at the thousands pouring in from the river, we'd intermittently make up strategies for getting closer for a shoot, most of which we abandoned. On our return to the city, my father would get around our failure as crane hunters by dusting off an old joke about the proper way to cook a wild turkey. You stew it in a pot along with an old boot. Boil for three days. Then pitch the turkey and eat the boot.

Without my knowing it, the wild, melancholic threnody of the crane that came to my ears on those hunting trips joined other sounds already stashed in my aural medicine bundle of prairie: wind through spear grass, a gopher's piercing whistle, a distant bittern's slough-pump, hard rain in an aspen bluff. The older I get, the more I treasure the solace of such sounds.

If any bird can be an elder, teach me some things about what it takes to settle into a mature life within family, tribe, and land, it is this graceful wader of northern bogs and prairie marshes. Each spring when I watch the northbound flocks as they pause on farmers' fields warming in the April sun, some of the adults are already stained red from the mud they use to paint their feathers. People who study cranes are not sure what the feather painting is for, but some believe it may have some purpose in serving their fierce pair bonds. Once two sand-hills become a couple, the bond is so tenacious that on the rare occasions when a pair does break up, biologists call it a divorce. They don't come into breeding age until their fourth or fifth year, but bonded pairs generally remain faithful to one another for life. And life is sometimes twenty-five years or more, making them among the longest-living birds. Staying together year-round, crane pairs migrate south with their off-spring each fall. They stop off at exactly the same locations going north and south, steadfast pilgrims in what may be the oldest wildlife migration in the New World.

One of the ways pairs of sandhill cranes renew and strengthen their nuptial commitment is by dancing together at sunrise. A couple of years ago, as I drove out from our cabin on an April morning to watch some sharp-tailed grouse at their dancing grounds, I came across a flock of eighty cranes just as the sky began to lighten in the east. When the sun appeared on the horizon, spilling its gold onto a thawing stubble field emblazoned with the grey and ochre forms of cranes, I noticed a pair on the near edge of the flock pulling themselves fully erect and facing one another. Simultaneously, they threw their heads back and pointed their bills skyward. One of them, the female I believe, initiated the proceedings by letting out an ecstatic cry. After she repeated her call, her partner responded on a lower pitch. They carried on in unison then, uttering a series of orchestrated calls back and forth, and filling the air with a loud trumpeting that made the furrows ring.

But this was mere prelude. They began, slowly, to dance, the two of them moving in deliberate, graceful bows, each prancing and spreading its wings. For how many springs have these two been enacting this ritual, I wondered. Ten? Fifteen? If God became a bird and danced, it would look like this. At one point the male crane, or the one I assumed was male, suddenly leapt into the air, higher than the head of his mate. She returned the gesture, but the wind caught hold of her outstretched wings and carried her right over him in a perfect buoyant arc. On her landing, the two began again, with more bill raising, bows, flapping, and strutting, as though the world's oldest truths might depend upon their ceremonies.

As the great survivor of nature's sorting out of what will work and what will fail here, the sandhill crane has good reason to decorate itself with ochre, stand tall, trumpet its triumph, and dance in the dawn light of spring. There were ancestral cranes here on this continent when the Miocene camels, rhinoceros, and mastodons had their brief grassland safari. Modern sandhills were here to witness the rise of the bison, the pronghorn, and the upright and naked primates who began to change everything. Nine-million-year-old fossils of an ancient crane that looks virtually identical to the sandhill have been found in Nebraska not far from the Platte River, where 80 percent of the sandhill population still gathers each year on migration to renew the rites that have made it a survivor.

The earliest fossils of modern sandhills are two and a half million years old, placing its genesis well before the Pleistocene and making it one of the longest-standing bird species on earth. Most of the other animals it shared the land with two million years ago we know only from their ghosts in the fossil record. "When we hear his heralding call," Aldo Leopold wrote in his *Sand County Almanac*, "we hear no mere bird. He is a symbol of our untamable past."

The crane I heard just now was in its own way trumpeting an untamed present, a wildness that may be reasserting itself in this great mystical bird. In the last decade, cattlemen with land near the Strawberry Lakes, a few miles ahead of me, have reported breeding pairs with young in the summer, when most of their kind are far to the north in isolated bogs. One man I know, Arden Kurtz, runs cattle by the largest of the Strawberry Lakes, where he has seen as many as eight cranes at a time, adults and young together, during breeding season. Ray Schaefer, a rancher whose son's cattle graze our pastures, has been paying attention to birds in the area for a lifetime. A couple of times a summer he stops by for tea and gives me a report on the cranes' whereabouts.

The sandhill is one of the only crane species on the planet that persists in abundance. Around the world, cranes are revered as birds of great spiritual and cultural importance, but that hasn't stopped the destruction of their wild breeding grounds on almost every continent. Eleven of our fifteen cranes are now on threatened and endangered lists. While populations of the Siberian crane and the whooping crane are perilously low, the sandhill population is estimated to be 650,000 and growing. The arctic and subarctic boreal populations are holding steady, and some populations in the more temperate mid-continental regions are actually increasing. Small pockets of the prairie population clung for decades to bogs and sloughs in southern Manitoba, northern Minnesota, and, in one spot a two-hour drive north of here, near the town of Yorkton. Now their offspring appear to be moving outward to recolonize prairie wetlands.

Even Leopold's Wisconsin sandhills, which declined sharply after settlement, have recovered. Where the Wisconsin population was down to twenty-five pairs in the 1930s, a count in the year 2000 found thirteen thousand breeding birds. Farther east, breeding sandhills are reoccupying their former range in small colonies from southern Ontario and Quebec through Illinois, New York, and Vermont.

But this kind of habitat I am walking through may be especially good for cranes. The aspen parkland's patchwork of agricultural land, wooded areas, and here and there large complexes of undisturbed wetlands seems to be attracting the cranes both on migration and in the breeding season. As well, fledgling rates may be higher in this eco-region. In Minnesota's Agassiz National Wildlife Refuge, in the southern reaches of the parkland, each pair of cranes has been raising on average 1.2 young per year, well above averages in other eco-regions.

As I make my way east, I check the skies now and then for the cranes. There are days in mid-summer when their voices blow into our piece of the valley, reminding me that I should get out again to look for them. So far I have only one breeding-season sighting for my efforts: two adults foraging in a seeded field in June just west of the lakes.

I watch and listen for this bird because the sandhill crane's persistence through to our denatured world today is a sign that the land is not as tamed and tamable as we assume. It is not enough merely to eyeball the local quotient of wildness by taking a quick look at the surface as I walk past. This land, stripped of natural cover and converted to crops, is impoverished and domesticated, but mercifully there are patches of wetland left, enough to keep the crane faithful to its long journey out of the primeval bursting-forth of life on this continent. It knows the long truths of a survivor. It knows that the deepest wild energies in the land remain: the sun, rain, air, and land cycling nutrients through organisms and soil. All of these and the crane have made it through the scouring force of mile-thick glaciers several times over. And when the glaciers melted back north, the remaining hunks of ice left pothole wetlands behind as compensation. If we can find it in our hearts to do likewise with our scouring of the surface, the sandhill crane might well see another million years.

If I had to guess what it is about cranes that has allowed them to rise above the ebb and flow of this land's many passing forms, and say what most signifies their tenacity and endurance as a species, I would look to their annual renewal of mating bonds within the presence of the larger community, to their attentive child-rearing, and to their fidelity to one another and to the places where they nest, stage, and winter. Choosing one and forbearing others, the bond of two cranes is a psalm written anew by the wind in river mud each spring. If we could listen, what would we hear? That community life protects the nuptial bond, shared well-being, and child-rearing? That life is served best when you are faithful to the partner and place you choose, when you guard the sanctity of your courtship, mating, and family, and dance now and then in the larger circle of your tribe?

The wisdom of their two-million-year witness penetrates all the layers that buffer us from the others who are less other than we thought after all. Out of such truth rises the seeded furrow, the blackbird song, the rank scent of a weasel gone through grass, the tang of balsam trees budding out in bottomland, and the better parts of any man or woman's path through this life. The illusion of eating alone finally fading to one banquet, we all have fire on our brows, that fierce golden eye, and legs and wings for dancing on the resurrection fields of spring.

Road Conditions: Other Two-Legged Walkers

The crane walk helps to strengthen the heart,
calm emotions, and ease anxiety.
—Deborah Davis, *Women's Qigong for Health and Longevity*

Birds are the other creatures who often walk on two legs, having saved their forelimbs for more elevated work. But they owe their walking skills to the branch of bipedal dinosaurs that survived extinction to become feathered fliers. Grassland larks and sparrows in particular are adept walkers and runners—in part because they retain the long hind claw of their Jurassic forebears. Many species of grassland birds, when returning to the nest, will land some distance away and then scurry mouse-wise along the ground between the grass stems to avoid disclosing their nest location. For a model of grace and economy of movement, though, the cranes are unsurpassed. Stepping across a muddy field, lifting and placing each foot with great care, a crane gives an impression of undistracted focus and patience. Qigong, a mindfulness and movement practice with roots in Chinese medicine and Taoism, includes an exercise based on the crane's walk. Teachers of qigong say that walking like a crane, slowly and deliberately shifting weight from one foot to the other, heals us by drawing ch'i, or life energy, up from the earth to lighten the heart.

17 Dust and Breath

Just up ahead I can see the first place where the road disappears at a T-junction, leaving me to make a two- or three-mile traverse across trackless terrain. In theory the road allowance continues east, slicing through some aspen bush, but when I arrive at the junction it becomes clear that there is no trail into the woods. I stand at the road edge peering ahead, trying to guess the best route to take around the bush and through the fields. The first half mile is about all I can see clearly and it has the hospital-green tones of swathed canola. As I ponder my options, a black pickup truck approaches from the north on the intersecting road. It slows to a stop and I walk over to the driver's window. A man in his sixties, wearing a ball cap more stylish than those you usually see on prairie farmers.

He asks me if I am hunting, the only activity that would explain someone on foot in this landscape. I say I am just out for a walk, and that makes me a curiosity worth engaging. I introduce myself, and describe where I am heading. He tells me his name, which I recognize as one of the original German families in the area. I ask him if he knows a friend of mine who has the same surname. Oh, yes, Dave, he's a cousin. He grew up just down the road. Dave's younger, though, he says. Just had his sixty-ninth birthday himself last week. Grew up on a farm nearby but has lived his adult life in the city. Had to take over the land when his brother died in 2001, but he still lives in the city. He's been renting it out to local guys. Just last year the guy who was farming it died in the tractor right over there (he points to the field where I will be walking). Heart attack, only thirty-eight.

You never know, he says. It just comes like a thief in the night. Then he tells me he spent the day cleaning up after a second break and enter at the farm. Last year he was robbed of thousands of dollars in tools and equipment, but this time it was more a mess than anything else. We commiserate over the risks of owning property but not being there to take care of it all the time. I ask him if he'd mind me walking across his fields to get to the next stretch of the road. He chuckles at this and admits he has no idea what might be the easiest route across. A lot of sloughs and bush in there, he says, but he doesn't walk on the land himself. I ask if he has seen any cranes in the area. No, he says, and we part ways—he to the west on the road I was walking and me into the field of cut canola.

The stubble leftover from swathing canola is stiff, sharp, and stout. Fall on it the right way and it might go right through you. I strike a rhythm of seven careful paces across stubble and then three over a windrow of canola pods down and ripening for harvest. Each swath, rising a foot or two above the ground, is springy as I walk over to the next stretch of stubble. After a half mile of this I veer south onto a field that has been turned and seeded to winter wheat. My sandals sink a few inches into soft clods with each step. A slough in the middle of the field explodes with a hundred mallards jumping from water to air as only mallards can, their wings making a startling thunder as they climb. Another explosion when I cross farther south into a weedy field: a jackrabbit bursting out of its form, bounding erratically away.

After the field left to weeds, I veer north to see if I can reckon my way back to where the road allowance becomes a road again. It can't be very far, but from here the east horizon is all bush. I decide to head toward what looks to be willows, hoping to find a way through what will likely be a network of small wetlands. Over a fallen fence left from days when someone ran cattle on the land, I enter a pasture of mostly tame grass. It reaches past my knees, quack and brome grass with a few of the more persistent natives—green needlegrass, goldenrods, smooth aster, and buffalo sage. With the sun now felling the long tree trunk of my shadow across the pasture, each step takes me down toward a great swale dotted with dark blobs of willow, sedge, and rush scattered among shining blue mirrors where water catches the evening light. Beyond, to the east, north, and south, are aspen woods that must be on higher land. I decide to head for the nearest patch of trees, back to the south, and east along the old fenceline.

The wind has fallen and a new stillness surrounds me. It's no more than a mile or two's slog through bush and bog to get to the nearest farmhouse, but with twilight cloaking the land, the world is gathering to a wildness that appears as remote as any I have walked through in forest or alpine. Reaching the woods, I find myself on the edge of a flooded thicket that disappears into the gloom. I could follow the edge south, but I am losing light and energy and don't relish the idea of having to backtrack north to get to my road. There must be a way through the willow bog. I turn back toward it again, telling myself I may find a crane there.

I locate a long bridge of drier sedge that looks promising, but it ends in a peninsula jutting out into open water. Two more blind alleys later, I back up to higher ground to get a picture of the way the land is flooded. Something about the low light deepening the contrast between the leads of water and the mounds of willow gives the labyrinth of marsh a pattern that looks familiar. What *is* this like? As I strain to remember, a pleasant sensation, the nerve endings at the base of my scalp and behind my ears coming to attention, lets me know that something in my body is responding before my brain can manage the retrieval. That's it. I had this same feeling two springs ago during our first controlled burn on our uplands. After putting out the flank of the fire at the spot where we wanted it to stop, I had reached a ridge and was taking a breather in a safe spot surrounded by remaining snowdrifts. All around me was burnt ground enclosed farther out by meandering lines of snow in low spots. At the edges of the blackened earth in the fore- and middle ground, smoke was streaming along the ground. It came from the fire's front and flanks, where I could see flames rise and fall according to the type of grass or brush they were passing through. In a dense patch of little bluestem they leapt, and the crackling sounds rose to a low roar for a few seconds until that fuel was gone. I was exhausted and had inhaled too much smoke, but a giddy feeling of being happily disoriented overcame me and I suddenly saw the hills as a lively presence, a fierce in-dwelling made manifest in everything now unified by ash and fire.

It is here too. Not fire but water, the convergence of lives in this maze work of pond and willow and sedge. I still don't know how I am going to get across, but it's the not knowing that has opened something up in my perception. I head down toward the cattails at the edge of a long slough that has inundated a fenceline in one of the only patches not surrounded by willows and wet sedge. The row of fence posts nearly disappears in the middle, but it emerges again on what looks to be dry ground on the far side. If the posts are of average height, I should be able to wade through without getting my pack wet. If the bottom is muddy, though, I could find myself in deeper water. I back up for one more look for a way through the willow bog to the east, but clouds have closed over the remaining twilight, making it harder than ever to talk myself into another foray into the maze. If I can make it across this one big slough, I should be able to get through the aspens to the north and east and then to the road again.

By the time I am back at the shore, mustering the courage to step into the cold water, the sky is all but dark. I consider setting up camp for the night, but that feels like more dithering, so I plunge in, feeling my way with the stave. The first few steps are encouraging. At the fourth fence post, though, I am already up to my thighs in water. The mud is holding on to my sandals with enough suction to get my heart going. I look back over my shoulder, but pausing to turn around only gives more time for the mud to grab my ankles. In three posts I will reach the deepest water at half-way. I can't see the far shore.

The next step takes me into softer mud well past my ankles, the water now at my waist. A sulphurous stench bubbles up as I pull that foot up and totter for balance, holding the stave and a wiggly fence post. I can hear a nighthawk working the willow bog east of me. I stop and turn instinctively toward the sound, but it's too dark to see the hunting bird. It calls again: a peculiar percussive rasp accentuating the silence. The shadows of bush against the blue-black sky make the contours of a sleeping herd of animals. A shiver runs up my spine from the slough water, and then I realize both my feet are stuck. There is no way to wiggle out of my sandals. I've done this enough to know that pulling on one foot and then the other just takes you deeper. This would be a bad time to fall. Standing as still as possible and facing northeast, I can just make out the first stars of Cassiopeia.

Each night on the hilltop in June, the stamping and whoofing sounds of the deer awoke me at the same time. I'd sit up and stare out at the dark prairie, seeing nothing but grass shadows and the odd firefly winking on and off, and then I'd fall back on the sleeping bag, looking up at the stars. And each night when I did that, directly overhead would be the constellation Cassiopeia—the beautiful and vain queen whose fall from pride turns her throne of stars upside down, tossing her into the void as the heavens wheel.

On the last night, though, the deer would not let me

sleep. It stayed for an hour, and then after it went away I spi-ralled down into a morass of dread and desire, until I thought I would run screaming from the hilltop or be devoured by lust and fear. The worst of it was the moment I felt sure that I was not alone, that something unbenign and appalling had come into the tent, something that wanted me to give up and admit that fucking and flesh is all there is, that the passing vaude-ville of nature in its ten thousand forms, the birthing, copu-lating, and dying carnality of it, contains all of the secrets, all of the salvation a man needs.

Holding the fence post, I place the end of my stave into the mud by my left foot and gently begin to pry against the suction. With that foot free, the plunge forward levers the other foot out and I carry on across the slough, not pausing now, steady toward the shore that I can just see in milky light from the new moon.

The dark, libidinal presence that kept me awake that final night on the hill, making the case for sex and death as the alpha and omega, went back and forth between cold rational-ity and a get-what-you-want sales pitch. It was a tag team of Christopher Hitchens and Mick Jagger, but Mick's offer was more compelling: You like nature, don't you? All you have to do is surrender to nature and its prime mover, the old limbic dance of impulse and satisfaction, and you can inherit the earth and transcend it all at once! Harness that deer stamp-ing outside your tent and it will take you to whatever heaven obsesses you.

Out of the slough, I sit down on a mound of grass and wring out my pants. I have thought of the deer often in recent weeks, wondering if it was flesh or spirit. On a night like this, though, with the earth so still and luminous, the moon-shadowed sedge at my feet and the stars overhead, that ambivalence surrounds me as the very signature of God. As I walk east toward the aspen woods that will take me back to the road, a small revelation circulates through me with the blood warming my legs: resigning to that paradox of inspirited flesh in a being just outside my shelter was finally what invited a more wholesome Spirit to come inside.

Like everyone else, I live within a prevailing sacrilege that dispirits the world, deflates it to a cosmos as thin as the film of slough water evaporating from my skin. The flesh-only deal on offer every day in this life had followed me up the hill and waited for the right moment to make the pitch, but the deer would not let me buy. It came a second time on the last night, and by then my layers of resistance had worn away enough for the message to begin to get through. I could feel the ground shaking as its hooves struck the sod. I knew it was just a deer pawing and snorting by my tent, a common-enough experience if you camp on the prairie, but this time something shifted as I tried to get up to look for it in the moonlight. My body felt heavy, the way it often will during a dream, though I am certain I was still awake. I felt something go out from me as I sat staring at the dark hillside, and then in my exhaustion I dropped back down and went immediately to sleep.

The snorting and stamping continued in my dreams, but instead of being on the prairie I was at home in the city. Annoyed at the deer for invading my world, I trudged out to the front yard to shoo it away, thinking as I went, *Even if the deer is large, it will be easy to intimidate.* Turning the corner, I found a small African antelope reclining on the grass. That unnerved me, but I tried to chase it off just the same. It stood and pointed the short spikes above its brow at me and said, "You don't frighten me." Not wanting to give in, I walked forward to call its bluff, but a second and much larger antelope rose to its feet, with a great arching set of horns sweeping back over its heavy shoulders. It looked more like a prehistoric cave painting of an ibex in the caverns of Niaux or Chauvet than any flesh-and-blood creature I have ever seen in waking life, but it lowered its head and stepped menacingly toward me. I raced back through our fence and shut the gate. The antelope spoke to me from the other side, saying, "Don't be afraid. If you feed us, we will graze your pastures." I ran into the house, cut up apples and other fruit, put it on a tray, and brought it out to the yard.

When I woke in the morning, the dream was there as vivid as the sunlit grass around me, and with it a word: *reciprocity.* At the time, I took that as a reference to what seemed like a bargain or two-sided exchange proposed in the dream: take care of nature and it will take care of you. An important ethic of conservation, one that appeals to our self-interest and sense of fairness, and to the scientific perspective that reminds us that human health comes from ecological health; but is our relationship to creation really a two-way, back-and-forth exchange, something we can weigh on the expense and income sides of a balance sheet?

The realm I walk through tonight is embraced by a much wider reciprocity. Not the static, thin line of a quid pro quo transaction, but the round fullness of the prairie dancing forward in uncountable interchanges as old as the stones, as new as the moist air rising from the undersides of grass leaves into the sky.

If you feed us, we will graze your pastures. When you live in a world of deal-making and commerce, everything sounds like a sales pitch. But the dream wasn't a proposition; it was an invitation to nurture and join the deeper, wider reciprocity that fills the earth with life. The wild paradox of pasture land is that to remain healthy over the long run, it must give part of itself away to be eaten or burned. The grasslands of the world evolved along with fire and natural grazing from buffalo, deer, and antelope, thriving in a circle of disturbance and recovery that depends on the dynamic, random gift of grass through time and space, cycling carbon and other essentials for life through the animals that eat it while storing the balance in the top layers of soil as a treasure of fertility. Soil, the agrologists tell us, is not an aggregate of lifeless dust; it is a community of *creatures*.

For me, this is where a pasture's circle of giving widens beyond science to embrace metaphysics. With the interchanges of the rhizosphere and glomalin administering the passing of energies from one open hand to the next, wholeness begins to look like holiness. In ancient Hebrew the word for a living creature is also the word for soul, *nephesh*, and it applies to all of us, from protozoan to leviathan, all beings made of dust quickened with the very breath of God. What is the liveliness in dust if not soul—the individuated pulse of spirit that is here holding a body together and then so obviously gone when that body becomes a corpse? How apt it is that, once that integrating principle is gone, the body falls apart and feeds the living community in the soil, and that the two words, soil and soul, are so alike.

To believe that we are *nephesh*, that creatures are made of dust inspirited by the creator, is to affirm that we are not *like* the soil but *are* the soil: a communion of beings, all of them ensouled by the breath/spirit of the One whose life in and through us connects the all in all. What would it be like to live in full awareness of that communion? Would the false binaries of commerce that divide body from soul, sacred from profane, religion from nature, and economy from ecology all give way to a wider reciprocity?

An hour later, I am back on the road, walking by the blue light of a moon over my shoulder, thinking about what it takes to travel with one foot in the physical world and the other in the spiritual precincts from which we draw breath, and about what it would mean to serve both the dust and the breath as one unified mystery. Reciprocity speaks to us in the oldest of spiritual maxims, versions of which are found in all traditions, providing variations on the law of karma, the golden rule, or *You reap what you sow.* But it is giving without any expectation of equal return that opens my soul to the holy interchanges that exceed and underwrite the superficial churn of matter.

Before the first mile is gone, I find a small aspen bluff in a field of baled alfalfa that will make a fair campsite. No sign of clouds, so I decide to sleep on the bivouac bag, without the plastic tarp, which is still damp and looking ragged from last night.

Road Conditions: Walking by Moonlight

After walking by night several times I now walk by day, but I
am not aware of any crowning advantage in it.
—from Henry D. Thoreau's journal, June 13, 1851

"Walking," Thoreau's great essay, was more or less drafted
in his journal during 1851 as he recounted experiences
and thoughts that arose on long walks through Concord.
Travelling through woods, along streams, fields, and rail-
roads, he moved across the land at all hours, but it may have
been his nighttime walks that most directly informed what
became his spiritual ethos of walking. He would sometimes
stay out all night, moving in the shadows of moonlight from
dusk to dawn. "The chaster light of the moon" (September 7)
allowed him to imagine a less civilized world, where he could
step into the mythic presence of nature, "nearer the origin of
things" (June 11). As Lewis Hyde argues in his introduction
to a collection of Thoreau's essays, moving in darkness has
always been a trick of those who seek spiritual knowledge,
from the author of *The Cloud of Unknowing* to mystics who

follow the *via negativa*. Away from "sunlit knowing," we are able to cast off our conventional categories and ideas and expose our souls to what is hidden in shadow.

PART THREE

Motherland

This terribly fraught area in Western Christendom, where the sexual meets the spiritual, urgently awaits the discovery of new paths to God.

—Charles Taylor, *A Secular Age*

18 *Imago Dei*

EVERY LANDSCAPE HAS ITS WAY of turning from twilight's interregnum to the supremacy of night. In this savannah land of aspen interspersed with fields and sloughs, the transition is seductively slow until the last moment, like a heavy door closing against its hydraulic arm. The final latch of darkness overtakes you, and suddenly the moist air carries a trace of alfalfa blooms' sweet-pea scent and the spicy bitterness of snowberry leaves. Unseen animals liberated by the night rustle in underbrush and pasture, looking for something to eat or someone to impregnate.

I listen from my sleeping bag, the stars overhead the only evidence that there will be an opposite and visible realm taking hold a few hours from now. The rustling stops around midnight when a great horned owl begins hooting from the next aspen bluff. Coyotes take up the watch and then a deer arrives and starts whoofing. I sit up to listen and look for shadows, but it seems to be hidden in the chokecherry understorey of the bluff. Each snort is a loud expulsion of air through nostrils, followed by the sounds of hooves striking the ground, which I can feel vibrating in my chest. After a minute or so I begin speaking in soft tones, and it stays nearby, snorting and stamping at intervals, moving restlessly from place to place in the bluff. This has to be a buck. I recognize his fear alloyed to aggression because I feel it so often in myself, the defensive male bluster that takes over when I think I am being challenged. Eventually the deer gives up or moves on and in the stillness I fall asleep.

Hours later, morning spreads its honeyed light across a bedewed world, droplets covering the shorn alfalfa and my sleeping bag. I dig an apple out of my pack, eat one half and place the other at the edge of the aspen woods. When I told Daniel about the nightly deer visits during my fast, he said I would have to prepare a gift for the deer as a sign of gratitude, as I had been instructed in the dream. I was to cut up some apples, place them in a wooden bowl, and then leave it by the circle of sage on the hilltop. At the time I wondered if the deer might be telling me something about the fear and aggression strategy I learned early in life, a two-sided coin of survival that has outlived its currency. When the deer came last night, though, he seemed more driven than before, half mad with the fire of autumn in his blood. I could not see him but imagined his outline in the shadows, the heavy throat and fresh antlers of a buck who in the weeks to come will do everything in his power to find and impregnate as many does as he can. At this time of year, deer exhibit some of the most pronounced sexual dimorphism in nature. Every male invests a good portion of his bodily health into the annual process of advertising his maleness. Starting in late winter he begins growing antlers big enough to give him a chance during the fall rut, while retaining enough vigour to undertake the rites of impressing, chasing, and mating with does and driving off other suitors. Mature males can be twice the weight of does, and look much broader and more muscled in the front body, while female deer are slender in front and wide in the hips. This difference in breadth allows a good tracker to identify a buck merely by the span of front hoofprints in a trail.

As I pack up camp, I look around for tracks, but without snow or mud I am not much of a deer stalker. Daniel would laugh at me for looking. When we met for coffee a few weeks ago, he made another of his napkin drawings to show me the intersection of the masculine and feminine energies in creation. He made a broad V shape to represent the space between the mountains where the sky touches the earth. At this joining of Father Sky and Mother Earth, he said, is the vortex where everything happens between Spirit and this world. He extended the lines, making it into an X, and, pointing to the centre, he said that spiritual knowledge travels in a straight line up and down through its axis. Your deer, he said, had to follow that line to come to you at night.

Through the field of alfalfa bales and back to the road, I think of the mule deer I know from our patch of prairie. We see more does than bucks, and last year I came upon a mother with twin fawns. Lifting her head, she froze and I did likewise. The young ones continued to browse on pea vine, and then their mother got a whiff of me and bounded off with a snort. After a couple more "man is on the prairie" alarms from Mom, the fawns went to her side a safe distance away.

Along the roadside there are small mounds of hay, each

a foot or so high and at regular intervals, as though the baler was leaking as it went along the windrow collecting the cut grass. I punt one and then another into the ditch, falling into a rhythm I developed as a boy kicking lumps of snow on the way to school and back. As a piece flies off one of the mounds, landing on the edge of the gravel, something brown above and pink below scurries out onto the road, giving a sharp, almost imperceptible shriek. I watch dumbly as the mother deer mouse, trailing her latched and naked nurslings, runs for cover to the far ditch.

The worst of it is that this is not the first time I have evicted a nursing mouse from her nest. I was forking through our compost heap last year and heard the same piercing alarm as a mouse leapt out with young dangling from her nipples and then disappeared into a corner of the pile. Then as now, I felt a surge of remorse at having exposed the sanctity of a mother's nest.

I resolve to step more lightly the rest of the way. Mouse nests are everywhere on the landscape, but I don't want to be kicking them into the ditch. If there is any place more blessed on this earth than the circle where a mother broods and feeds her young, I have not seen it. The old Hebrew verses tell us that we were both, man and woman, made in the image and likeness of God. An honest man possessing a mirror will imbibe that poetry with a grain of salt, but one look at his naked wife nursing a child and he becomes a believer. When a young father stands just outside that embrace for the first time, his job is to see his wife and child for what they really are in that moment: an image of the circle of giving from creator to creature and back again. I remember marvelling at a woman's biological capacity to offer a gift that is both generative and profoundly relational. At how that possibility— never mind achieving it perfectly—sets women aside from the profane world. How it consecrates motherhood, trans- forming every pregnant woman, every nursing mother, into the *imago Dei*.

What I recall most from Karen nursing our children, apart from that transcendent beauty and the moon-eyed bliss flowing back and forth between her and the baby, was the frightening intensity of a newborn's latch. Once a baby has discovered that her mouth and the nipple have something good going on, getting attached and staying attached are all that matters. In the first few days of nursing, as her breasts adjusted to the task, Karen would often wince and let out a small gasp as the baby latched on. It looked painful, but within seconds she was smiling.

Maybe that pang from the suckling child was small beside the rest. Despite the best efforts of medical science, a woman's body still comes with tribal initiation ceremonies included. She matures through a series of earthy, body-scarring trials from adolescence onward: the monthly ebb and flow of blood and hormonal tides, the accompanying moon-phases of fertility and infertility, then pregnancy moving through an arc of discomfort that culminates in a final act of new life breaking forth on waves of water, blood, and wrenching pain. And though the denouement leaves her marked and aching, she is somehow able to smile with the wisdom of mystics as she feels the warm and painful letdown of milk from her breast that lets her know her baby has taken hold of life.

A dog is barking up ahead, so I take a short detour into a tame pasture. Arcing back toward the road past a small pond, I see three spotted sandpipers with the flawless feathers of shorebirds born this summer. Only weeks ago they were inside eggs cradled in a scrape lined with moss, grass, and feathers next to a body of water. As much as I may like the sandhill crane's model of fidelity and family values, birds provide many more examples of promiscuity. Males usually lead the way, but the spotted sandpiper, an abundant species across the continent's temperate zone, is part of the 1 percent of birds who rely on a strategy of the female mating with several males and never brooding any of the eggs she lays. Once she has attracted one mate and laid eggs from their coupling, she leaves him to do the brooding and heads off in search of another male, often battling other females to gain his favour. Before the breeding season is over, she may have mated with as many as five males, laying eggs for each of them to tend.

From our perspective as a species that depends on maternal fidelity as a minimum for survival, a mother who drops her eggs and then moves on to the next rendezvous seems a shameless hussy. But her sacrifice, like a nursing mother's, is energetic. The female spotties I see picking bugs along the shores of our lake are making new sandpipers at a ferocious pace in part to keep up with a low survival rate for their offspring. Each of the eight to twenty eggs a female lays in a summer weighs an astounding 20 percent of her body weight, which means she is cycling through the equivalent of her own biomass two to four times each breeding season. The price tag for all this energy-intensive egg dispersal may include a truncated lifespan. Though female spotties come early to breeding age, they average only about three summers before they die.

A mouse running with nurslings attached, a sandpiper developing a huge egg in her oviduct, or a woman smiling at the painful latch of her nursling: every kind of motherhood is formed in a crucible of attentive giving. Where does that leave fathers? Why is it that any giving by human fathers seems to require a greater exercise of will and presence to take it beyond sperm donation? Our offspring are the opposite of sandpiper chicks. Human babies are not born with insulative covering and legs that can run to find food and shelter within hours of birth. The sandpiper strategy of maximizing production to overcome a low survival rate doesn't work when your babies are born helpless and naked with big brains barely protected by a skull that has not yet hardened.

Even though we are no longer defending them from sabre-toothed tigers, our children have become the most vulnerable and demanding critters on the planet. The two to four years of breastfeeding is but a start. Getting enough protein into their oversized brains and keeping them healthy and alive to reach breeding age is an investment of fourteen years that goes better with two parents participating. You can double that figure in this anomalous era of delayed parenthood, but whatever the number of years of dependence, the presence or absence of good fathering is an important wild card of human culture and evolution.

The taboos of culture and religion we now regard as superstitions that restrained our autonomy and made us fearful and unfulfilled also played a role in keeping a lid on human eros. Knowing that the mystery in charge of life and death will see and perhaps even punish a father's failure had the benefit of marshalling some of that necessary willpower and presence to draw male sexual energies closer to his family's hearth. Removing that lid, necessary though it may have been, seems to have scattered us to the winds of sexual liberty, where the public forum makes room for STDs, human trafficking, pornography, and armies of orphans, while private life becomes crowded by secrets of obsession, dysfunction, and pharmaceutically boosted performance.

I have seen two cars on the road since I started out this morning. The death toll so far has included a couple of garter snakes, a wood frog, an American coot, and a grey patch of fuzz with small recurved incisors that looked to be the jaw of a barn cat.

I can see a monument of some kind just up ahead on the south side of the road. It's a stone cairn with a few feet of mown grass around it, setting the space aside from the farmer's field. *St. Paul's Cemetery—1899–1905* says a brass plaque. I look around for headstones or evidence of graves, but there are none. The monument lists twenty German names, with birth and death dates, from Busch to Zerr. A six-year cemetery, but the bodies are no longer there? Are they lost under the sod somewhere, in the cultivated field, or were they exhumed and moved to a town cemetery to make room for wheat and canola? The oldest person in this plot was Anton Zerr, born 1821 and buried 1899. His wife, Frances, born 1842, was buried three years later.

What a restless, scattershot civilization has taken hold of these buffalo plains. A German man and woman, living in a first exile in Russia, flee to North America to escape fresh persecution, only to die a couple of years later within its vast heart of grassland. It's no surprise that the displacement continued even after they were put in the ground. For good or ill, that scattering, centrifugal force throwing us outward from home is bound up with the restless wayfaring urge that we all share, men in particular, as we look for new worlds or new roads through them. Take away that *homo viator* longing and we'd be some other hominid still on the mother continent, Lucy's lost cousin enduring in the natal circle of our primate origins.

Without a centripetal force to counter our drive to flee the centre, however, without someone tending each new hearth along the way, how far would our wandering ancestors have made it before dying out? As the counterpart to our centrifugal energies, we seem to need the pull of a home that can raise each generation of healthy wanderers.

I have always thought of the urge to foster a stable centre for child-rearing as an archetypically female characteristic, and the outward movement as male, but last night's visit from the deer has left me with a sense that today's walking task is to ponder the overlap and interplay of those complementary energies. I woke up thinking about what Daniel said about the deer having come to me down that line where the masculine and feminine converge.

My marriage has been almost thirty years of living that rhythm, of being propelled outward and drawn back inward toward the heart centre of our relationship. Somehow the systole of the soul, sending me forth, contracting with a restless desire to do more, be more than another married man with children, has always had its corresponding diastole, the in-between pause when I circulate back to settle into home and everything that flourishes there. I like to claim some credit for that flourishing, certain that at least part of it comes from my magnanimous sacrifice in keeping my day job instead of heading off to be a naturalist-guide on the *Lindblad Explorer*. But the truth is that the tree at the heart of our home is rooted in the soil of motherland: a small subculture of mothering, birthing, and that most local of food movements, breastfeeding advocacy.

If the phone rings and it isn't someone in early labour or wanting advice on nipple shields, it will be for a prenatal yoga class or a recipe for making your own placenta capsules to ward off postpartum depression. A few weeks back, the phone call was for me, a radio reporter asking me to comment on a proposed coyote cull. "I think we met once," he said. "Your wife, Karen, was the doula for our first birth. Say hi to her for me, will you?"

Strangers beaming with bashful smiles introduce themselves to me at readings or writers' festivals and I muster my modesty for the impending adulation only to hear, "Karen was our doula. She saved our lives. Your wife is a miracle worker. If it wasn't for her, I don't know what would have happened. Can you tell her we said hi?"

I do a lot of saying hi on behalf of others. Others who regularly remove the miracle worker from my bed in the middle of the night. The word *doula* is Greek for "handmaiden," but women like Karen who use the term to describe the labour support they offer are in fact practising a kind of shamanism in the age of skeptics.

If there is value in keeping pregnancy, labour, and birth as natural as possible, it is in helping young couples be awake as they undergo the one remaining ritual we have not been able to entirely expunge from our passage into child-rearing adulthood. To help that transformation along, Karen likes to see the naked baby going directly from birth to the mother's breast. She dims the lights to create a cocoon experience as the mother smells and touches her child for the first time. There are crucial bonding hormones swirling in the room from baby to mother and back again. They affect the father too, so she makes sure he comes into the circle to bring on the transformation he will need to cross the gap between all that draws him outward and all that brings him home.

When you live with someone who can manage that kind of high-wire act, escorting terrified mothers- and fathers-to-be across the minefields of modernity and medicine to a place where they can remember they are not machines but living souls connected to other souls and to the earth itself, you'd be wise to shut up and not question her methods or calling. You would be, but I haven't been. "That's just stupid" sprang to my lips far too easily in our early years as parents. I was skeptical the first couple of times I saw her avoid a trip to the hospital by staunching a child's inch-long cut with a magnet pressed on the gash. Now I do it to my own cuts when she isn't looking.

I laughed at her squirting breast milk in our children's eyes to cure conjunctivitis until she snuck some into a dropper and fixed my own eye infection with it. I was equally dubious about her other eye remedies. As a toddler, our son, Jon, would run into the house crying and pointing to his eyes covered in sand. Karen, with only the barest of pauses in her conversation, would take the little face in her hands and lick both eyes in a sideways stroke, spitting out grit before sweeping him to her breast for consolation. I thought I had her when one of our pure, never-to-be-immunized children contracted whooping cough, but then we learned it came from a kid who had been inoculated but got sick anyway.

Getting used to the voodoo medicine, and having to admit it usually works, has been easier than letting go of my ideal of what a stay-at-home wife should or should not do. I clock forty hours a week at my corporate writing job but still spend more time at home than Karen. I don't think I expected to be regularly coming back from the office to discover a tidy kitchen and living room filled with the aroma of fresh baking, but the first few times that actually happened I got in trouble. Now I know the drill. Don't touch the muffins, they are for the La Leche League meeting, and oh, would you mind retreating to the bedroom early tonight? Some of our younger moms are shy nursing with men around. There's some chili to warm up for supper if you like, but don't leave a mess.

As long as I have known Karen, I have been trying to get her to ease up on her women-who-do-too-much schedule. I start off sounding magnanimous, very concerned for her peace of mind and health: this madness is not good for you or for the family. In a few moments, though, we are both angry because she knows it's mostly about me wanting a more orderly home life, more attention from her, and less warmed-up chili. If the argument goes badly for me, I offer to quit work and be the domestic caregiver. Someone should be at home, I say, making a threat that long ago lost its capacity to scare anyone other than me.

That dance has been the primary tension between us for years: Karen wanting to do all she can for the women who appreciate her wisdom and skill, and me casting about for some way to get her to be the kind of wife I think she should be. In my worst self-pitying moments I have convinced myself that my stay-at-home wife is more at home in the circles of women she created with her friends than she is with our family. Doula workshops, Friends of the Midwives committee meetings, "blessing way" gatherings to prepare a woman for her birth, La Leche League meetings, and women's spirituality circle on Saturday mornings. To be fair, she misses a lot of these gatherings, but with her doula work, yoga teaching, volunteer commitments, and friends to keep up with, she has a calendar that would send the White House chief of staff away in tears.

If I had a wife who wasted her time at Botox parties, wine

bars, and shopping malls, I might have a case, but the truth is that Karen is giving her days and nights, for meagre pay or none at all, to work that quietly and bravely builds social cohesion in the face of everything else madly tearing it down.

Over the last twenty-five years, I have watched my wife and her closest mothering friends make a community where there wasn't one before. I don't think they knew they were going to make a community; it just happened as they were swept up in an old way of doing things, a mysterious process that is a little like women passing a sourdough starter from household to household and generation to generation. Beginning with the leavening they received from an older group of nursing, stay-at-home mothers in the city, Karen and a handful of other women, all in their twenties, created new circles, some formal, others less so. And in their turn these women have passed on the leaven to dozens of younger moms just starting their families. The basic recipe is the same one that has been bringing women together and fostering community for thousands of years: attend and celebrate one another's births, meet to exchange information and support one another in nursing and child-rearing, and laugh, cry, and commiserate to make sense of the stories they carry as mothers and wives.

One story in particular expresses the kind of bonds formed in such circles. A young mother Karen knows was having trouble breastfeeding her newborn after a home birth. Her milk had not come in yet and after several days the baby was not looking well. The doctor recommended artificial formula, but some of the woman's friends with their own nursing children intervened and began breastfeeding the child themselves, bridging the baby over until its mother's milk supply was up to the task.

Like any community, this one has its conflicts. There have been online flame wars over who gets to meet with the local midwives, and meetings where two of the LLL leaders avoided one another. Women are just as moved by rivalry, desire, and envy as men, though perhaps more sophisticated in the expression.

At first I thought this emphasis on breastfeeding and birth was merely women's business, interesting enough but nothing I had to think about as a new father. About ten years in, though, amid the blur of managing life with three small children, a job, a house, and a writing career, it suddenly dawned on me that all of my closest friends are married to the women from these mothering circles. To a man, we were conscripted by our wives into a community we did very little to build. Whether we recognize it or not, most of the people we share our lives with—the ones who celebrate milestones with us, show up for work bees, travel with us, share land with us, drop food off on the doorstep in times of crisis—come from the subculture our wives have nurtured out of their bonds as mothers who want to raise healthy families.

These days, Karen and a handful of her friends, all in their late forties and early fifties, are mentoring a generation of younger women as they figure out what mindful mothering might look like in the era of the smart phone and Facebook. This new peer group of moms, having come to motherhood bearing a more sophisticated and ironic regard for media and consumer culture, stride into the role with some branding awareness and an unapologetically self-conscious flair for leaving their mark on what mothers should or should not be. They follow hip mothering blogs and post YouTube videos on their Facebook pages, laughing at the expense of their own cohort, the "crunchy mama," who buys organic cotton diapers, wears her baby all day, sleeps with her all night, gets raw milk from an anonymous farmer in a back alley, and makes her own fruit leather and gluten-free teething biscuits.

What these young mothers seem to share most, though, is a burning desire to do better than their own mothers, women who were among the first to step outside the social norms of what is feminine or motherly. Given some sexual freedom, the permission to divorce, and the usual misdeeds of men, that first step often meant poverty and confusion for children as parents split and then formed new relationships. The women who watched their mothers walk away from one adolescent man only to fall into the arms of another are now in their thirties and forties, raising children of their own. A big piece of their self-worth is measured against a desire to not go through the same struggles, to give their children the financial and emotional security they never had.

The young women Karen works with are striving for a new kind of mothering that can go two ways. Many try to have it all—healthy children, solid marriage, successful career, organic food, Caribbean vacations, terrific sex, yoga practice, spiritual fulfillment—running themselves ragged in a competitive/comparing mode, hoping to outdo their mothers and measure up to their overachieving peers. A few women of the same generation, however, manage to get beyond the urge to become have-it-all mothers by doing two things that, for better or worse, have long been associated with motherhood.

First, they make sacrifices. Against all the rules of what an intelligent, self-determined woman is supposed to do, they set aside career plans for a few years because they want to give their children more of their lives than maternity leave plus evenings and weekends. They choose a single-income marriage even though it means they may never have what some of their working-mom friends have: the two-thousand-square-foot home with two new cars in the garage, the clothing and shoes, and a tropical vacation every winter. The second thing they figure out is that it is a lot easier to make that kind of countercultural choice when you do it in the company of like-minded souls. Once they find one another, and discover that there are other creative, educated women staying at home because they want to, a circle of giving and borrowing begins to take form. Food, advice, clothing, recipes, child care, furniture, and labour begin to move from household to household, often without any money changing hands. And circulating within all of that material and energy is a spirit that moves and holds them and their families together against the marketplace and its scattering forces, almost as though it were possible to be a tribe again.

This may be a faint echo of one of the oldest kinds of community: women acting in concert with other women to achieve the mutual benefit of improved conditions for child-rearing, including stable relationships with men. A few weeks ago I was reading about a radical group of anthropologists who speculate that deep in our hominid past, girls became women by experiencing the power of this solidarity in the earliest initiation rites. They argue that hunter-gatherer women trying to get men to form lasting pair bonds may have been the first socialists. Extrapolating from first-contact accounts of African hunting tribes, they speculate that in early cultures women may have used menstrual synchrony—real and faked (painting themselves with red ochre)—to render the clearest indicator of imminent fertility all but useless to philandering men. By initiating young girls at the onset of menstruation, taking collective control of the blood signal, amplifying it with cosmetics, and instituting a monthly sex strike based on those signals, they were able to secure greater fidelity from their men while forming community bonds that led to co-operative child care. By collectively refusing sex to their partners at the same times of the month, they found a way to encourage their wandering men to be more attentive and return to semi-permanent settlements with the meat that their children needed to be healthy.

One of the more speculative but interesting propositions in this line of anthropology posits that it was this collective action of women getting men to commit to tribe and hearth that ultimately brought about language, religion, symbolic representation, art, and other cultural advances.

The settler women buried in the roadside cemetery behind me were the culture-bearers who tried to hang on to the traditions, music, literature, and morals they brought with them to the New World. Books, piano lessons, and religious celebrations have always been the purview of women's circles whenever the wayfaring urge brings us to a new land. The granddaughters of those first women are married to men who work the canola and wheat fields I walk beside. They are thousands of years away from a hunter-gatherer life and its first women's collectives, but they no doubt have had their own reasons to gather from time to time.

I wonder if part of what has made us such adaptive creatures, forming elaborate cultures and inhabiting every possible niche on the planet, is our capacity to shift from competitive to co-operative strategies. The only other animals that have evolved complex social forms of co-operation are the colonial insects, the ants, bees, and wasps who also rely on a sisterhood to make their cultures thrive. There is no way to prove that women showed us the way first in their circles of nursing mothers, but I have trouble imagining men banding together without direction from the feminine energies that obsess us.

Not long after the fast, I had the unmanliest of dreams. I was nursing a child. Even in the dream it was embarrassing. I can still remember the feeling of the flow, warm like tears leaving my chest, pleasant but painful all at once. Then the story shifted and I was escaping from a building where my family and I were held captive by an ogre. He was an angry, cruel man whom I feared for his violence and his controlling, manipulative ways. While he was out, I packed my bags and snuck away. I was relieved to be free of his anger, but saw his suffering and felt sorry for him too. I wish it were that easy. I have packed those bags in my mind several times, but in real life, when you leave, the resident ogre usually comes with you.

Men like to walk out the door dramatically, because the threat of abandonment has a powerful effect on our partners. If part of that power comes from knowing that fathers are today more than ever walking away from home and leaving their families for good, the rest of it comes from the sad truth that sometimes the men who stay aren't really there either.

In the early years of our marriage, the centrifugal pull of the world had me leaving the house every time Karen and I had a big fight. I never got to actually packing a suitcase, but it crossed my mind. Instead, I would just walk out the door without saying where I was going or when I would return. I rationalized my angry departures as a way of cooling off, until one time I came back into the house and found Karen playing a game on the floor with our two small children. She was nursing our son, who was maybe two at the time. Over his mother's breast, he looked up at me with the sad philosopher gaze he had perfected by then, and that was it. I knew I could never go out the door again without saying exactly where I was going and when I would return.

Karen tells me that when she talks to young women, helping them to cross the threshold into motherhood, she will sometimes say that breast milk is the salve that heals a mother from the wounds of pregnancy and the tearing apart that happens at birth. It's not much of a stretch to say that it helps too with the wounds that come from trying to get men to grow up.

It has taken me far too long to figure this out, but here I am at the age of fifty-two reluctantly admitting that the best thing I can do to mature, the best thing I can do for my family, is to be man enough to be there, to respect the circle my wife has made, and to either help or get out of the way when she is doing the work of expanding and nurturing it.

Road Conditions: Walking in Childbirth

There is a woman with us, belonging to one of our men,
who has walked the whole day, in the snow and water,
and who, this evening, gave birth to a son.
—from Daniel Harmon's journal, March 24, 1804

In the early spring of 1804, Daniel Harmon, trader and partner with the North West Company, was walking north across aspen parkland prairie with a party of Cree and Nakota people. He kept a journal, which constitutes one of the most vivid accounts of life on the northern Great Plains before the plough. When he wrote the above passage about a woman in their party giving birth, they still had three days of trudging through wet snow to get to their destination of Fort Alexandria, near the present-day town of Sturgis, Saskatchewan. Harmon went on to write in his journal that the next day the woman took the child on her shoulders and "continued on her march, as though nothing unusual had occurred. It is a very happy circumstance, that the women of this country are blessed with such strong constitutions." A year later Harmon, following the custom of the northwest, received one of those hardy women as a country wife. Lisette Laval, half French, half Snake Indian, was fourteen and Harmon was twenty-seven. She travelled with him through Canada's unsettled interior until 1819, when Harmon returned home to Vermont. Unlike most adventurers who came to the northwest, however, he took Lisette back with him, wedding her in a formal ceremony at Fort William during their trip east across the continent. They remained together for life and had many children.

19 The Vineyard

I HAVE ALMOST RUN OUT OF WATER, but my next cache is only a mile ahead. I know that only because I recognize the farmyard I am walking past, its machinery and agricultural detritus scattered in an explosion pattern radiating outward from the buildings. Two large black dogs are sleeping on the gravel driveway at ground zero. A twenty-acre slough separates us, but I do my best to step quietly. The dogs snooze on. Just above the surface of the water, young black terns are trying out their wings and a dozen barn swallows plane through the air after midges. I stop to watch the terns and swallows, two bird families that have always seemed like congeners to me, though taxonomy has placed them in entirely different orders.

The looping flight of sickle-winged birds has a way of settling me. This is the kind of thing I do to take comfort: stare at a slough, sorting through the patterns of nature to find things that curve in ways much more inspirited than I feel, grab one with my gaze, and hold it against my desire. A more socially acceptable use of beauty than allowing my eyes to linger on the curve of a woman's torso, perhaps, and almost as effective.

I wish I could say that living with a breastfeeding advocate has taught me that the breast is not a sexual object for male pleasure, but I am as happy as most men to "behold the circummortal purity" of a well-formed bosom. Karen is convinced there is something infantile in the male obsession with breasts, says we didn't get enough time there as babies. That has a certain ring of feminist truthiness, but I think our fixation might also have something to say about our approach to feminine energies in general, both in our sexual encounters with women and in our interchange with the land.

I came across a handy pseudo-mystical justification for my obsession with the female form in a tantric sexuality book (not mine—I'm just keeping it for a friend). The author says that men are drawn to a charge coming from women, a current of relationality that is alluring perhaps because it is so alien to our own natures. That latent relationality is natural, familial, and often communal, carrying the potential to bind us to woman, family, community, and the earth itself. In our better moments, the book claims, we recognize that for our own fulfillment we need to access those generative, relational, and nurturing energies. Yet there is something in a man, some kind of congenital flaw, that must be overcome or else we devolve into the grabbiest of lovers, mindlessly serving our own gratification. Most of the time we get stuck seeking pleasure as an end in itself, completely missing the truth that the bonds a woman can choose to offer a man are about a whole lot more than letting off sexual tension in a few seconds of neural fireworks.

This kind of highfalutin thinking has led me to conclusions that will sound quaintly old-fashioned, even retrograde to some ears, but now that I have two daughters of marrying age and a third getting close, I have some licence to contrive elaborate moral theories about the responsibilities of men in the face of that female choice.

I turn off the road and cross the ditch to look for the three wine bottles filled with water I left at the foot of an aspen tree. There they are, two Mouton Cadet and an Australian Gewürztraminer, in the dark green of brome grass next to a field of flax ripening to a rich brown.

Finding a cache of water right where you left it is one of those small satisfactions of outdoor travel, like soaking your feet in a puddle or adjusting the straps on your pack to shift the load. I return to the open sunlight of the ditch, settle into the brome grass, and down half of one bottle, then transfer the rest of the water into the lighter bottles I am carrying with me.

The water droplets remaining on the palm of my left hand have made snow-globe microcosms of my surroundings. Each one contains the green arc of the aspen bluff, the sky holding blue, and a dark spot that could be me. When I shift my focus from the droplets to the trees thirty feet away, light bounces back through the leaves, forming gold and green embroidery underpainted with indigo shadows. The effect is exactly like one of Courtney Milne's more abstract images made during his final years. Though I met Courtney only a couple of times before his death last year, the photos he created toward the end, as he suffered the indignities of cancer with great equanimity and wisdom, have been coming into my thoughts as I walk through aspen and slough country.

After decades of travelling the planet to photograph its most compelling landscapes and sacred places, Courtney came home again through the daily practice of paying attention to the light and colour reflected in the water of a pool on his acreage near Grandora, Saskatchewan. I had seen some of these poolside photos before—contemplative images of trees and sky reflected in the wind-stirred or calm surface of the pool taken in all seasons of the year—but I didn't fully appreciate what he had achieved until I saw them afresh during a performance celebrating Courtney's life and art this past spring.

It was at the university, several months after he died. Not sure what was to come, I waited in the half-light of a small theatre with about a hundred others gathered for the memorial. The room fell to darkness, then a choir of twenty-four men and women walked on and began to sing canticles to heaven and earth, plunging all of us into a symphony of light, shadow, colour, movement, and song. My hair stood on end as great projections of Courtney's photos filled the space with their shimmering, crystalline presences. Here was art given freely to the community in a way that mirrors the creator's original generosity: life celebrating itself in conscious awareness. In his last years, with infirmity and mortality as his teachers, Courtney broke through and became transparent enough to join in that celebration each day.

The choir, focused, balanced, moving and singing with great mindfulness and accord, was conducted by Jean-Marie

Kent, a visiting professor at the university. The music she selected worked seamlessly with the dance of Courtney's soul-stirring photography as it played before our eyes on a large screen. A luminous spirit moved through the whole experience, a spirit familiar to those who knew Courtney as he came into the full bloom of his life as a mystic and artist. I looked around at the others, the eyes glistening in the dark, taking in light and colour, our hard edges blurring just a bit. I felt a flow of energies we don't often acknowledge binding us together in a shared experience that seemed liturgical and, in that broadest sense of the word, erotic.

The moment I recall most vividly was when the choir paired up in man-woman couples and began to sing a choral arrangement from the love poetry near the opening of the Song of Songs.

Rise up, my love, my fair one, and come away.
For, lo, the winter is past, the rain is over and gone;
The flowers appear on the earth;
The time of the singing of birds is come,
and the voice of the turtle-dove is heard in our land.

If there is a piece of sacred text that expresses the essential, paradoxical nuances of female sexual giving and receptivity and its analog in the bountiful life of the earth, it is this unusual and erotic eight-chapter canticle making up one of the shortest books in the Hebrew scriptures. Later in the second chapter of the Song, the woman declares, "My beloved is mine, and I am his." Then she describes him feeding "among the lilies," and invites him to turn and become like "a roe or a young hart."

First the rich images of spring bursting forth from the earth in all of its eros and fecundity, then the declaration of her covenant with her beloved ("my beloved is mine, and I am his"), and finally the invitation every man longs to hear whispered in his ear.

Later in the Song of Songs, the verses show female sexual giving to be a subtle paradox with wider lessons for how we treat the fertility of the land. In chapter eight, after saying she wants to be kissed, the woman qualifies the invitation with a caution, saying, "But my own vineyard is mine to give." There is a lot contained in that "but." Man, it is implied here, has no right to just take the vineyard. Her beauty and fertility are not his to possess or exploit for his own purposes. She is fully constituted in herself as a spiritual being, a child of God, possessing her own inviolable freedom to bestow the gift of herself. And that gift, expressed in receptivity, is bestowed only after the two lovers have formed a bond of trust, a covenant of mutual respect and love.

The image of the private vineyard is joined in the man's regard for his lover: earlier in the song he acknowledges and praises her for being a "garden locked up . . . a spring enclosed, a sealed fountain." But it is the bride who seems to understand that the depth of their bond is formed in mutual giving and belonging. "My lover belongs to me and I to him," she says, describing the reciprocity and communion formed in the self-gift of nuptial life. A woman giving herself to a man is offering the possibility of more life, a way to nurture it within family and the larger community, and a way for a man to become fully a man by receiving it in a spirit of service, sacrifice, and commitment worthy of such a bestowal.

Cranky fathers who want their daughters to guard their vineyards are almost alone in thinking of sexual energy in such lofty, utopian terms. Worse yet, most of us are hypocrites. The comfort of knowing that the oldest moral and religious traditions on earth would back me up in an argument for greater continence and fidelity fades entirely when I think of how I have a thousand times let the prevailing pragmatism of our day—lust is natural and good for you— excuse my thoughts when I am faced with the perplexities of feminine allurement.

"I was born twenty years too early," a friend said to me at work the other day. "Look at the young guys around us. Most of them are just goofballs, nothing special to look at, going bald at twenty-five, low-paying jobs, and they go through a string of gorgeous, intelligent women with professional careers. They get all the sex they want and they don't have to get married. What the hell is going on?" Married, with three kids, he was expressing something that a lot of men in committed long-term relationships find themselves thinking in moments of weakness.

My answer probably wasn't that convincing. I said, do you want to grow up or do you want to have sex with lots of women? You can't do both. Okay, don't answer that, I said. It's supply and demand. There's a shortage of grown-up men. Or men who even have the potential to grow up. And, yeah, it's the open access to commitment-free sex in the flesh and in high-def video that is keeping men adolescent right into their forties. A woman's maturing, some would say, is bound up with the process of opening herself up to a committed sexual relationship—which in former times usually led to motherhood—but a man grows up by becoming *worthy* of a woman choosing to open herself up to him in the bonds of a committed sexual relationship that could well lead to that motherhood. You want to be one of these younger men because they are getting lots of sex, but think about that for a moment. If women had been offering you plenty of sex, free of any commitments or expectations, and all you had to do was be reasonably charming and take a shower now and then, would you have done what you know you needed to do to become the kind of man a self-respecting woman would want to marry? And what if you weren't terribly charming or outgoing, and you had endless access to the most erotic and varied visual stimulation online? We underestimate the power of women to regulate the things that motivate a man to finally grow up, to remind him that if he wants regular sex, he has to broaden his horizons and start thinking beyond his groin.

The work-in-progress we call gender equality complicates the sexual economics that are helping to suppress male maturity. It is increasingly easy for a young man to convince himself that the lesser offers he sees women make in the marketplace—sex uncomplicated by any real bond or connection—are the actions of liberated and fully realized women. To assume otherwise is to risk an accusation of paternalism. Women are autonomous creatures with their own weaknesses and free wills, and can seem just as eager for recreational or transactional sex as the men they meet. If we are honest with ourselves for a moment, though, we might remember that most of the rules of the game in which women seem to have become more relaxed about recreational sex have been set by men. Never mind that we are also responsible for the immediate vectors of birth control availability and Internet porn. Our legal systems, the nature of our economy and food production, and every other contrivance holding up the edifice of modern civilization—the autonomous individual, science, the nation-state, and the concept of private property—were all forged in the smithy of the male heart. Granted, to secure a measure of economic stability and comfort in the game, women have learned how to harness the carnal desires in that male heart. But if one gender's hindbrain longings have determined the playing field and most of the rules, the "freedom" of the other one to act with power and self-determination is always going to be compromised and reduced to the limited choices of an underclass, no matter what many of its members may believe about their own bold expressions of autonomy.

The reigning pragmatism of our day tells us that male desire will always exploit the feminine in a woman's body or in the gifts of the earth. Once that brand of realism takes hold, the verities of innocence, communion, love, and respect for creation become no more than impossible ideals muttered by those we can dismiss as religious, mere dreams a practical people cannot afford to serve. Dreamless and hopeless, we settle instead for the banal consolations of more achievable "truths" endorsed by the marketplace:

lust is a natural appetite, we are all consenting adults, we all need to make a living, don't we?

A man sustains his weakness with such stale bread, devising elaborate schema that will hide his failure to regard a woman's receptiveness in its full moral and spiritual implications, to honour it in the spirit of respect and fidelity it deserves. In our self-serving pragmatism, conducting the "realistic" transactions that degrade everyone involved, we scatter masculine energies into the world in a thousand deleterious ways, turning away from the mounting evidence that our collective failures as men are at the heart of much of the economic, social, and environmental disarray hurtling us nearer to apocalypse.

Alternatively, when a woman's choice is truly autonomous and not distorted by male commodification and control of resources, it becomes a powerful force for transformation and justice in our world. Over the last decade, women in Africa and Latin America have implemented sex strikes to wake men up and recruit their energies to social causes in their communities. In Colombia, one group of women who had nearly given up trying to get a road repaired finally saw some results after refusing to bed their husbands. In another case, the wives and lovers of a Colombian gang used the same strategy to reduce violence in their community by more than 25 percent. Most famous of all was the sex strike organized by Nobel Peace Prize–winner Leymah Gbowee and her coalition of Christian and Muslim women in Liberia. Like the Greek women in Aristophanes's *Lysistrata*, they turned their men aside to get them to end a fruitless and protracted war.

The warlords of Liberia would still be hacking at each other today if Gbowee and her co-leaders in the women's peace movement had not organized women to withdraw from the game and set some new rules. Under the chaotic and corrupt leadership of Liberian men fractured into several "liberation" groups employing boy soldiers, peace was thought to be an impossible ideal, but these women managed to bear it into the light of day by praying in their various spiritual traditions and finding new ways to steward their feminine energies.

Gbowee would say later that their strike was aimed at waking up "good men" who had become complacent. At the very least, their unorthodox strategy brought media attention from around the world, ultimately shaming the warlords into sitting down with one another to hammer out a peace deal. The talks, held in a hotel in Ghana, quickly turned into a melee, but Gbowee and a couple of hundred women travelled to the site and surrounded the negotiation room, linking arms in a circle. Finally, when all hope for an agreement seemed lost and the men were on the verge of forcing their way through the circle to leave, the women played their final card by threatening to remove their clothing. In much of sub-Saharan Africa, an older woman disrobing herself in public is the most powerful curse a woman can invoke, one to be used only in the direst of circumstances. The men of Liberia stopped in their tracks and went back to the negotiation tables with renewed motivation, reaching terms for peace that led to the end of the war a few weeks later. Within two years, Charles Taylor, the former president infamous for stirring up horrific violence, was gone from power. One of

Gbowee's cohorts in the women's peace movement, Ellen Johnson Sirleaf, became the first woman elected to lead an African nation.

It is a wonder men do not experience more collective refusals from and withdrawals by women. Not merely to provide sex, but the food, beauty, organization, and nurturing that our households, communities, and institutions depend on. Some women, of course, are hooked up with men who would only respond to refusal with more violence and infidelity. They need other women and men to help them get free. But not all men are beyond redeeming; many are merely sad and lazy. What changes would we see if women began to organize acts of forbearance to wake good men up from their slumber? How many refusing women would it take to get some legislation banning the fire retardants and other toxins that accumulate in breast milk and tissues? What kind of refusal from nuns and laywomen would grind the Catholic Church to a halt and force it to face up to its misogynist policies?

Female choice and receptivity are much simpler matters for birds. The male barn swallows I see at farmyards along the road merely have to wait for the right signals from a female who knows when she is ready to invite courtship from the particular male she chooses. No subtlety, no paradox required. A long tail, strong singing voice, and extensive rusty wash on his breast let her know that he has the vigour and health her offspring will need. The male swallow may drive interlopers away from his bonded mate, but otherwise he harbours no illusions of controlling and exploiting her or the earth that produced the bugs that brought him and the object of his desire into breeding condition. Nor does it matter whether he sees his bonds with her or the land as sacred.

Somewhere after we came down out of the trees, we traded in that kind of simplicity for our big brains and the freedom to choose. The descent brought us face to face with a choice: either we regard our bodies and the earth as autonomous properties to be owned, subdivided, and used for our own private gain, or we see them as confluent creations whose interdependencies resist all claims of possession. Choosing the first has distorted the masculine and dishonoured the feminine energies in the earth and our bodies. Disprivileging the feminine, the mother force that cradles us in nature, has tossed us into an androcentric world that has made this road and the fields beside it into functionaries of the marketplace. The Song of Songs was written for a people already immersed in that world, where the choice had been made in ways that favoured entitlement over respect, ownership over gift. Then as now, the old boys overseeing the imbalance were afraid of the fecund mysteries and gifts of the mothering land even as they converted them into commodity and capital.

The metaphors in verse after verse associating the sacred feminine with the generativity and receptivity of nature are not coincidental or merely poetic. The woman speaking so erotically in the enchanted language of Song of Songs is fully a woman, but she is also a figure of the feminine both in our bodies and in the earth; her gardens are the sacred ground of all creation, which no man is to take without proper courtship and bonds of deep respect. The bride's freedom to give or not give herself is featured in opposition to the usual way of the world where, high-ho the derry-o, the farmer takes a wife and whatever else he needs. Amplified to a broader moral voice, "My own vineyard is mine to give" is a warning from the good earth bridling against the commodifying grip of humanity.

The Song proposes that we all become lovers and invites us to revisit in our own souls that anthropological moment of deciding how we will look upon our bodies and the earth. These cannot be objects to be used for selfish pleasure and gain—not if we are lovers. To love life, love another, love a place, is to know that the flesh of the body and the flesh of the earth are one, and that this unity is good and holy, testifying to a truth uttered in our very language of the body. Our generativity and our genitals are set within sacred ground. We call that region at the core of our bodies the "sacrum" for reasons that did not evaporate with all the constraints we got rid of in the sexual revolution of the last fifty years.

Thoreau believed that a man's connection to the earth could not be divided from his own moral purity. "If I would preserve my relation to nature," he wrote, "I must make my life more moral, more pure and innocent . . . I must not live loosely, but more and more continently." In another passage he referred to "the generative energy" having the capacity to dissipate or invigorate depending on how it is channelled, saying that through continence it inspires us, bearing fruits of "genius, heroism, holiness and the like." In nineteenth-century New England, this was about as close as any writer, no matter how iconoclastic, was going to come to saying outright that the way a man governs his sexual energy will affect his character and his relationship to the earth.

On a walk such as this, in solitary steps past farms and duck ponds, I am free to let myself believe or imagine a further flowering of the body's generative meaning, pitched beyond even the ideals of Thoreau. A feather flutters to earth from the wing of one of two phoebes in their spiralling ascent above the cut grain, and I step off the road to pluck it from the grass. It is veined and curved in my hand, grey-brown like a shaving of rare hardwood. I wonder if my body too was formed in such gracious innocence, whether there is a way to rediscover the nuptial potential that was given flesh in the form of the human—female and male and all of the intergrades in between. Some ambitious conclusions fall from those premises, assertions I do not have the authority or courage to defend: that perhaps, just perhaps, we too were given to the earth as a gratuitous donation, a gift for its own sake, and to the degree that we betray our promise, that gift becomes a curse; but inasmuch as we embrace that original freedom, which is not licence but a natural mastery of the self, we can also make of ourselves a disinterested gift to our beloved ones. And when that happens, then love really is made; or, perhaps more accurately, grown. Grown the way grapes grow on the vine and, further than that, offered to and uniting the wider community in the wine of blessing and Spirit that inevitably escapes the garden walls.

Road Conditions: Slow Walking

*So long as man practises the sex act in instinctual blindness, that
is to say like any other animal, the light remains hidden.*
—Mircea Eliade, *The Two and the One*

*To the extent that present-day conditions are different from
ancestral conditions, the ancestral genetic advice will be wrong.*
—Richard Dawkins, *A Devil's Chaplain*

To meditate while walking is to learn the value of slowing down and letting go of the need to get anywhere. To
do anything mindfully that we *usually* do instinctively or
reflexively—whether it is walking, eating, or making love—
is to elevate that activity to prayer. As far as we know, *Homo
sapiens* is the only species that aspires to mindfulness or
prayer. The human brain, with all of its capacity for awareness, reason, adaptation, and choice overlaying its core of
limbic responses, gives us all we need to map a better way
through abundance conditions (widely available junk food
and opportunities for sex) that are entirely different from

the scarcity conditions that gave rise to the opportunistic urges and instincts encoded in our DNA. Instead of mindlessly following the genetic advice that often leads us astray in an age of ever-present stimulation and opportunity, we can wake up and use our attention and choice to decouple the meaning of a step, a morsel, or a kiss from our blindly compulsive, genetic programming. Like walking, making love can be spiritual work. Most spiritual traditions that attempt to foster the creative, spiritual meaning of the conjugal embrace offer variations on the same points: go slow, find the energy in stillness, breathe, be open and gentle, and, most important, pay more attention to the way than to the destination.

20 Listening to Aspen

THE RUMPLED FORM OF A DEAD OWL appears on the roadside as I near the last trackless portion of the walk. A short-eared. The buff-yellow swirls that edge its facial discs flow in sinuous lines like water weeds in a creek. Whether it was sound gathered by those dished forms or movement caught by its mascara-framed eyes, the mouse was too absorbing for the owl to notice the truck or car that would intersect its line of attack. Placing the body in high grass far from the naked road, I turn it over to let the insects work on the other side. In a few days it will be gone from here, its bones cleaned and carried off by larger scavengers and, in the leaner days of winter, nibbled on by the rodents it once hunted.

When the road disappears into a standing crop of canola edged by a half mile of aspen bush, I head south along a muddy track following the north-south road allowance. Ahead, a rise of rolling land looks like native pasture. From there I should be able to find a way to get farther east and back to where the road resumes.

At the corner of the fenced grass, pondering the route

I will take, I hear the growl of a quad or all-terrain vehicle growing louder as it comes from the south. I watch the horizon and in moments the quad appears, bearing a man and his boy. He lets off on the accelerator to coast down the hill to where I stand waving.

His name is Duane and he is out checking his electric fence with an ohmmeter. Tanned face beneath the ball cap, dirty-blond hair, forearms and hands that have been used for most of the days in his thirty-some years. I admire his pasture and ask if I could walk through it to get back to the road. Duane doesn't ask why or where I'm headed, just casts an assessing eye my way and then out over the fence.

"I've got a bull in there, but he probably won't bother you. After the first mile, though, you'll hit some sloughs. You might want to head north and east a bit through the next quarter. That's a big corporate operation. No bulls. Nothing but feeders."

"Nothing but feeders" is part put-down and part lament for a passing way of life. The traditional culture of the family cow-calf operation is dying out and giving way to a system that applies the standard management methods of big business to the process of putting meat on the hoof and getting it to market. Feeder cattle companies buy heifers in spring, fatten them all summer on mostly tame grass, and then ship them to feedlots in the fall. No bulls, no calving, no wintering. They thrive by specializing in one part of the conveyor belt that takes an animal from conception to meat on the dinner plate. Raising capital to get big and benefit from economies of scale, they hire and lay off staff as needed, taking advantage of the latest information technology to manage dollars, animals, people, and other inputs.

Traditional cow-calf men tend to have more native grass and keep bulls and breeding stock to develop the quality of their own herd. They calve in spring, rotate their herd through their pastures, shipping some heifers and all the steers in the fall, and overwintering their breeding stock on hay, typically in a corral. The tribe of cattlemen has its code of honour and set of acceptable practices, and anyone who comes from outside and gets big fast by investing a lot of dollars to buy land away from his own home is going to be suspect no matter how successful his business practices may be. And successful they are. Operations like this one have found a way to squeeze a dollar out of a beef market tilted in favour of the feedlots and meat processors and increasingly stingy to anyone trying to graze their own cattle in a small-scale, cow-calf system.

At the east end of the section of native grass, I cross the fence onto the corporation's alfalfa field. The heifers are well off to the north and I reckon my way back toward where I think the road will start again. Up ahead is a small knoll that escaped the plough. I find it hard to resist this kind of agricultural nunatak, so I climb it, tripping on abandoned farm machinery before I reach the top, where a small glacial erratic rests, altar-wise to consecrate the land it overlooks. Eastward on the horizon, the road slices across the aspen-sloughed broadloom of field and pasture. I will be on gravel again in less than half an hour.

When you step onto a road after walking through trackless farmland for a spell, you come out grateful for the sloughs, sedge meadows, and bush, but grateful too for a straight path where you can stride ahead with nothing grabbing at your legs.

Our stepping matters. The absence of the farmer's footsteps from furrow and pasture is first among the evils wrought by the scaling up of our agriculture. The old saying about the farmer's footsteps being the best fertilizer is on one level a simple assertion that someone who pays attention to his land will yield more or healthier produce. But there is also a spiritual just-so wisdom in associating fertility and mindfulness. Just as the good farmer focuses his attention and labours on the soil to feed and awaken its natural fertility—that is, its own capacity to attend to the needs of the plants—so we must all feed and awaken our own spiritual fertility gone dormant in our souls if we hope to mature within and attend to the needs of family, community, and place.

I have met old farmers and cow-calf ranchers whom the years of working with soil, seeds, animals, and grass through flood and drought have given the bearing of natural mystics. They would be hard put to say much about the stirrings they feel in their bones, the decisions they make with their hands and feet. How to graft an apple branch, when to sow barley, whether that cow is going to have trouble delivering her calf—all of it arises from relationships, interchanges that cannot be corralled with words.

It strikes me that if any remnant of humanity will make it through the population bottleneck we seem headed for, it may well be those who have learned to make their footsteps fertile for the soil and the soul. Walking through this pasture land, it is possible to imagine a mycorrhiza of the spirit that comes to life in us if we are stepping in the right way in the right places—mindfully in garden, field, forest, and prairie. In contact with the soil and its community of relationship-tending beings, we might have a chance to foster our own inner community of receptivity. What exercise could we undertake to become over time exquisitely attuned to signals in our bodies, in others, and in the whole matrix of life around us, developing the ear, eye, and touch that might let us perceive what our children and spouses need from us; to awaken resources in ourselves and in others to help a neighbourhood struggling with housing problems and poverty; or to restore a creek suffering from upstream agricultural residues and urban sewage?

A mile and a half along the road, I realize the ditch has changed. Instead of brome grass I see the glistening awns of the original native spear grasses, June grass, and buffalo sage mixed with asters and goldenrod, all of it spilling over from the wild pastures flanking the road. I step off the gravel and sit down near a slough almost entirely surrounded by large, straight aspen. Leaning on my pack, I dig into the dirt and bring a handful up to my face. Not a lot of clay, mostly sand, but something is holding it together just the same. Grains of feldspar glint in the sun and I imagine I can smell the *Actinobacteria* that give soil its lively tang when it rains. I wonder if glomalin participates in the scent of earth. These aspen trees seem grander than the average prairie poplar. The ones nearest the water have died back from flooding, but even in death they stand like warriors on a windswept plain. The bark of their surviving neighbours is shining as white as the bundled cumulus passing overhead. No sign of cattle damage, but that isn't enough to explain their vigour. There must be something in this sandy soil keeping these trees happy.

I stand up with the fistful of dirt and walk over to the shade of the nearest poplar, pressing my back against its bole and staring across at a larger trunk, the base grey and creviced with black trenches that look much like aerial images of prairie river breaks in a dissected plateau. An orange crustose lichen is spattered here and there amidst the breaks, but at chest level the darker tones give way suddenly to chalky white bark scarred with charcoal markings aligned horizontally.

The tree I am facing may well be another part of the aspen I am leaning against. Aspen poplar grow in clones, their stems connected underground. Each "tree" appears to be separate but is in fact connected to many of its neighbours in a single massive organism. This surprise came to me one autumn when a botanist friend pointed to a patch of aspen on the hillsides by our cabin where the leaves had all turned orange at the same time. "There," he said, "the fall colours sometimes let you see the boundaries of the clonal colony." He explained, saying that the trees in a colony all draw from the same shared root structure.

I was dubious. Aspen trees stand there like people, autonomous and self-determined. When I cut one down for my woodpile, its neighbours don't seem to mind. They carry on with their vital breath work, making food and oxygen out of starlight. But when I consulted Wikipedia a couple of days later, the story was confirmed and got even stranger. Apparently, there is a single clonal colony in Utah that includes forty-seven thousand trees covering forty-three hectares. It is estimated to weigh six million kilograms and could be as much as eighty thousand years old, making it the largest and longest-living organism known on the planet.

Right now, though, sitting here amidst these white-skinned spirits, the monastic community of the parkland world, I wonder if the illusion is that aspen trees appear independent and therefore seem like people, or is it that people appear to be separate but are actually like aspen trees: latent Buddhas who share a support system hidden from their own awareness? If I cut a stem from a colony of aspen and detect no response, the matter may be less about indifference on its part than insensitivity on mine.

Something is rustling through the chokecherries at the edge of the bluff thirty yards south of me. I hold still, staring in the direction of the sound. One pointed ear slips out of the grass understorey, turns, and then disappears with a swish. The bronze and grey tones are right for a coyote.

Coyote and the aspen trees. I used to tell my kids a Nakota trickster tale that I found in a book of Plains Indian stories for children. Coyote is out walking over the prairie one day, bragging about his greatness to the sun, the grass, the stones—anyone who will listen. Suddenly, he begins to hear a quiet voice coming from the earth, someone singing softly, "We are the strongest people in the world." Coyote, who has never heard such effrontery before, is incensed and scoffs, "Bah, who is this talking, who is this who dares to brag of his strength but won't show himself? I, Coyote, am the strongest and smartest animal under the sun."

But the singing continues: "We are the strongest people in the world," getting a bit louder and a bit louder until Coyote realizes it is coming from the grass. The grass people are singing. At this, Coyote collapses in laughter and rolls all over the prairie, guffawing and snorting at the thought that grass might be strong. After a long laugh he gathers his wits and declares, "I will show you who is strong. I will eat you who say you are so strong, and then we will see!"

Coyote greedily stuffs himself with as much grass as he can hold and then lies back on an aspen tree to rest. Immediately he hears the singing again, but this time it is coming from inside him: "We are the strongest people in the world . . . because we will make you fart!" More laughter from Coyote. "Hah, that is nothing for me. I am not afraid of anything. . . ." But then he feels his stomach begin to bloat. A great explosion lifts his tail and sends him high into the air. He crashes down on the hard ground with a bruising oopmph! And then another blast and another blast send him even higher, each bringing a more painful landing, and soon he is in a panic trying to find something to anchor himself to the earth. He grabs the base of an aspen tree and holds on tight. As the blasting continues, his grip pulls the aspen a short way out of the ground, exposing the base of its roots. Even today, the story ends, large aspen trees often show their roots, proving that Coyote was there, passing on the humble power of the grass people.

Beneath the humour of this story, and the lessons about the lowly grass having its power and pride having its dangers, lies a hunting people's ecological and spiritual understanding of the communion of creatures whose roots, whether they are visible or not, are interconnected. In the life of aspen parkland prairie, the coyote, the grass, the aspen, and many others support one another in roles and pathways that intersect. As one of the top predators, the coyote is eating an array of smaller mammals, especially rodents. Some of them eat grass, others eat and store seeds, others gnaw on tree saplings, some of them till the soil and eat roots. All of these activities influence plant growth and soil. At the same time, the presence of coyotes affects the populations and success of smaller predators, including skunks and foxes, helping to regulate their relationships to prey as well. It is impossible to calculate the influence of coyotes within the community of a stretch of aspen parkland grass and bush, but it would be safe to assume that it is intricate and vast.

Five years ago, a few sheep ranchers north of here talked the provincial government into offering a twenty-dollar bounty on dead coyotes. Truckloads were killed that winter, their paws cut off and turned in to rural municipality offices, where women more accustomed to handling tax notices had to process the bloody claims, dipping each severed paw into red dye to prevent anyone from bringing it back for a second bounty. By spring, seventy thousand coyotes had been killed. The scale of the massacre surprised even its political sponsors, who sheepishly announced that the bounty had been such a success it was no longer needed. No doubt the $1.4 million paid out also had something to do with their new restraint.

The evening chorus of yips we hear from the aspen coulees and grassy hilltops near our cabin disappeared for a year or two, but it is nearly back to full voice now. The trick of this trickster is that it outflanks most of our efforts to limit its populations simply by increasing the number of pups whelped in each den.

This kind of palaver about a creature like the aspen tree or the coyote only goes so far. If it is soul I am after here on the roadside, if the wildness I sense here is more than an assemblage of facts and stories, where does it live in me? I am pretty certain that the one thing I share with these aspen trees is being. I don't know for sure, but I want to believe that we travel together in the same orbit around a centre of radical generosity, an infinite giving that is the Being in charge of beingness. And if I were wiser, if I could walk a thousand of these miles in solitude, I might arrive at a place where I would stop longing to be dissolved within that ground because I would know, really know, that I am already there, already united anyway with everything spinning through the starlit reaches of creation.

Tell me, fellow travellers, aspen, dirt, and coyote—what is needed if we are to become more alive to the great openness, the expansive web of earthbound spirit within, around us, and beneath our feet? To gain the intuition that will allow us, in our temporary, provisional lives, to touch the hem of the garment of that infinite generosity?

The wind and crickets offer up their standard responses

and, lacking the patience to wait for more than that, I decide it's time to head back to the road. My palms are white with the chalky powder or bloom that protects the south sides of aspen trees from the sun. The thin outer skin of an aspen performs some of the photosynthesis that feeds it in summer, but in winter it needs to reflect the light away and remain dormant. I can't remember whether the bloom increases in winter, but someone once told me that it has enough wild yeast in it to make a sourdough starter. Skiing through aspen woods with our children when they were small, I would often smear their cheeks with the white bark bloom, leaving two or three streaks from my fingers. They rode the hills on fibreglass skis and carried nylon backpacks full of grocery store food, but with slashes of white on their cheeks they were wilder for the moment, and they loved it.

Remembering my children, I feel a lift in my chest at the thought that I am not always alone—that it isn't up to me and my little soul to extract the secrets from an aspen tree. Yes, it takes solitude and time, but that aloneness is held in a net formed by the community of pilgrims, a net made of the intuitions, interpretations, and visions of uncounted hearts who have also sat in the presence of an aspen tree.

If I listen alone beneath a tree, any insights that enter my awareness might get me to a place of pleasing daydream, but to move from private reverie to a deeper reverence it helps to reckon the experience within a community of believers and listeners, within the subjectivity of other souls gathered through time and space. Over generations any subjectivities that turn out to be less helpful or "true" reveal themselves to the honest heart as maladaptive and fall away in a natural selection of spiritual intuition.

I look back at the slough, straining to see if the coyote is in view. At the far shore the water suddenly stirs into sharp dancing peaks and the willows bend down as a soft roar rises, shaking leaves that drown out all other sounds in the amphitheatre of aspen and pond. I watch in anticipation as the zephyr picks up pace and races across the water toward me, rippling the still surface on its way. It rushes up the near cattails and through the aspen trees in front of me. I close my eyes to meet the wind, waiting to be shaken too, and it blows right through me, my trunk and limbs more alive than they were a moment before, than they will be when the wind has passed on.

Road Conditions: Forest Walking

Man is an outdoor animal. He toils at desks and
talks of ledgers and parlors and art galleries but the endurance
that brought him these was developed by rude ancestors, whose
claim to kinship he would scorn and whose vitality he has
inherited and squandered. He is what he is by reason of
countless ages of direct contact with nature.
—James H. McBride, MD,
Journal of the American Medical Association, 1902

Those lines, written more than a century ago by an American doctor, are the epigraph at the beginning of a recent book called *Your Brain on Nature.* The authors, Harvard physician Eva M. Selhub and naturopath Alan C. Logan, use research on the health benefits of the Japanese practice of *shinrin-yoku* to demonstrate that walking through a forest (or any natural landscape with some depth and variety) lowers one's blood pressure and cortisol (a stress hormone) levels. Though *shinrin-yoku* is translated simply as "forest bathing," it refers to walking through a natural environment with one's senses open to its gentle stimuli. In the introduction to their book, Selhub and Logan speak of the "videophilia" and other forces that keep us indoors, suggesting that there are personal, social, and environmental consequences that fall to a civilization buffered from the healing tonic of time in nature. The Japanese research they detail suggests that the immune and stress-response systems are affected, but their wider thesis is that the less we are exposed to nature, the less we care about policy and reform that will protect wild places and healthy ecosystems.

21 Taking Steppes

THE SILENCE OF THE ROAD GIVES WAY to the snarl of a high-compression engine. It's another quad, approaching from the north where a road intersects with this one. I stop and watch it coming, its rider straddling the seat, holding on to handlebars in a posture not that far from a man astride a quarter horse. But a quad is not a horse. In time-is-money agribusiness, an all-terrain vehicle with roll bar and winch has the power of sixty horses, none of which have to be fed, watered, or ridden until you need them. You just turn the key and there they are.

These horses are running along at more than twenty miles an hour, carrying a young man who looks as if he has a job to do. He pulls to a stop beside me, dropping his machine down to a low idle.

"Nice day for a walk," he says loud enough for me to hear above the engine. The smile comes from a shaven face in the shade of a camo-patterned ball cap. Work boots, a green hooded sweatshirt, and jeans.

"Yes, it is. You have cattle out here?"

"Nope. I just work for some people who do. They run feeder cattle on all this land around here."

I ask about the test well on the north horizon where some prospector is looking for potash and he tells me that it too is on company land.

"So what are you doing today?"

"Killing gophers and burrweed." He shows me the pail of poison bait in the back and a spray-pack of 2,4-D, a weed killer that has been linked to non-Hodgkin's lymphoma. I ask if the gopher poison is strychnine, but he does not know for sure. He tells me he is a university student and this is just a summer job.

"Should go. I might see you on my way back," he says, before putting his machine into gear and waving as he departs up the road to the west. Another smile, this one as innocent as the first, but not unintelligent. This kid seems to know how lucky he is to get eleven dollars an hour to be out here on a day like this travelling from pasture to pasture. Definitely the kind of young man you wouldn't mind dating one of your daughters. A vain, deluded thought, but in my defence I would not be near so keen on making decisions for the women around me if I had even the merest inkling of how they come to make their own decisions.

I was reassured when I read a *New Scientist* interview with Stephen Hawking on the occasion of his seventieth birthday. The interviewer asked him what occupies his thoughts most at this stage of life. A new way to measure black holes? Perhaps a refinement of his quantum theory of gravity? No, the greatest cosmologist of our age has something else on his mind: "Women," Hawking said without hesitation, "they are a complete mystery."

Hawking knows that trying to say what any woman is or is not will get him in a lot more trouble than guessing at the way the mass of the sun curves space-time. It would be wise to follow his lead and renounce all former claims to knowing anything about women, but who can resist pondering one of creation's most confounding and enthralling mysteries? Fifty years of watching and thinking about women and I haven't a clue whether they are as blameless as they seem or why so many seem to choose men who are violent and controlling.

In the end there may be nothing to be gained from calculating just how much of the world's problems we can place on the shoulders of this gender or that one. Right now, for this mile of the road at least and maybe more, I am entertaining another possibility. What if the root of our sinfulness is not in the failure of men, but in the way masculine and feminine energies have come together and been expressed in the world?

Sometimes when we are alone at the land on warm summer mornings, Karen and I will dispense with our clothes as we make our rounds from cabin to lake to garden. One of us will make a joke about our scrawny bodies helping to scare land developers away from the valley, but after a while we forget that we are naked. Sometimes, in that forgetting, I see it: for just a heartbeat I catch a sideways glimpse of the life that comes from the original donation of the creator. With the sun low in the east, we ease off the platform of our twin canoe barge and into the silvered realm of the lake. I dive to the bottom, come up for air, and there is Karen shining beneath a veil of water droplets. And it flashes before me like a seldom-seen animal, a kit fox caught in the open, this sudden apprehension of the paradox of how much she is like me but not like me, separate but connected to me—a wild something arising from the polarity of who we are, the complementarity of our bodies as freely given as the first to walk in the green shade of Eden. One of us speaks and the spell evaporates. We get back into the canoe and paddle to shore, merely naked again in our aging skins.

What is it about the opposition of masculine and feminine that is unifying instead of divisive in an age when we are discovering that the traditional binaries of gender are not nearly enough to encompass all of human experience? Even if you don't hold truck with religious thinking, West or East, any reasonably thoughtful, open-minded person has to admit that there is something compelling in the yin-yang representation of reality. Before corporations appropriated the black-and-white emblem to sell everything from cars to charm bracelets, the contemplative mind could ponder the simple truths of a hill in shadow and a valley in light; the sun above the valley, the moon illuminating the hill, each interpenetrating and containing something of the other. Beyond any symbols or words, yin-yang expresses a cosmic embrace, a complementarity of opposites woven into the fabric of creation. Regardless of whether this form or that is identified as 100 percent male or female, the dynamic of giving and receiving from opposite poles is the dance that moves in the matter of this universe, from the subatomic particle's orbit to the pull of stars. Not antagonistic or even dualistic, the yin and yang of life are interdependent forces that breathe and couple like lovers, creating a harmony that is more than mere balance or back-and-forth reciprocity, that moves in an oscillating, dynamic interchange which over time ensures the equal influence of both polarities.

As fruitless as it may be to make statements about where any place or time rests within such a far-flung metaphysical spectrum, all it takes to tempt me is a glance ahead where the road, dry and stony, slices east through the hidden, softer realm of grass and water vanishing over the edge of the earth. You don't need Lao-tzu as a walking companion to see that the yang energies of road and fence, oil well and gas line, corral and windrow, have run roughshod over the yin nature of prairie.

Five more miles to go. With or without a sage at my side, if I kept walking east on this latitude, maintaining a pace of forty miles every three days even across the Atlantic, after about one year I would pass through northern Europe into Asia and come to another kind of prairie where the yin-yang emblem is on the national flag. The grasslands of Mongolia, like this part of the northern Great Plains, came to life in a mid-continental steppe just a few degrees north of the fiftieth parallel.

Years ago, with a TV channel changer in my hand, I flipped to a station that carries British nature documentaries and found images of familiar-looking low, soft-curved hills covered with grass. It was a rare delight to see our northern grasslands on the screen, the distinctive tones and wind-ripple of the native grass, the glaciated landforms repeated across the horizon, all of it bathed in a quality of light I have known all my life and can usually recognize when I see it projected on a screen. As the camera panned, though, a yurt with a bright blue door hove into view with two Mongolian herdsmen mounted on sturdy ponies. *What are they doing here?* I thought, but then it became clear that this was not a documentary about remnant grasslands in Saskatchewan or Alberta or the Dakotas. It was a show about the changes to traditional herdsman life on the Mongolian plains. If the film had been set almost anywhere on the North American Great Plains, it is likely that the camera would have chosen angles to avoid showing the edges of the grassland remnant where cropped farmland takes over dominating the view. The Mongolian grasslands, on the other hand, have so far survived the insults of industrialized agriculture. From horizon to horizon and beyond there is more grassland, for the Mongolian steppe is one of the largest contiguous expanses of intact native grass in the world.

The film said that until the privatization movement of the 1990s, for more than twenty-two hundred years of statehood in Mongolia, land had never been privately owned. The entire place, including one million square kilometres of grassland, was a vast commons used by everyone without price, and yet somehow the "tragedy of the commons," the capitalist's boogeyman, never played on that stage. Instead, the rolling plains of sheep fescue and stipa have reigned over human enterprise, each nomadic family dwelling in a yurt they call a *ger*, answering the call of grass and water and moving with their sheep, ponies, yaks, and two-humped camels through an unfenced world. Despite the oncoming tragedy of progress,

40 percent of Mongolia's 2.4 million people continue to live the herdsman life. They occupy an ecological niche increasingly distorted by the modern market and its digital fripperies, but their way of life has allowed the signature species of grassland to persist into the twenty-first century. There are still wolves, Corsac foxes, steppe eagles, saker falcons, and several rare species of crane living on the Mongolian grasslands. Their undammed rivers are said to be relatively clean and alive with fish in healthy numbers. The iconic takhi, or Przewalski's horse, the only wild (i.e., not feral) horse species left on earth, was extirpated from the plains but is now being reintroduced. Perhaps most remarkable of all, millions of Mongolian gazelles still move in massive herds across the steppe each year, enacting one of the planet's last remaining great ungulate migrations.

How has this Asiatic grassland, so similar to what we once had here, managed to escape the forces that parcelled, ploughed, and fenced the plains I am walking through? The difference has something to do with the conversion of land to property, of taking the gifts of a place that grows grass and making them into commodities to be tossed into the great furnaces of production and wealth. Somehow, the degenerate gospel of success and progress missed Mongolia until the Soviet empire collapsed. In the last twenty years, though, international capital has helped the Mongolian people make up for lost time. Mining companies, including Canadian ones, have discovered gold and other hidden treasures beneath the steppes, and liberalized trade along with a privatization rush is bringing the requisite forms of ugliness. As the economy modernizes and becomes more dependent on distant capital and trade, cities nestled in grassland are now surrounded by shantytowns filled with ex-herders who burn tires and coal in their stoves. Some work in official mines, making the wages that are drawing people off the land. Others simply dig for gold on their own, creating improvised mines that leave the land scarred with open pits and the miners contaminated with mercury and other chemicals used to extract gold from the overburden.

Last year, a Saskatchewan trade-and-export mission travelled to Mongolia to look for opportunities to "improve agriculture" there while finding fresh markets for our farm-machinery industry. The Mongolian Ministry of Food welcomed the visit as a way to modernize food production, "secure its food supply, and protect its environment." They hosted a trade show where most of the exhibitors were from Canada, Saskatchewan in particular. None were from Mongolia.

There may be some good in having our businessmen fly there to trade, but just now I have trouble imaging what that might be. If I could walk there on this latitude, I would ask what Mongolia has to give us other than market opportunities. For trade I would offer some cautionary tales describing what we have learned in subduing this mid-continental steppe. If the exchange went well, and my heart was open enough, perhaps I would in return learn something from people who are just now emerging from a culture where land was always shared as part of the commons. I would ask how

the interplay of yin and yang has survived the onslaught of
the modern marketplace so far. Does it persist in their sha-
mans, in their traditional diet, in their throat singing, and in
the people still living the simple nomadic life, packing up the
ger and following cues in nature that have yet to disappear?
Are there ways to honour the balance of yin-yang even as
more land is owned by individuals and subdued to human
wilfulness, or is it inevitable that one day someone will take
the sweetness of grass, the freshness of milk, and claim it too
as possession?

Road Conditions:
Walking to Convert the Barbarians

*The interplay of yin and yang within
the womb of the Mysterious Mother creates the
expansion and contraction of nature.*
—Lao-tzu, *Hua Hu Ching*

In 1258 CE, Tibetan Buddhists and Taoists were battling one another to gain the favour of the Mongol court. To settle the matter, the Great Khan Kublai sponsored a series of debates between their best scholars. Things quickly came down to origins—who lived first, Lao-tzu or the Buddha? The Buddhists said that Lao-tzu was merely one of the Buddha's many lesser incarnations, and the Taoists claimed that the Buddha was an incarnation of Lao-tzu who, they said, walked to India and watered his teachings down to convert the barbarians there. They produced a document whose authorship is contested in Taoism to this day: *Hua Hu Ching*, or "Classic on Converting the Barbarians." Khan decided in favour of the Buddhists, and Buddhism today is stronger in Mongolia than Taoism.

If you could walk back through humanity's religious history with Lao-tzu at your side, you might want to ask him who was right—the Buddhists or the Taoists—but it might be good to know too who did write the inspired and controversial verses of the *Hua Hu Ching*. A version by British poet Brian Walker, based in great part on the Taoist oral tradition, speaks of a "Mysterious Mother" whose fertility dance created the universe, which is merely one small element of her entire being. Likewise, the text says, the reproductive function is but one aspect of human life. Though many become distracted by the generative impulse for their entire lives, to countenance the universal heart and mind of the Mother one must refine the fire of yin and yang that is felt in sexual desire and draw it upward. Chapters 69 through 71 are surprisingly direct in advising the "self-cultivation" discipline of celibacy or the "dual-cultivation" practice of a sexual tai chi to integrate yin and yang. Either path, the *Hua Hu Ching* counsels, can be effective though dangerous to those who have not cultivated the required virtue and self-mastery.

22 Our Lady of the Journey

I HEAR A HIGH, RAPID series of notes, a shining, silver string of lark song drifting on the wind over the bare field to my left. When I do my annual breeding-bird survey on the plains just south of here, I have to estimate numbers of unseen birds singing from the grass. Identifying the species by ear is easy enough; reckoning the number of each species vocalizing, though, is another matter.

I look out to the sky but cannot see the horned larks to count them. The eye is an organ of exactitude and possession. Pictures are taken. The times I have found myself chasing a grasshopper sparrow down a fenceline, camera in hand, forcing it to fly from perch to perch seeking a safe distance, even if I get the picture, I come away feeling the wrong kind of gratification. And it doesn't last any longer than it did when I was nine and had just got my hands on a Stan Mikita hockey card. What next, the hunger asks?

I close my eyes and stand with my face up to the sky trying to receive the plaintive contact calls of the larks going by. This is how John does it. John Neville does not get to see birds, but he records their sounds almost every day of his life. I once spent a day birding with him at his home on Saltspring Island. We stood in his garden overlooking the Salish Sea and listened to the whizz of rufous hummingbirds passing from one rhododendron to another, and the falsetto *Chi-ca-go* whistle-stop announcements of California quail moving through the lower hedges. I fussed with binoculars, my eyes darting from the golden-crowned sparrows on the patio to the hummers at the feeder to a towhee flying past. John stood still, facing the sky, hands in his pockets, smiling most of the time and speaking now and then in his soft, Welsh-tinged voice to direct my hearing to a new sound. "There, that was a surf scoter out on the bay. If we go down later, you'll hear it better."

While he is excited to find new bird sounds to record, John seems to have nothing of the birder's acquisitive twitch. His gentle, equanimous bearing reminded me of another visually impaired friend, Lawrence, who is officially a reflexologist though I think of him as an intuitive healer. Lawrence does his listening in the darkness of his studio where people come with every ailment from general unhappiness to terminal carcinoma. He takes in their immediate suffering, the physical or emotional condition that brought them, often finding it with his hands on their feet. But that is merely the first stage. As he works, he asks questions that let him listen for the underlying tenor of the spirit and mind. After that, he begins to tell stories to illustrate what might be happening and how to get back to health. Everyone goes home with advice on how to bring healing and ease into their lives: drink more water, be gentle with yourself, and consider that you might need to examine some of your beliefs; do this simple thyroid test with iodine; the most important part of regularity is just showing up; go easy, everything in moderation. Some of us are cured; all are comforted.

When I meet men like John or Lawrence who have had to learn how to listen, I realize how vision dominates my apprehension of the world. Instead of listening, I live through my eyes, seeing what is happening, what is needed, what I need, what will bring me pleasure, comfort, or esteem. Instead of nurturing others, I want to direct them, to have them see what I see, know what I know. And if they can't, I get impatient. "There, can't you see it? It's in the top right-hand corner of the ash tree. Two feet in from the edge. Are you blind?"

No one else is here to see this weasel scampering across the road, a capital *L* with legs beneath, the black-tipped tail wagging to and fro like a flag on a boy's bike. As my eyes try to pull it back into view, the act of witnessing veers off toward the urge to capture. *That would have made a great photo*—and suddenly witness gives way to desire. The moment I lapse into my default mode of groping for pleasure and comfort, whether it is the ellipse of a tern in flight or the sweep of a woman's thigh, any given image becomes a billboard for satisfactions that can never really be delivered on. Witness, the attentive presence of soul, is as weak as the breath we draw, an inhalation easily overwhelmed by the winds of desire.

A man doesn't start off this way, his eye a scandalizing organ, turning the gifts of creation into obstacles to be tripped over in his daily road. Like anyone else, my first sensory experiences had nothing to do with the eye. It would have been sound, not sight—feminine sounds, the beating of my mother's heart, the sloosh of her blood, the pleasing tones of her voice.

The last time I had coffee with Daniel, we swapped stories about our aging mothers. I had asked him again about the role of feminine energy in creation. "I've never asked that question in the lodge, so I can't say exactly," he said, "but I know this: the Sun Dance cannot begin unless there is a young girl, about seven years old, who can start the cutting down of the tree with an axe. She takes four blows, like that, before others can take over and turn it into the Sun Dance's main pole."

He said that, among most Plains peoples, women were valued more than men. Men were expendable, he said, but not women, whose hand skills were particularly vital for the survival of the clan. Then he started talking about his mother.

"She's ninety-four now. She was always tough, a strong woman. She still lives by herself here in the city, but we all take care of her. My siblings and I take turns staying with her. We get some respite help now and then, but mostly we look after her ourselves. She has lost a lot of her speech, but the one thing she can still say is 'I want to go home.' I thought she was saying she wanted to die, but it wasn't that. So in the lodge my brother and I asked what does she mean and they told us, she wants to go back to where she was born and lived as a child. So now, every so often, I take her back to the reserve and we go out to the cemetery to see the graves of her parents. But there is no going back to the kind of place where she grew up, to what her parents had: eighty head of horse, sixty head of cattle, chickens, pigs, a big garden. That is all gone now." As Daniel spoke, I imagined his mother in the passenger seat, looking out over the reserve where she grew up, and I did not ask what I wanted to ask: was she ever that seven-year-old girl taking those first four whacks at the Sun Dance pole?

It was my turn, so I told him how my mother had grown up with that kind of farm too, and that I have taken her back to the old homestead and to the cemetery where her siblings and parents are all laid to rest. But no one would ever say my mother is strong. As a girl she saw her mother, my grand-mother, abused and betrayed by a philandering bounder who extended his rights as a property-owning lord of the New World to include poaching the valley's deer and his eldest son's bride. My grandmother kept chickens, milked the cow, hauled the firewood, fed the family from game and garden, and washed laundry in the river without complaint, but her quiet suffering marked all of her children in one way or another. Leaving home at seventeen, my mother, born Olive Jeanne, became Jeanne, had her imperfect teeth replaced with perfect dentures, took catechism from the Catholic Church, and mar-ried my father. Though he never raised his hand against her, I heard my father raise his voice far too often at my mother.

In the towns where we lived, the closest thing to a liber-ated woman was one with a job and a driver's licence. "That's it," my mother would say. "I'm going to learn how to drive." But she never did.

Once, when my brother and I were giving her grief about something—I no longer remember what—she announced she was leaving, but the best she could do was to run out the front door and down the street. After a dumb moment looking at our now motherless kitchen, I followed, catching her a few blocks away. I apologized and brought her back knowing only that we had pushed her forgiving nature too far that time. I may also have felt sorry that her escape from our juvenile cruelty had been so ineffectual, but I didn't know how amazing it was that she chose to leave when she well might have thrashed us. No matter how we taunted or mistreated her, she would never even consider smacking one of us. My best friend lived next door and his mother was gone because of one bad day—or at least that was how I understood it. People said she pitched something big through the picture window and now she was "in North Battleford," which was where fractious mothers were sent in those days. Doctors signed papers and whoosh, off they went. We were fortunate that the only doctoring papers signed for our mother were to prescribe Valium, the solution for less serious cases of misbehaving women.

In her forties she did eventually begin to take part-time work outside the home, though we all complained, particularly if her shift at the store was anywhere near supper hour. The years she worked in drugstores and at Sears may have been her happiest. She had her own spending money, time away from housework, and people who appreciated the way she would hold their hand and simply receive their stories of struggle, failure, or betrayal with an open heart.

When I visit Mom now in the nursing home, she will remind me that she is a valued staff member. "I like working here," she'll say, or sometimes, "They need me here." And in a way she is right. Some poor, tormented soul will be crying softly from down the hall, "Help me . . . someone help me." No response from staff, who hear it every day, but Mom, who does not remember whether the woman was crying out yesterday or an hour ago, hears it afresh. Someone is in need, so Olive Jeanne draws herself up onto her unsteady feet and heads down the hall to the ailing woman's side.

She may not remember that she put salt on her potatoes two minutes ago, but she has not lost her knack for establishing instant bonds with everyone in her midst. A wink in the direction of a handsome nurse walking past, a joke at my father's expense, or just a look from those faded periwinkle eyes is usually enough. But stirred into that bottomless well of charm and empathy are the waters of a life marked by fear and sadness.

The nursing home is named after Saint Anne, who, according to Christian apocrypha, was the mother of Mary and grandmother of Jesus. When I visit, if the weather is good, I walk my mother out to a small courtyard in the centre of the building. I wrap her in a quilt and we sit on a garden bench looking out toward a small bronze statue. I am the first to go look at any statue. It might be a Joe Fafard, a Henry Moore, or just one of those figures mounted in city parks—it doesn't matter. I am there, touching it, looking for the eyes, the hands, the feet.

The statue in the St. Anne courtyard depicts a skinny teenager wearing a rough tunic with a belt at the waist, and carrying a satchel slung over the shoulder. The figure, caught in mid-stride, is walking with a confident air, one arm swinging forward and the other back. It has the angularity and sketchbook gesture of child characters from the heyday of Disney's animated films. In fact, the hair cut in a bob and the boyish swagger put me in mind of Wart, the young King Arthur in *The Sword and the Stone*. When I first examined the statue, I knew it had to be a figure from Christian tradition, but I could not imagine who—Isaac following his father up the mountain, David on his way to face Goliath, a young Saint Francis? Glancing down at the brass plate on its base for some help, I read the small inscription: *Our Lady of the Journey, Luke 1: 39.*

Lady? Maybe a girl, but you can see in the angle of her chin, the set of her mouth, that she knows something and that the thing she knows is making her step toward her destination with more than the usual adolescent mix of innocence and confidence. Last week, driving down a street in our neighbourhood, I overtook a slender schoolgirl striding along the sidewalk, blond hair swinging in a squirrel's tail sine wave behind her. Free but self-aware, knowing a bit more of her own charms perhaps than her innocence, the not-yet-hurt part that is the treasure of a fourteen-year-old girl. I did my best not to stare as I passed and then discovered that it was my youngest daughter, Maia, walking back from a friend's house.

Our Lady of the Journey. When I looked up that passage in Luke, it described her journey in one line: "At that time Mary got ready and hurried to a town in the hill country of Judea." She was in a rush to see her cousin Elizabeth to give her the news. Elizabeth, who thought she was barren and beyond child-bearing, was pregnant with the child who would become John the Baptist. The subsequent verses say the two expectant cousins embraced and then Mary, teen-aged unwed mother of God, spielled off a speech that begins with one of the boldest opening lines in the Bible: "My soul magnifies the Lord." The rest of the monologue is rich with some of the promises that have been hardest for Christendom to keep—dethroning unjust kings, feeding the hungry, send-ing the rich and proud away empty.

As presumptuous as it sounds for anyone to claim that their soul magnifies the Lord, is that not the potential that every pregnant mother bears inside her? Women have every right to be excited, to burst with bold claims, when they discover they are pregnant. They are bearing into the world a person who at least for now has unlimited potential to upset princes, feed the poor, chasten the proud. That word *bearing* speaks in three common usages that converge on *gift* as a fundamental characteristic of human experience. We take it for granted that mothers will be good at bearing all three—pregnancy, gift, and burden—and children of course are all three at once.

For twenty years after I left home, my mother would bake my favourite cake, an impossibly fudgy and dense chocolate edifice, and send it by bus to arrive on my birthday. She was excited to send it, and its journey from her was part of that expectancy. These days Maia has taken over responsibility for the recipe, and eating it reminds me more than ever of the unconditional generosity of the one who bore me, and the potential of my own daughters to manifest in their very flesh the reciprocity and communion of persons. But where does that leave my son, and the rest of us who are so gobsmacked by these creatures whose souls magnify the Lord, who especially in pregnancy come closest to the giving that is truly free, to the giving of life that allows us to walk our days here without any interference from the One who created all of this?

The answer has to be in a man's freedom to choose. In the face of the gift of life in all its glorious diversity, will we be takers or receivers? Rapists or lovers? How do we guard and husband our own body's most intimate giving? Our flesh too must be a witness to creation as a fundamental gift, to the Love from which all giving springs. The quality of our decisions on what we do with our bodies, particularly in response to femininity and its gifts, is our most direct path to living that original generosity with the awareness and strength that leads to mutual giving in relationship.

If the creator's very love for the world is hard to see in couplehood, most of us can usually find it reflected in our mothers, nature and nurture confluent in their unreserved giving and attention to relationship. My mother still cannot eat beside her husband or children without offering a piece of bread or meat from her plate. She does it whenever I am with her at mealtime at the nursing home, the habit of feeding me remaining in her heart much deeper than any dementia can touch. Pinched between two fingers and her thumb, the morsel comes my way. In my confused shame I usually refuse it, feeling unworthy or angry that her life has been so reduced to its barest instincts. I will not be surprised if her last conscious gesture will be those three digits pressed together, offering life to loved ones near at hand.

~

My stomach is suggesting I dig into my pack to see what remains of the larder. A chunk of beef jerky, the sardines I have been avoiding, and a handful of gorp. This will be my last meal of the walk. As I chew on a mouthful of sardines, the muffled purr of a quad approaches from the west. It is the young hired hand again. He pulls over and shuts the engine down beside my ditch-grass picnic where I am surrounded by little bluestem and the seed heads of gaillardia long past bloom. We talk for a while, this time about his parents selling their cattle when the bovine spongiform encephalopathy crisis hit in 2003. "Now they just have an acreage," he says.

He is studying to become a teacher, he tells me, because you have to be crazy or rich or both to get into cattle these days. I ask him what he does on rainy days and he says he goes into the office and does some accounting work on the computer or drives an asphalt truck for the boss. Before he leaves, he digs into his lunch kit and produces a bagel and a small Tetra Pak of grape juice, handing them to me. I thank him. He starts the motor again and against that noise I shout, "What's your name?"

"Joseph."

"Thanks, Joseph," I say, but now the thing is in gear and revving too loud for words to make it through.

Road Conditions: Walking in Gratitude

If you want to see where you are, you will have to get out of your space vehicle, out of your car, off your horse, and walk over the ground. On foot you will find that the earth is still satisfyingly large, and full of beguiling nooks and crannies.
—Wendell Berry, "Out of Your Car, Off Your Horse"

How can there be no God, when there are all these beautiful things?
—Dorothy Day, *The Long Loneliness*

Wendell Berry begins his essay on local versus global thinking by inviting readers to look at a photograph of the earth taken from outer space and see if they can recognize their neighbourhood. One of the benefits of thinking locally is that you have to be here walking the real ground of the real world to do it, and that increases the chances that you may look closely enough to see its gifts. If that happens, gratitude becomes at least a possibility. And where there is gratitude, can generosity be far behind?

Dorothy Day, Catholic social activist, anarchist, and spiritual writer, walked the poor neighbourhoods of Chicago's South Side as a girl and was astonished by the beauty she found amid suffering and deprivation. The cover of the 1985 edition of her autobiography, *The Long Loneliness*, shows her as an old woman walking through the woods. Several times in her life she walked her way into jail while protesting injustice. In 1917, she picketed with forty others in front of the White House to demand the vote for women. That was her first jail term. Her last one came at the age of seventy-eight, when she received ten days for walking along with César Chávez to support farm workers. From the 1930s to the 1970s, she travelled the streets of New York to bring justice and relief to the poor, but she also walked the beaches and marshes of Staten Island whenever she could spend time at her cottage there. Her gravestone at a cemetery near the cottage reads *Deo Gratias*—thanks be to God.

23 Give Away

Down the road a mile I come to some wetlands that have sloshed through the ditch and right up to the edge of the gravel. With water lapping against the grade ten feet on either side for three hundred paces, the road has become a long bridge through a flooded world. The bottoms of my sandals are only an inch or two above the surface of the slough. On the one side I see clumps of cattail and mud where black terns and coots hatched out their young a few weeks ago. A snipe flushes in front of me, and young coots with bad hairdos skitter ahead as I make my way along.

A half mile past the slough, I hear a vehicle slowly drawing near, popping gravel behind me as it advances, so I pull off to the left side. Seconds later I see a new SUV draw up alongside me, the window down, the driver's arm dangling against the side of the door.

"Helluva day for a walk," says the sixty-year-old man, not likely a farmer, grinning a grin that wavers somewhere between indolence and curiosity. He wants to talk.

"Uh-huh." Walking over to his window, I nod to his buddy in the passenger seat. They introduce themselves. Alec and

Mert, harmless good ol' boys from a town a few miles south, are taking the back roads to Indian Head, driving slow and drinking road pop: orange-flavoured rum coolers nestled between their thighs. I tell them about our place at Cherry Lake and they pass me a Coors Light from under the seat. In a minute or so I learn that Alec knows some of the characters who camp at another lake nearby. I've met them too. People with camper trailers, quads, and Jet Skis. We exchange news about bear and moose sightings. Alec passes on some gossip about a marriage breaking up over an affair that started at the camp. "Yep, those two hooked up. So now he's liquidating alla his stuff—'cause of the divorce."

The beer tastes better than I remember Coors ever tasting, but everything is better on the last two miles of a forty-mile walk. As the sound of Alec and Mert pulling away fades, I hear a Swainson's hawk overhead giving one long cry. I look up and find three then four of them circling right above me. A few raindrops fall from the darkening midday sky. The hawks drift lower and scream louder, repeatedly. I take off my pack to cover it with the poncho. "All right, I hear you. What is it?"

My feet are sore, but I don't want the walk to end yet, so I sit in the ditch and watch the hawks circling. They flap hard to stay aloft in the drizzle, and my beer-borne thoughts follow. My head feels odd, emptied out, a bowl licked clean. It was a bit like this on my final morning on the hilltop. After a third wretched night, the darkness passing in horned dreams and little in the way of sleep, I crawled out of my tent at dawn to sit and look over the bottomland below. Something had shifted. My thinking was slower. For a few moments in a row it seemed I could see each thought rise and pass, etched against the white void of my unknowing. The fear, aggression, and self-loathing had evaporated for the time being, and in their place remained the residue of the night's visitors and their promise of reciprocity. *Don't be afraid. If you feed us, we will graze your pastures.*

That last daybreak, as I thought about the deer coming every night, Karen walked into view far away on the valley bottom, stepping along the road to the place where she turned to look up to my hilltop each morning. The first two days she just sat for a half hour or so facing my direction, but this time she was bending over something on the ground. After a few seconds she sat back and lifted one arm, releasing a narrow wisp of smoke, edged with silver from the sun spilling into the valley behind her. She had lit a sage smudge and it was billowing into a shining cloud of incense rising in the still dawn air. The cloud grew until it lifted well above the valley rim, and suddenly I felt a pressure build in my chest and then a laugh bursting out of me like water through a breached dam. I fell back on the grass, weak from the surge of whatever it was that was making me laugh.

A flock of teal whistled overhead toward the lake. "Ducks!" I said out loud, and laughed again. "Clouds!" Gratitude was suddenly something I could feel in my flesh, just as vivid and palpable as anger or fear have always been. I don't know if gratitude is an emotion, I remember thinking, but if it is, I am short on it.

～

My hawk escort is moving east. Hauling myself up out of the ditch, I follow, listening to their sharp cries drift above me. It dawns on me that they are, in their own way, regarding me as I am regarding them, each of us from within our own world. Days like this, they know freedom and obedience both, held elegantly in the tension between the openness of the air and the direction of autumn's ancestral pull to the south. In a month's time they will be swirled within ecstatic kettles of a thousand hawks or more, spiralling over the Isthmus of Panama on their way to the Pampas of Argentina. Two of the hawks appear to brush past one another, primaries nearly touching as they circle. One breaks away and comes by for another pass. Its head swivels to look my way. That eye is not as haughty as it might be for a creature who lives in upper realms. Freedom within obedience, obedience within freedom. I decide to ask the hawk my question: *how do we touch the hem of that garment, that infinite generosity in creation?*

Immediately, my thoughts go back to the candy wrapper I found on the hilltop. I can see it, written on the crinkled plastic: *GIVE AWAY!* Okay, so what have I got that I must give away? My great wealth? I'm assuming this is not an injunction to throw off my worldly goods and walk barefoot, Francis-wise, into the world. Becoming a shoeless beggar is fine for a medieval monk, but I've got a family who still need me to keep the fridge stocked and the furnace going. It must be something else. What do I treasure most, fear losing most? No great pondering required there. It's the same thing everyone holds on to with white knuckles. When I wake in the middle of the night and think, *Holy smoke, I am going to die someday*, what is it that I am afraid of losing but the very I who is moved by fear of death? The fragile cocoon of identity and roles I have spun from a thread of inheritance braided with experience: the fearful, defensive, insecure, angry, obsessive, judging, impatient, soft-headed dreamer who claims to be a son, husband, father, naturalist, artist, and activist. And for all that, the one thing I am starting to understand is that none of this precious cargo is any more permanent or substantial than a single blade of grass along this road.

I have been standing in a doorway for far too long now and the view over my shoulder is less comforting every day. The unease of this year has been in coming to know that the self I have made has turned out to be something of a golden calf that no soul would bow down to. Might as well give some of it away now rather than have it wrenched away all at once later. Whether in grief, failure, sickness, or death, eventually my treasured, seemingly insoluble self will be washed in just the right solution to let it flow away into wider rivers. Not that I imagine there is some kind of giving away in this life that dissolves the ego completely into that perfect union. But perhaps I can taste something of it in giving, in the preemptive giveaways that help us prepare for those inevitable inundations of loss and death when they come. A three-day walk is not on its own enough to tell me exactly what that means for me, but it has been enough to show me that this next phase of life is about giving my life away, and staying awake and watchful for paths that will take me there.

～

Moments ago, as I ate the bagel and drank the juice Joseph left me, I was thinking of my friend Joseph when he was that same age. We'd meet between classes in the students' lounge at St. Thomas More. He'd flop down on the couch and begin lecturing me with his own gonzo mélange of philosophy he'd inhaled during long hours on the fourth floor of the library, tossing in quotations he'd memorized from the Tao or the theologian who was his current favourite. One of these I remember now, perhaps because I have heard it repeated by others so often in the intervening thirty-five years: "In the torment of the insufficiency of everything attainable we eventually learn that here, in this life, all symphonies remain unfinished."

Joseph grudgingly admitted his respect for Karl Rahner— "for his mental rigour, not all of its fruits." At the time, the concept of nothing coming to perfection in life would have appealed to my sophomore's sense of the tragi-poetic, but I doubt I had an inkling of what Rahner was going on about. Decades of looking for consummation in the wrong places has helped a bit, though I am not quite ready to give up the quest. Wiser men may say it ain't possible in this too fleshly existence, but the juvenile inside me is still holding out for an ultimate union. As long as I am looking to the Logos of the billboard for transcendence, as long as there is a chance that my desires might finally make good on the promises they advertise, I am apt to keep shaking apples from the tree of life.

Funny how that works, though. The more I eat mindlessly from that tree, the more tasteless it all becomes. Give away? The first gift from the fruits hanging within our reach in life is the freedom to choose how and what we take, receive, give, and give up. To give away may be to live more mindfully by finally and really receiving the primordial gift-blessing of freedom, which is not licence but self-mastery within a wider obedience, the capacity to live in fidelity and continence as I husband my generative energies. Any aspirations I may have to safeguard wild places, grow gardens, and build community stand little chance of success if I cannot do a better job of tending to the holiest of connections, my sexual bond with the feminine (a bond with one woman in fidelity is a bond with all women in forbearance), and then, falling out of that primary bond, all of the others: with family, community, land. If I can set aside transcendence and union on some other plane, I might find ways to receive the gift of peace hidden within forbearance and continence on this plane, the gift of freedom hidden within the paradox of self-sacrifice.

Thoreau was on to something when he said that we "must converse much with the field and woods" if we would imbibe such health into mind and spirit as we covet for the body. His imbibing suggests an intimacy that is much deeper than conversation, but arising from a childlike purity of heart. "If I would preserve my relation to nature, I must make my life more moral, more pure and innocent . . . I must not live loosely, but more and more continently."

A child is created to be conversant that way, to be open in all of his senses to the banquet of delights surrounding him. Coming of age, as a young man fired with the eros that made him look for connection and fulfillment, Thoreau, like any man, saw himself fall into habits that dulled his sensitivity and capacity for delight. His pure relation to nature began to fall away, as it does for every child of God, the moment he entitled himself to all that is meant as gift, the moment pleasure became something to be taken. The more a man possesses, the more he is possessed, the more his faculties for appreciating the numinous and beautiful fade. Where else can he relearn the child's purity of heart if not among the gifts that come from gardens, forests, and prairies? To the extent that he receives them with a pure and open heart, he retains at least the potential for taking part in a chaste, bonding intimacy. Like all intimacies, our deepest exchanges with the otherness of our world involve physical gestures, touch, and sustained stillness within a mutual embrace. Any glance, squeeze, hug, or kiss we give or receive bears a weight of intention or energy. If we are awake, we will know exactly where the gesture rests on the spectrum from formality through manipulation, betrayal, lust, gift, and love.

Our most intimate moments happen when we are quiet in the bosom of a place we love or in the arms of our beloved, times when we feel we have been touched by something we cannot quite hold on to yet, but the touch is lovely nonetheless, a bestowal of sweetness undeserved and therefore truly a gift, one that bears with it an invitation to carry ever so lightly that exquisite not-yetness.

Tomorrow, a dozen of our closest friends are arriving at the land to help us properly receive the summer's bestowal of sweetness. If everything goes according to plan, my bee-keeping partner, Jordan, and I will pull frames dripping with honey from the two hives, brushing the bees off before we transfer them to the honey house. Once we have the building heated to about eighty-five degrees Fahrenheit, the honey should begin to flow. It will be tempting to lick our fingers, but we will do our best not to, not yet. When we gather to begin the extraction, we make a pact that before anyone tastes it, we are going to give the first bit of honey back, back to the bees and the land they gathered it from.

In the heat of the honey house, we are stripped to the waist by the time we have spun out the first four frames. Then we fill a wooden bowl with some strained honey and take it outside, where Karen places it on a mat woven of cattail leaves and decorated with wildflowers and fruit from our gardens. We gather in a circle around the youngest child and the oldest of our guests, who together hold the gifts. I improvise a short prayer of thanksgiving before giving Sean, a yoga teacher friend, the signal to fire up the bagpipes. He begins walking toward our highest hill in solemn kilt-wise steps and the gift bearers and the rest of us follow him through the spear grass and wolf willow to the crest, where we offer up the first fruits of the summer harvest.

Sean plays a raucous skirling tune from other highlands to take us back down the hill, where we begin the celebration. We dip fingers and spoons into a bowl of honey and slather it on fresh buttered cornbread, washing all of it down with drafts of the mead Jordan made with last year's harvest.

Between the sun glinting on gold dripping from spoons, the laughter that runs among us, and the mead in our bellies, we know the rightness of giving thanks in this way. For once in my yearly round, the earth becomes its enchanted self again, and I stop to remember that even on these harsh plains where the very wind can take my life, everything that falls into my hands is unmerited grace. No man deserves the sweetness this life, this land, this woman offer. The only way to receive any of it, to be able to appreciate any gift, is to give it back saying no, I cannot accept this. I am not worthy. The miracle is that I usually get a second chance to receive it, and the gesture of giving it back makes the gift all the sweeter in the end. Ritual and gesture alone will not be enough to polish my soul into something finer, but over time and in the company of others who help me receive and be grateful for what is given, letting it break down my mistrust and through my selfish hide, I may get there yet. On this last rise in the road before the descent toward our pastures, the hope I hold on to is the possibility that, in the sharing of all that is broken, imperfect, and human, I will find in gratitude a wider embrace, a bonding and a fidelity that points me toward the ultimate union that the human longing to connect can never quite manage in this life.

I can see the hills that surround our piece of the Upper Indian Head Creek watershed now. The road gives way to a muddy track for the last two miles to our fenceline. On the north side of the track, a pea field already combined. Looks like Mr. Larmenaux has been busy. On the south, the rolling kame and kettle moraine that folds into the coulees and springs feeding the creek, its chain of beaver ponds, and our small lake. The anticipation is almost too much. How good it will be to slip into its bottle-green waters, to lunge and roll like a trout among the slippery weeds.

The hawks pull up and away a half mile before I reach our fenceline. I stop to watch them diminish down to specks and then step over the barbed wire and into the old growth of June grass and fescue still pining for the buffalo. Chokecherries, almost a month ripe now, dangle between weary leaves. The trail drops down through our northern coulee, taking the air temperature with it, to cooler, damper precincts where mule deer and coyotes wait out the day.

The rain is starting again. Slowing my steps, I fall into the trochaic cadence of an old canticle I found once in a breviary. It belonged to a woman I know only through the testimony of her friends and children.

The rhythm more than the words of the canticle have stayed with me, so I am improvising:

shower and dew (bless the Lord), sun and moon (bless the Lord), stars of heaven (bless the Lord), all you winds (bless the Lord), fire and heat (bless the Lord), cold and chill (bless the Lord), ice and snow (bless the Lord), nights and days (bless the Lord), lightnings and clouds (bless the Lord), prairies and hills (bless the Lord), bushes and sloughs (bless the Lord), creeks and rivers (bless the Lord), birds of the air (bless the Lord), cattle of the fields (bless the Lord), everything growing from the earth (bless the Lord), sons and daughters . . . bless the Lord.

I walk down into the valley and through the yard site, the buildings and gardens. Tree swallows, barn swallows, house wrens, a late oriole, and ruby-throated hummingbirds the only residents today. After dropping my pack next to the cabin, I take off my sandals and head for the shore. The dock feels slick from the rain as I look out to the surface of the lake, still but for the circles rippling outward from a million droplets of water. The susurration, barely audible, is achingly sad and lovely. The rain speaking, the lake answering, and I am not the only one listening. Two bufflehead are bobbing against the far banks, their white heads lit by the warm rays of late afternoon light. I watch their small forms fade and darken in the first pangs of dusk that will bring more rain tonight.

I was sweating a minute ago, but now, with the rain streaming down my back, I am cold enough to have second thoughts about the swim. More discouragement from the heavens, as a low rumble follows the flare of lightning over the valley to the west. Suddenly the rain shifts into a steady pour, and the lake begins to dance. The hell with it. I dive in anyway.

Coming up through the green gloom, I make a circuit out to the middle of the lake and back, then wade into the shallows and stand with my feet planted in eight inches of black, organic muck. An assembly of whirligig beetles is skating loops on the surface of the water near my knees. Young blackbirds squabble in the cattails.

Back at the cabin, I grab an old quilt and roll, bone-tired, into the string hammock we keep on the outdoor porch. The sun has sliced low through an aperture in the western cumulus, casting a complete rainbow over the lake and hills, granting the landscape the naive grace of a child's crayon drawing.

"How was your walk?"

I come to with Karen's hand on my cheek, the scent of her skin, twilight caught in her hair. "It was a good walk," I say, "but it's good to be here too."

"And the hawks? Did you talk to them?"

I start to answer but, between the spirits of my nap now fading and the warmth of the woman who holds a place for me, something conjures up a memory of the look on her face when she found me on my back next to the ladder, winded and groaning.

Is there a way to love, I wonder, without ever scaring one another? Without the descent off rooftops and into old age, without knowing the fear in one another's eyes? Somehow in this life, it is the heaviness that lets a bird launch into flight, and the uncertainty ahead that makes us walk new pathways.

Over Karen's shoulder, a flock of five birds comes into view. Too large for hawks, their great draping wings flap slow and deep as they pass high above the lake. Look, I say, and she turns and together we watch the first cranes of autumn heading for their night roost.

Acknowledgements

While this book is non-fiction and a personal account in which I have done my best to re-create conversations and actual events faithfully, I plead all the usual exemptions about memory's imperfection. I have changed many but not all of the names of characters in the story to protect the privacy of people who may not want to appear in a book.

Walking a prairie road for a couple of days might inspire some gratitude, but writing about it works even better. My heart was warmed, my spirit stirred, and my mind pried open by so many people as I worked on this book that I hesitate to try listing all of them for fear of the inevitable omissions. Nonetheless, there are a few people I wanted to be sure to acknowledge:

Trevor and Ruth McMonagle and the rest of the folks who run the Haig-Brown House Writer-in-Residence Program in Campbell River let me work in a place where fine naturalist writers have been writing for nearly a century. The bigleaf maple trees, the view from the kitchen, the inestimable library, and the river running past—all haunted by the genial spirits of Roderick and Ann Haig-Brown—breathed life into my little walking narrative and continued to inspire me long after I had returned home. The five months they and the Canada Council gave me in the Haig-Browns' historic home produced a first draft of the manuscript I could take to my publisher.

Many friends read a version of the manuscript and provided helpful insights and comments: Etienne Soulodre, Shelley Banks, Leanne Armstrong, Brian Bartlett, Kevin Van Tighem, and Michael Cichon. As well, the good men of the fire, who make me laugh and keep me sane, were in my thoughts, peering over my shoulder as I wrote. (I apologize for changing your good names to the ones I found in a list of chartered accountants, but it was either that or the 1922 Roughriders roster and then one of you would have been "Piffles.")

The good counsel of my friend "Daniel," who also had to be renamed in the book, showed me how to make sense of sitting and walking and much else. Emma Korkola, week in, week out, inspired me with the discipline that is 99 percent practice and 1 percent theory. Hamilton Greenwood, always generous with his astonishing photographs of prairie landscapes and birds, let us use one of his images of a Swainson's hawk for the cover. Jackie Kaiser of Westwood Creative Artists, early in the writing process, helped me shape and reshape the concept for this book into something that might work for readers and publishers. Phyllis Bruce, who edited my last book, was enthusiastic and encouraging from the outset, willing to take on a book about a man walking on an unremarkable road. For that confidence and for bringing me initially to HarperCollins, I am very grateful. Patrick Crean,

Noelle Zitzer, and John Sweet at HarperCollins guided the manuscript through to publication with editorial grace and unfailing good cheer.

Karen, who lets me indulge in regular vacations away from the real world of parenthood and household maintenance, shows no signs of smartening up. Against all good reason, she actively encourages me to write books while the subfloor upstairs remains naked and the ceiling downstairs remains leaky. When a man awakens each morning to one so beguiling, generous, and true, he might begin to imagine that his bond with her is whispering intimations of heaven. And if she loves him and has given him her life and children out of that bond, then he is right and there is nothing left for him to do but be still and listen.

Sources

This book borrows lavishly from many of the insights of other writers who have given much more thought than I have to the ecological and spiritual impasse of our time. I am particularly indebted to Bill Plotkin, Ron Rolheiser, and Rob Bell. Rather than interrupt the text with a lot of names, titles, and footnotes, though, I have placed them in the following chapter lists of source material, citing them here with deep gratitude and admiration for their work.

Epigraph

Kierkegaard, Søren. *Provocations: Spiritual Writings*. Farmington, PA: Plough Publishing House, 1999.

An Introduction: *Homo Viator*

Plotkin, Bill. *Soulcraft: Crossing into the Mysteries of Nature and Psyche*. Novato, CA: New World Library, 2003.

Rilke, Rainer Maria. *Book of Hours: Love Poems to God*. Translated by Anita Barrows and Joanna Macy. New York: Riverhead Books, 1975.

Thoreau, Henry D. *Thoreau on Man and Nature: A Compilation by Arthur B. Volkman from the Writings of Henry David Thoreau*. Mount Vernon, NY: Peter Pauper Press, 1960.

Part One: Outdoor Complaints
Forster, E.M. *Howards End.* New York: G.P. Putnam's Sons, 1910.

1. On the Road Allowance
Whitman, Walt. *The Complete Writings of Walt Whitman.* New York: G.P. Putnam's Sons, 1902.

2. By Fire
Thoreau, Henry D. "Walking." *The Essays of Henry D. Thoreau.* New York: North Point Press, 2002.

3. Every Road
Berry, Thomas. *The Dream of the Earth.* San Francisco: Sierra Club Books, 1988.
White, Lynn. "The Historical Roots of Our Ecological Crisis [with discussion of St. Francis; reprint, 1967]." In *Ecology and Religion in History.* Edited by David Spring and Eileen Spring. New York: Harper and Row, 1974.

4. Shadows
Rilke, Rainer Maria. *Letters to a Young Poet.* Translated by Reginald Snell. Mineola, NY: Dover Publications, 2002.
Stegner, Wallace. *The American West as Living Space.* Ann Arbor: University of Michigan Publishing, 1987.
Weil, Simone. *Waiting for God.* Translated by Emma Craufurd. New York: Harper Colophon, 1973.

5. Pathways
Brewer, J.A., P.D. Worhunsky, et al. "Meditation Experience Is Associated with Differences in Default Mode Network Activity and Connectivity." *Proceedings of the National Academy of Sciences* 108 (2011): 20254–59.

Main, John, OSB. *Word into Silence*. London: Darton, Longman, & Todd, 1980.

Nhat Hanh, Thich. *Buddha Mind, Buddha Body: Walking Toward Enlightenment*. Berkeley, CA: Parallax Press, 2007.

Oliver, Mary. *New and Selected Poems: Volume Two*. Boston: Beacon Press, 2005.

Steindl-Rast, David, OSB. "Sacramental Life: Take Off Your Shoes!" www.gratefulness.org/readings/dsr_Sacramental_Life.htm (accessed October 4, 2013).

6. Of Stones and Rivers

Haig-Brown, Roderick. *Measure of a Year: Reflections on Home, Family Life, and a Life Fully Lived*. Toronto: Collins, 1950.

Haig-Brown, Roderick. *A River Never Sleeps*. New York: William Morrow, 1946.

Woodcock, George. *Gabriel Dumont*. Toronto: University of Toronto Press, 2003.

7. Joining the Dance

Berry, Wendell. *Sex, Economy, Freedom, and Community: Eight Essays*. New York: Pantheon Books, 1993.

Hartmann, Thom. *Walking Your Blues Away*. Rochester, VT: Park Street Press, 2006.

Rolheiser, Ron. *The Holy Longing: Guidelines for a Christian Spirituality*. New York: Doubleday, 1999.

8. Little Queens

Bell, Rob. *Sex God: Exploring the Endless Connections between Sexuality and Spirituality*. Grand Rapids, MI: Zondervan, 2007.

Bharati, Swami Jnaneshvara. Yoga Sutras Interpretive Translation. www.swamij.com/pdf/yogasutrasinterpretive.pdf (accessed October 4, 2013).

Farhi, Donna. *Yoga Mind, Body & Spirit: A Return to Wholeness*. New York: Henry Holt, 2000.

Rilke, Rainer Maria. *Book of Hours: Love Poems to God*. Translated by Anita Barrows and Joanna Macy. New York: Riverhead Books, 1975.

Rolheiser, Ron. *The Holy Longing: Guidelines for a Christian Spirituality*. New York: Doubleday, 1999.

9. Monk or Beast

Kierkegaard, Søren, to Henriette Lund, 16 May 1844. Printed in *Breve og Aktstykker vedrørende Søren Kierkegaard*. Translated by Josiah Thompson. Copenhagen: Munksgaard, 1953.

Percy, Walker. *Love in the Ruins*. New York: Farrar, Straus and Giroux, 1971.

10. Better Signs

Seton, Ernest Thompson. *The Gospel of the Red Man*. Garden City, NY: Doubleday, Doran & Co., 1936.

Thoreau, Henry D. "Walking." *The Essays of Henry D. Thoreau*. New York: North Point Press, 2002.

11. Retreat

Thoreau, Henry D. "Walking." *The Essays of Henry D. Thoreau*. New York: North Point Press, 2002.

Part Two: Small Deaths

Balzac, Honoré de. *The Physiology of Marriage*. Translated by J. Walker McSpadden. New York: Liveright, 1932.

Chesterton, G.K. *Orthodoxy*. London: John Lane Company, 1909.

12. Greater Beings

Rilke, Rainer Maria. "The Man Watching." *Selected Poems of Rainer Maria Rilke*. Edited and translated by Robert Bly. New York: HarperCollins, 1981.

Whitman, Walt. *The Complete Writings of Walt Whitman*. New York: G.P. Putnam's Sons, 1902.

13. Lilies, Grubs, and Slough Hockey

Kelsey, Henry. *The Kelsey Papers*. Regina: Canadian Plains Research Centre, 1994.

Lawrence, Bonnie, and Anna Leighton. *Prairie Phoenix: Lilium philadelphicum, the Red Lily in Saskatchewan*. Regina: Nature Saskatchewan, 2005.

Rogers, Robert Dale. *Rogers' Herbal Manual*. Edmonton: Karamat Wilderness Ways, 2000.

Thoreau, Henry D. *The Journals of Henry D. Thoreau*. Boston: Houghton Mifflin, 1949.

14. Sirens

Berry, Thomas. *The Great Work: Our Way into the Future*. New York: Bell Tower, 1999.

Robinson, Marnia. *Cupid's Poisoned Arrow: From Habit to Harmony in Sexual Relationships*. Berkeley, CA: North Atlantic Books, 2009.

Siebert, Charles. "How TV's Nature Shows Make All the Earth a Stage." *Harper's Magazine* 286 (February 1, 1993): 43.

Sigman, Aric. "Visual Voodoo: The Biological Impact of Watching TV." *Biologist* 54, no. 1 (February 2007).

15. Tilth

Hawley, Jack. *The Bhagavad Gita: A Walkthrough for Westerners*. Novato, CA: New World Library, 2001.

John Paul II, Pope. *The Theology of the Body: Human Love in the Divine Plan.* Boston: Pauline Books & Media, 1997.

Lao-Tzu. *The Teachings of Lao-Tzu: The Tao Te Ching.* Translated by Paul Carus. New York: St. Martin's Press, 2000.

Suzuki, Shunryu. *Not Always So: Practicing the True Spirit of Zen.* New York: HarperCollins, 2003.

16. First Dancers

Davis, Deborah. *Women's Qigong for Health and Longevity.* Boston: Shambhala, 2008.

Leopold, Aldo. *A Sand County Almanac, and Sketches Here and There.* New York: Oxford University Press, 1949.

17. Dust and Breath

Hyde, Lewis. *The Gift: Imagination and the Erotic Life of Property.* New York: Vintage, 1983.

Hyde, Lewis. "Prophetic Excursions." Introduction to *The Essays of Henry D. Thoreau.* New York: North Point Press, 2002.

Thoreau, Henry D. *A Year in Thoreau's Journal: 1851.* New York: Penguin, 1993.

Part Three: Motherland

Taylor, Charles. *A Secular Age.* Cambridge, MA: Belknap Press of Harvard University Press, 2007.

18. *Imago Dei*

Harmon, Daniel Williams. *A Journal of Voyages and Travels in the Interior of North America.* New York: Allerton Book Company, 1922.

Harmon, Daniel Williams. *Sixteen Years in the Indian Country: The Journal of Daniel Williams Harmon 1800–1816.* Macmillan, 1957; collector's edition, Victoria, BC: New Caledonia House, 2006.

Knight, Chris. *Blood Relations: Menstruation and the Origins of Culture*. New Haven, CT: Yale University Press, 1991.

19. The Vineyard

Bell, Rob. *Sex God: Exploring the Endless Connections between Sexuality and Spirituality*. Grand Rapids, MI: Zondervan, 2007.

Dawkins, Richard. *A Devil's Chaplain*. New York: Houghton Mifflin, 2003.

Eliade, Mircea. *The Two and the One*. Translated by J.M. Cohen. London: Harvill Press, 1965.

Richardson, Diana. *The Heart of Tantric Sex*. Alresford, Hampshire, UK: O Books, 2003.

Thoreau, Henry D. *The Journals of Henry D. Thoreau*. Boston: Houghton Mifflin, 1949.

20. Listening to Aspen

McBride, James H., MD. "Some Points in the Management of the Neurasthenic." *Journal of the American Medical Association* 38, no. 14 (1902): 855–61.

Selhub, Eva M., and Alan C. Logan. *Your Brain on Nature: The Science of Nature's Influence on Your Health, Happiness and Vitality*. Mississauga, ON: John Wiley & Sons, 2012.

Strauss, Susan. "Coyote and the Grass People (Assiniboin)." In *Coyote Stories for Children*. Hillsboro, OR: Beyond Words, 1991.

21. Taking Steppes

Lao Tzu. *Hua Hu Ching: The Unknown Teachings of Lao Tzu*. Translated by Brian Walker. San Francisco: HarperSanFrancisco, 1992.

22. Our Lady of the Journey

Berry, Wendell. "Out of Your Car, Off Your Horse." *Atlantic*, February 1, 1991.

Day, Dorothy. *The Long Loneliness.* New York: Harper & Row, 1952.

23. Give Away

Rohr, Richard. *Immortal Diamond: The Search for Our True Self.* San Francisco: Jossey-Bass, 2013.

Rolheiser, Ron. *The Holy Longing: Guidelines for a Christian Spirituality.* New York: Doubleday, 1999.

Rolheiser, Ron. *Our One Great Act of Fidelity.* New York: Doubleday, 2011.

Thoreau, Henry D. *The Journals of Henry D. Thoreau.* Boston: Houghton Mifflin, 1949.